Linux Shell Scripting Cookbook

Second Edition

Over 110 practical recipes to solve real-world shell problems, guaranteed to make you wonder how you ever lived without them

Shantanu Tushar

Sarath Lakshman

[PACKT] open source *
PUBLISHING   community experience distilled

BIRMINGHAM - MUMBAI

Linux Shell Scripting Cookbook
Second Edition

First published: January 2011

Second edition: May 2013

Production Reference: 1140513

Published by Packt Publishing Ltd.
Livery Place
35 Livery Street
Birmingham B3 2PB, UK.

ISBN 978-1-78216-274-2

www.packtpub.com

Cover Image by Parag Kadam (paragvkadam@gmail.com)

Credits

Authors

Shantanu Tushar

Sarath Lakshman

Reviewers

Rajeshwari K.

John C. Kennedy

Anil Kumar

Sudhendu Kumar

Aravind SV

Acquisition Editor

Kartikey Pandey

Lead Technical Editor

Ankita Shashi

Technical Editors

Jalasha D'costa

Amit Ramadas

Lubna Shaikh

Project Coordinator

Shiksha Chaturvedi

Proofreader

Linda Morris

Indexer

Hemangini Bari

Production Coordinator

Shantanu Zagade

Cover Work

Shantanu Zagade

About the Authors

Shantanu Tushar is an advanced GNU/Linux user since his college days. He works as an application developer and contributes to the software in the KDE projects.

Shantanu has been fascinated by computers since he was a child, and spent most of his high school time writing C code to perform daily activities. Since he started using GNU/Linux, he has been using shell scripts to make the computer do all the hard work for him. He also takes time to visit students at various colleges to introduce them to the power of Free Software, including its various tools. Shantanu is a well-known contributor in the KDE community and works on Calligra, Gluon and the Plasma subprojects. He looks after maintaining Calligra Active – KDE's office document viewer for tablets, Plasma Media Center, and the Gluon Player. One day, he believes, programming will be so easy that everybody will love to write programs for their computers.

Shantanu can be reached by e-mail on shantanu@kde.org, shantanutushar on identi.ca/twitter, or his website http://www.shantanutushar.com.

I would like to thank my friends and family for the support and encouragement they've given me, especially to my sweet sister for her patience when I couldn't get time to talk to her. I am particularly thankful to Sinny Kumari for patiently testing the scripts to make sure they function properly and Sudhendu Kumar for helping me with the recipe on GNU Screen.

I must also thank Krishna, Madhusudan, and Santosh who introduced me to the wonderful world of GNU/Linux and Free Software. Also, a big thanks to all the reviewers of the book for taking the time to painfully go through every minute detail in the book and help me in improving it. I am also thankful to the whole team at Packt Publishing, without whose efforts and experience, this second edition wouldn't have happened.

Sarath Lakshman is a 23 year old who was bitten by the Linux bug during his teenage years. He is a software engineer working in ZCloud engineering group at Zynga, India. He is a life hacker who loves to explore innovations. He is a GNU/Linux enthusiast and hactivist of free and open source software. He spends most of his time hacking with computers and having fun with his great friends. Sarath is well known as the developer of SLYNUX (2005)—a user friendly GNU/Linux distribution for Linux newbies. The free and open source software projects he has contributed to are PiTiVi Video editor, SLYNUX GNU/Linux distro, Swathantra Malayalam Computing, School-Admin, Istanbul, and the Pardus Project. He has authored many articles for the *Linux For You* magazine on various domains of FOSS technologies. He had made a contribution to several different open source projects during his multiple Google Summer of Code projects. Currently, he is exploring his passion about scalable distributed systems in his spare time. Sarath can be reached via his website http://www.sarathlakshman.com.

About the Reviewers

Rajeshwari K. received her B.E degree (Information Science and Engineering) from VTU in 2004 and M. Tech degree (Computer Science and Engineering) from VTU in 2009. From 2004 to 2007 she handled a set of real-time projects and did some freelancing. Since 2010 she has being working as Assistant Professor at BMS College of Engineering in the department of Information Science and Engineering. She has a total of five years' experience in teaching in Computer Science subjects.

BMS College of Engineering, Bangalore is one of the autonomous colleges running under VTU with high acclamation nationwide.

Her research interests include operating systems and system-side programming.

John C. Kennedy has been administering Unix and Linux servers and workstations since 1997. He has experience with Red Hat, SUSE, Ubuntu, Debian, Solaris, and HP-UX. John is also experienced in Bash shell scripting and is currently teaching himself Python and Ruby. John has also been a Technical Editor for various publishers for over 10 years specializing in books related to open source technologies.

When John is not geeking out in front of either a home or work computer, he helps out with a German Shepherd Rescue in Virginia by fostering some great dogs or helping with their IT needs.

I would like to thank my family (my wonderful wife, Michele, my intelligent and caring daughter Denise, and my terrific and smart son, Kieran) for supporting the (sometimes) silly things and not so silly things I do. I'd also like to thank my current foster dogs for their occasional need to keep their legs crossed a little longer while I test things out from the book and forget they are there.

Anil Kumar is a software developer. He received his Computer Science undergraduate degree from BITS Pilani. He has work experience of more than two years in the field of Web Development and Systems. Besides working as a software developer, Anil is an open source evangelist and a blogger. He currently resides in Bangalore. He can be contacted at `anil.18june@gmail.com`.

Sudhendu Kumar has been a GNU/Linux user for more than five years. Presently being a software developer for a networking giant, in free time, he also contributes to KDE.

> I would like to thank the publishers for giving me this opportunity to review the book. I hope readers find the book useful and they enjoy reading it.

Aravind SV has worked with various Unix-like systems and shells over many years. You can contact him at `aravind.sv+shellbook@gmail.com`.

www.PacktPub.com

Support files, eBooks, discount offers and more

You might want to visit www.PacktPub.com for support files and downloads related to your book.

Did you know that Packt offers eBook versions of every book published, with PDF and ePub files available? You can upgrade to the eBook version at www.PacktPub.com and as a print book customer, you are entitled to a discount on the eBook copy. Get in touch with us at service@packtpub.com for more details.

At www.PacktPub.com, you can also read a collection of free technical articles, sign up for a range of free newsletters and receive exclusive discounts and offers on Packt books and eBooks.

http://PacktLib.PacktPub.com

Do you need instant solutions to your IT questions? PacktLib is Packt's online digital book library. Here, you can access, read and search across Packt's entire library of books.

Why Subscribe?

- ▶ Fully searchable across every book published by Packt
- ▶ Copy and paste, print and bookmark content
- ▶ On demand and accessible via web browser

Free Access for Packt account holders

If you have an account with Packt at www.PacktPub.com, you can use this to access PacktLib today and view nine entirely free books. Simply use your login credentials for immediate access.

Dedicated to my parents who taught me how to think and reason, and to be optimistic in every situation in life

—Shantanu Tushar

Table of Contents

Preface

GNU/Linux is one of the most powerful and flexible operating systems in the world. In modern computing, there is absolutely no space where it is not used—from servers, portable computers, mobile phones, tablets to supercomputers, everything runs Linux. While there are beautiful and modern graphical interfaces available for it, the shell still remains the most flexible way of interacting with the system.

In addition to executing individual commands, a shell can follow commands from a script, which makes it very easy to automate tasks. Examples of such tasks are preparing reports, sending e-mails, performing maintenance, and so on. This book is a collection of chapters which contain recipes to demonstrate real-life usages of commands and shell scripts. You can use these as a reference, or an inspiration for writing your own scripts. The tasks will range from text manipulation to performing network operations to administrative tasks.

As with everything, the shell is only as awesome as you make it. When you become an expert at shell scripting, you can use the shell to the fullest and harness its true power. *Linux Shell Scripting Cookbook* shows you how to do exactly that!

What this book covers

Chapter 1, Shell Something Out, is an introductory chapter for understanding the basic concepts and features in Bash. We discuss printing text in the terminal, doing mathematical calculations, and other simple functionalities provided by Bash.

Chapter 2, Have a Good Command, shows commonly used commands that are available with GNU/Linux. This chapter travels through different practical usage examples that users may come across and that they could make use of. In addition to essential commands, this second edition talks about cryptographic hashing commands and a recipe to run commands in parallel, wherever possible.

Chapter 3, File In, File Out, contains a collection of recipes related to files and filesystems. This chapter explains how to generate large-size files, installing a filesystem on files, mounting files, and creating ISO images. We also deal with operations such as finding and removing duplicate files, counting lines in a file collecting details about files, and so on.

Chapter 4, Texting and Driving, has a collection of recipes that explains most of the command-line text processing tools well under GNU/Linux with a number of task examples. It also has supplementary recipes for giving a detailed overview of regular expressions and commands such as `sed` and `awk`. This chapter goes through solutions to most of the frequently used text processing tasks in a variety of recipes. It is an essential read for any serious task.

Chapter 5, Tangled Web? Not At All!, has a collection of shell-scripting recipes that talk to services on the Internet. This chapter is intended to help readers understand how to interact with the Web using shell scripts to automate tasks such as collecting and parsing data from web pages. This is discussed using POST and GET to web pages, writing clients to web services. The second edition uses new authorization mechanisms such as OAuth for services such as Twitter.

Chapter 6, The Backup Plan, shows several commands used for performing data back up, archiving, compression, and so on. In addition to faster compression techniques, this second edition also talks about creating entire disk images.

Chapter 7, The Old-boy Network, has a collection of recipes that talks about networking on Linux and several commands useful for writing network-based scripts. The chapter starts with an introductory basic networking primer and goes on to cover usages of `ssh` – one of the most powerful commands on any modern GNU/Linux system. We discuss advanced port forwarding, setting up raw communication channels, configuring the firewall, and much more.

Chapter 8, Put on the Monitor's Cap, walks through several recipes related to monitoring activities on the Linux system and tasks used for logging and reporting. The chapter explains tasks such as calculating disk usage, monitoring user access, and CPU usage. In this second edition, we also learn how to optimize power consumption, monitor disks, and check their filesystems for errors.

Chapter 9, Administration Calls, has a collection of recipes for system administration. This chapter explains different commands to collect details about the system and user management using scripting. We also discuss bulk image resizing and accessing MySQL databases from the shell. New in this edition is that we learn how to use the GNU Screen to manage multiple terminals without needing a window manager.

What you need for this book

Basic user experience with any GNU/Linux platform will help you easily follow the book. We have tried to keep all the recipes in the book precise and as simple to follow as possible. Your curiosity for learning with the Linux platform is the only prerequisite for the book. Step-by-step explanations are provided for solving the scripting problems explained in the book. In order to run and test the examples in the book, a Ubuntu/Debian Linux installation is recommended, however, any other Linux distribution is enough for most of the tasks. You will find the book to be a straightforward reference to essential shell-scripting tasks, as well as a learning aid to code real-world efficient scripts.

Who this book is for

If you are a beginner, or an intermediate user, who wants to master the skill of quickly writing scripts to perform various tasks without reading entire man pages, this book is for you. You can start writing scripts and one-liners by simply looking at a similar recipe and its descriptions without any working knowledge of shell scripting or Linux. Intermediate or advanced users, as well as system administrators or developers and programmers, can use this book as a reference when they face problems while coding.

Conventions

In this book, you will find a number of styles of text that distinguish between different kinds of information. Here are some examples of these styles, and an explanation of their meaning.

Code words in text are shown as follows: "We create a function called `repeat` that has an infinite `while` loop, which attempts to run the command passed as a parameter (accessed by `$@`) to the function."

A block of code is set as follows:

```
if   [ $var -eq 0 ]; then echo "True"; fi
can be written as
if   test $var -eq 0 ; then echo "True"; fi
```

When we wish to draw your attention to a particular part of a code block, the relevant lines or items are set in bold:

```
while  read line;
do  something
done  < filename
```

Any command-line input or output is written as follows:

```
# mkdir /mnt/loopback
# mount -o loop loopbackfile.img /mnt/loopback
```

New terms and **important words** are shown in bold.

 Warnings or important notes appear in a box like this.

 Tips and tricks appear like this.

Reader feedback

Feedback from our readers is always welcome. Let us know what you think about this book—what you liked or may have disliked. Reader feedback is important for us to develop titles that you really get the most out of.

To send us general feedback, simply send an e-mail to feedback@packtpub.com, and mention the book title via the subject of your message. If there is a topic that you have expertise in and you are interested in either writing or contributing to a book, see our author guide on www.packtpub.com/authors.

Customer support

Now that you are the proud owner of a Packt book, we have a number of things to help you to get the most from your purchase.

Downloading the example code

You can download the example code files for all Packt books you have purchased from your account at http://www.packtpub.com. If you purchased this book elsewhere, you can visit http://www.packtpub.com/support and register to have the files e-mailed directly to you.

Errata

Although we have taken every care to ensure the accuracy of our content, mistakes do happen. If you find a mistake in one of our books—maybe a mistake in the text or the code—we would be grateful if you would report this to us. By doing so, you can save other readers from frustration and help us improve subsequent versions of this book. If you find any errata, please report them by visiting http://www.packtpub.com/submit-errata, selecting your book, clicking on the **errata submission form** link, and entering the details of your errata. Once your errata are verified, your submission will be accepted and the errata will be uploaded on our website, or added to any list of existing errata, under the Errata section of that title. Any existing errata can be viewed by selecting your title from http://www.packtpub.com/support.

Piracy

Piracy of copyright material on the Internet is an ongoing problem across all media. At Packt, we take the protection of our copyright and licenses very seriously. If you come across any illegal copies of our works, in any form, on the Internet, please provide us with the location address or website name immediately so that we can pursue a remedy.

Please contact us at copyright@packtpub.com with a link to the suspected pirated material.

We appreciate your help in protecting our authors, and our ability to bring you valuable content.

Questions

You can contact us at questions@packtpub.com if you are having a problem with any aspect of the book, and we will do our best to address it.

1
Shell Something Out

In this chapter, we will cover:

- Printing in the terminal
- Playing with variables and environment variables
- Function to prepend to environment variables
- Math with the shell
- Playing with file descriptors and redirection
- Arrays and associative array
- Visiting aliases
- Grabbing information about the terminal
- Getting and setting dates and delays
- Debugging the script
- Functions and arguments
- Reading output of a sequence of commands in a variable
- Reading n characters without pressing the return key
- Running a command until it succeeds
- Field separators and iterators
- Comparisons and tests

Introduction

Unix-like systems are amazing operating system designs. Even after many decades, Unix-style architecture for operating systems serves as one of the best designs. One of the important features of this architecture is the command-line interface, or the shell. The shell environment helps users to interact with and access core functions of the operating system. The term **scripting** is more relevant in this context. Scripting is usually supported by interpreter-based programming languages. Shell scripts are files in which we write a sequence of commands that we need to perform and are executed using the shell utility.

In this book we are dealing with **Bash** (**Bourne Again Shell**), which is the default shell environment for most GNU/Linux systems. Since GNU/Linux is the most prominent operating system on Unix-style architecture, most of the examples and discussions are written by keeping Linux systems in mind.

The primary purpose of this chapter is to give readers an insight into the shell environment and become familiar with the basic features that the shell offers. Commands are typed and executed in a shell terminal. When a terminal is opened, a prompt is available which usually has the following format:

username@hostname$

Or:

root@hostname #

or simply as $ or #.

$ represents regular users and # represents the administrative user root. Root is the most privileged user in a Linux system.

> It is usually a bad idea to directly use the shell as the root user (administrator) to perform tasks. This is because typing errors in your commands have the potential to do more damage when your shell has more privileges. So, it is recommended to log in as a regular user (your shell will denote that as $ in the prompt, and # when running as root), and then use tools such as `sudo` to run privileged commands. Running a command such as `sudo <command> <arguments>` will run it as root.

A shell script is a text file that typically begins with a shebang, as follows:

```
#!/bin/bash
```

Shebang is a line on which #! is prefixed to the interpreter path. `/bin/bash` is the interpreter command path for Bash.

Execution of a script can be done in two ways. Either we can run the script as a command-line argument to `bash` or we can grant execution permission to the script so it becomes executable.

The script can be run with the filename as a command-line argument as follows (the text that starts with # is a comment, you don't have to type it out):

```
$ bash script.sh # Assuming script is in the current directory.
```

Or:

```
$ bash /home/path/script.sh # Using full path of script.sh.
```

If a script is run as a command-line argument for `bash`, the shebang in the script is not required.

If required, we can utilize the shebang to facilitate running the script on its own. For this, we have to set executable permissions for the script and it will run using the interpreter path that is appended to `#!` to the shebang. This can be set as follows:

```
$ chmod a+x script.sh
```

This command gives the `script.sh` file the executable permission for all users. The script can be executed as:

```
$ ./script.sh #./ represents the current directory
```

Or:

```
$ /home/path/script.sh # Full path of the script is used
```

The kernel will read the first line and see that the shebang is `#!/bin/bash`. It will identify `/bin/bash` and execute the script internally as:

```
$ /bin/bash script.sh
```

When a shell is started, it initially executes a set of commands to define various settings such as prompt text, colors, and much more. This set of commands are read from a shell script at `~/.bashrc` (or `~/.bash_profile` for login shells) located in the home directory of the user. The Bash shell also maintains a history of commands run by the user. It is available in the `~/.bash_history` file.

> ~ denotes your home directory, which is usually `/home/user` where `user` is your username or `/root` for the root user.
>
> A login shell is the shell which you get just after logging in to a machine. However, if you open up a shell while logged in to a graphical environment (such as GNOME, KDE, and so on), then it is not a login shell.

In Bash, each command or command sequence is delimited by using a semicolon or a new line. For example:

```
$ cmd1 ; cmd2
```

This is equivalent to:

```
$ cmd1
$ cmd2
```

Finally, the # character is used to denote the beginning of unprocessed comments. A comment section starts with # and proceeds up to the end of that line. The comment lines are most often used to provide comments about the code in the file or to stop a line of code from being executed.

Now let us move on to the basic recipes in this chapter.

Printing in the terminal

The **terminal** is an interactive utility by which a user interacts with the shell environment. Printing text in the terminal is a basic task that most shell scripts and utilities need to perform regularly. As we will see in this recipe, this can be performed via various methods and in different formats.

How to do it...

echo is the basic command for printing in the terminal.

echo puts a newline at the end of every echo invocation by default:

```
$ echo "Welcome to Bash"
Welcome to Bash
```

Simply, using double-quoted text with the echo command prints the text in the terminal. Similarly, text without double quotes also gives the same output:

```
$ echo Welcome to Bash
Welcome to Bash
```

Another way to do the same task is by using single quotes:

```
$ echo 'text in quotes'
```

These methods may look similar, but some of them have a specific purpose and side effects too. Consider the following command:

```
$ echo "cannot include exclamation - ! within double quotes"
```

This will return the following output:

`bash: !: event not found error`

Hence, if you want to print special characters such as !, either do not use them within double quotes or escape them with a special escape character (\) prefixed with it, like so:

`$ echo Hello world !`

Or:

`$ echo 'Hello world !'`

Or:

`$ echo "Hello world \!" #Escape character \ prefixed.`

The side effects of each of the methods are as follows:

- When using `echo` without quotes, we cannot use a semicolon, as it acts as a delimiter between commands in the Bash shell
- `echo hello; hello` takes `echo hello` as one command and the second `hello` as the second command
- Variable substitution, which is discussed in the next recipe, will not work within single quotes

Another command for printing in the terminal is `printf`. It uses the same arguments as the `printf` command in the C programming language. For example:

`$ printf "Hello world"`

`printf` takes quoted text or arguments delimited by spaces. We can use formatted strings with `printf`. We can specify string width, left or right alignment, and so on. By default, `printf` does not have newline as in the `echo` command. We have to specify a newline when required, as shown in the following script:

```
#!/bin/bash
#Filename: printf.sh

printf  "%-5s %-10s %-4s\n" No Name  Mark
printf  "%-5s %-10s %-4.2f\n" 1 Sarath 80.3456
printf  "%-5s %-10s %-4.2f\n" 2 James 90.9989
printf  "%-5s %-10s %-4.2f\n" 3 Jeff 77.564
```

We will receive the formatted output:

```
No      Name        Mark
1       Sarath      80.35
2       James       91.00
3       Jeff        77.56
```

How it works...

`%s`, `%c`, `%d`, and `%f` are format substitution characters for which an argument can be placed after the quoted format string.

`%-5s` can be described as a string substitution with left alignment (- represents left alignment) with width equal to 5. If - was not specified, the string would have been aligned to the right. The width specifies the number of characters reserved for that variable. For `Name`, the width reserved is 10. Hence, any name will reside within the 10-character width reserved for it and the rest of the characters will be filled with space up to 10 characters in total.

For floating point numbers, we can pass additional parameters to round off the decimal places.

For marks, we have formatted the string as `%-4.2f`, where `.2` specifies rounding off to two decimal places. Note that for every line of the format string a newline (\n) is issued.

There's more...

While using flags for `echo` and `printf`, always make sure that the flags appear before any strings in the command, otherwise Bash will consider the flags as another string.

Escaping newline in echo

By default, `echo` has a newline appended at the end of its output text. This can be avoided by using the -n flag. `echo` can also accept escape sequences in double-quoted strings as an argument. When using escape sequences, use `echo` as `echo -e "string containing escape sequences"`. For example:

```
echo -e "1\t2\t3"
1   2   3
```

Printing a colored output

Producing a colored output on the terminal is very interesting and is achieved by using escape sequences.

Colors are represented by color codes, some examples being, reset = 0, black = 30, red = 31, green = 32, yellow = 33, blue = 34, magenta = 35, cyan = 36, and white = 37.

To print a colored text, enter the following command:

```
echo -e "\e[1;31m This is red text \e[0m"
```

Here, `\e[1;31m` is the escape string that sets the color to red and `\e[0m` resets the color back. Replace `31` with the required color code.

For a colored background, reset = 0, black = 40, red = 41, green = 42, yellow = 43, blue = 44, magenta = 45, cyan = 46, and white=47, are the color codes that are commonly used.

To print a colored background, enter the following command:

```
echo -e "\e[1;42m Green Background \e[0m"
```

Playing with variables and environment variables

Variables are essential components of every programming language and are used to hold varying data. Scripting languages usually do not require variable type declaration before its use as they can be assigned directly. In Bash, the value for every variable is string, regardless of whether we assign variables with quotes or without quotes. Furthermore, there are variables used by the shell environment and the operating environment to store special values, which are called **environment variables**. Let us look at how to play with some of these variables in this recipe.

Getting ready

Variables are named with the usual naming constructs. When an application is executing, it will be passed a set of variables called environment variables. To view all the environment variables related to a terminal, issue the `env` command. For every process, environment variables in its runtime can be viewed by:

```
cat /proc/$PID/environ
```

Set `PID` with a process ID of the process (`PID` always takes an integer value).

For example, assume that an application called **gedit** is running. We can obtain the process ID of gedit with the `pgrep` command as follows:

```
$ pgrep gedit
12501
```

You can obtain the environment variables associated with the process by executing the following command:

```
$ cat /proc/12501/environ
GDM_KEYBOARD_LAYOUT=usGNOME_KEYRING_PID=1560USER=slynuxHOME=/home/slynux
```

 Note that many environment variables are stripped off for convenience. The actual output may contain numerous variables.

The aforementioned command returns a list of environment variables and their values. Each variable is represented as a name=value pair and are separated by a null character (\0). If you can substitute the \0 character with \n, you can reformat the output to show each variable=value pair in each line. Substitution can be made using the `tr` command as follows:

```
$ cat /proc/12501/environ  | tr '\0' '\n'
```

Now, let us see how to assign and manipulate variables and environment variables.

How to do it...

A variable can be assigned as follows:

```
var=value
```

`var` is the name of a variable and `value` is the value to be assigned. If `value` does not contain any space character (such as space), it need not be enclosed in quotes, Otherwise it is to be enclosed in single or double quotes.

Note that `var` = `value` and `var=value` are different. It is a usual mistake to write `var` =value instead of `var=value`. The later one is the assignment operation, whereas the earlier one is an equality operation.

Printing contents of a variable is done using by prefixing $ with the variable name as follows:

```
var="value" #Assignment of value to variable var.
```

```
echo $var
```

Or:

```
echo ${var}
```

We will receive an output as follows:

```
value
```

We can use variable values inside `printf` or `echo` in double quotes:

```
#!/bin/bash
#Filename :variables.sh
fruit=apple
count=5
echo "We have $count ${fruit}(s)"
```

The output will be as follows:

```
We have 5 apple(s)
```

Environment variables are variables that are not defined in the current process, but are received from the parent processes. For example, HTTP_PROXY is an environment variable. This variable defines which proxy server should be used for an Internet connection.

Usually, it is set as:

```
HTTP_PROXY=192.168.1.23:3128
export HTTP_PROXY
```

The export command is used to set the env variable. Now any application, executed from the current shell script, will receive this variable. We can export custom variables for our own purposes in an application or shell script that is executed. There are many standard environment variables that are available for the shell by default.

For example, PATH. A typical PATH variable will contain:

```
$ echo $PATH
/home/slynux/bin:/usr/local/sbin:/usr/local/bin:/usr/sbin:/usr/bin:/
sbin:/bin:/usr/games
```

When given a command for execution, the shell automatically searches for the executable in the list of directories in the PATH environment variable (directory paths are delimited by the ":" character). Usually, $PATH is defined in /etc/environment or /etc/profile or ~/.bashrc. When we need to add a new path to the PATH environment, we use:

```
export PATH="$PATH:/home/user/bin"
```

Or, alternately, we can use:

```
$ PATH="$PATH:/home/user/bin"
$ export PATH

$ echo $PATH
/home/slynux/bin:/usr/local/sbin:/usr/local/bin:/usr/sbin:/usr/bin:/
sbin:/bin:/usr/games:/home/user/bin
```

Here we have added `/home/user/bin` to `PATH`.

Some of the well-known environment variables are HOME, PWD, USER, UID, SHELL, and so on.

> When using single quotes, variables will not be expanded and will be displayed as is. This means:
>
> **$ echo '$var' will print $var**
>
> Whereas, `$ echo "$var"` will print the value of the `$var` variable if defined or nothing at all if it is not defined.

There's more...

Let us see more tips associated with standard and environment variables.

Finding the length of a string

Get the length of a variable value using the following command:

```
length=${#var}
```

For example:

```
$ var=12345678901234567890$
echo ${#var}
20
```

The `length` parameter will bear the number of characters in the string.

Identifying the current shell

To identify the shell which is currently being used, we can use the SHELL variable, like so:

```
echo $SHELL
```

Or:

```
echo $0
```

For example:

```
$ echo $SHELL
/bin/bash

$ echo $0
/bin/bash
```

Checking for super user

`UID` is an important environment variable that can be used to check whether the current script has been run as a root user or regular user. For example:

```
If [ $UID -ne 0 ]; then
    echo Non root user. Please run as root.
else
    echo Root user
fi
```

The `UID` value for the root user is `0`.

Modifying the Bash prompt string (username@hostname:~$)

When we open a terminal or run a shell, we see a prompt string such as `user@hostname:/home/$`. Different GNU/Linux distributions have slightly different prompts and different colors. We can customize the prompt text using the `PS1` environment variable. The default prompt text for the shell is set using a line in the `~/.bashrc` file.

> ▸ We can list the line used to set the `PS1` variable as follows:
>
> ```
> $ cat ~/.bashrc | grep PS1
> PS1='${debian_chroot:+($debian_chroot)}\u@\h:\w\$ '
> ```

> ▸ To set a custom prompt string, enter the following command:
>
> ```
> slynux@localhost: ~$ PS1="PROMPT>"
> PROMPT> Type commands here # Prompt string changed.
> ```

> ▸ We can use colored text using the special escape sequences such as `\e[1;31` (refer to the _Printing in the terminal_ recipe of this chapter).

There are also certain special characters that expand to system parameters. For example, `\u` expands to username, `\h` expands to hostname, and `\w` expands to the current working directory.

Function to prepend to environment variables

Environment variables are often used to store a list of paths of where to search for executables, libraries, and so on. Examples are `$PATH`, `$LD_LIBRARY_PATH`, which will typically look like this:

```
PATH=/usr/bin;/bin
LD_LIBRARY_PATH=/usr/lib;/lib
```

This essentially means that whenever the shell has to execute binaries, it will first look into /usr/bin followed by /bin.

A very common task that one has to do when building a program from source and installing to a custom path is to add its bin directory to the PATH environment variable. Let's say in this case we install myapp to /opt/myapp, which has binaries in a directory called bin and libraries in lib.

How to do it...

A way to do this is to say it as follows:

```
export PATH=/opt/myapp/bin:$PATH
export LD_LIBRARY_PATH=/opt/myapp/lib;$LD_LIBRARY_PATH
```

PATH and LD_LIBRARY_PATH should now look something like this:

```
PATH=/opt/myapp/bin:/usr/bin:/bin
LD_LIBRARY_PATH=/opt/myapp/lib:/usr/lib;/lib
```

However, we can make this easier by adding this function in .bashrc-:

```
prepend() { [ -d "$2" ] && eval $1=\"$2':'\$$1\" && export $1; }
```

This can be used in the following way:

```
prepend PATH /opt/myapp/bin
prepend LD_LIBRARY_PATH /opt/myapp/lib
```

How it works...

We define a function called prepend(), which first checks if the directory specified by the second parameter to the function exists. If it does, the eval expression sets the variable with the name in the first parameter equal to the second parameter string followed by : (the path separator) and then the original value for the variable.

However, there is one caveat, if the variable is empty when we try to prepend, there will be a trailing : at the end. To fix this, we can modify the function to look like this:

```
prepend() { [ -d "$2" ] && eval $1=\"$2\$\{$1:+':'\$$1\}\" && export $1 ;
}
```

In this form of the function, we introduce a shell parameter expansion of the form:

`${parameter:+expression}`

This expands to `expression` if parameter is set and is not null.

With this change, we take care to try to append `:` and the old value if, and only if, the old value existed when trying to prepend.

Math with the shell

Arithmetic operations are an essential requirement for every programming language. In this recipe, we will explore various methods for performing arithmetic operations in shell.

Getting ready

The Bash shell environment can perform basic arithmetic operations using the commands `let`, `(( ))`, and `[]`. The two utilities `expr` and `bc` are also very helpful in performing advanced operations.

How to do it...

1. A numeric value can be assigned as a regular variable assignment, which is stored as a string. However, we use methods to manipulate as numbers:

   ```bash
   #!/bin/bash
   no1=4;
   no2=5;
   ```

2. The `let` command can be used to perform basic operations directly. While using `let`, we use variable names without the `$` prefix, for example:

   ```bash
   let result=no1+no2
   echo $result
   ```

   - Increment operation:

     ```bash
     $ let no1++
     ```

   - Decrement operation:

     ```bash
     $ let no1--
     ```

   - Shorthands:

     ```bash
     let no+=6
     let no-=6
     ```

These are equal to `let no=no+6` and `let no=no-6` respectively.

❑ Alternate methods:

The [] operator can be used in the same way as the `let` command as follows:

```
result=$[ no1 + no2 ]
```

Using the $ prefix inside [] operators are legal, for example:

```
result=$[ $no1 + 5 ]
```

(( )) can also be used. $ prefixed with a variable name is used when (( )) operator is used, as follows:

```
result=$(( no1 + 50 ))
```

`expr` can also be used for basic operations:

```
result=`expr 3 + 4`
result=$(expr $no1 + 5)
```

All of the preceding methods do not support floating point numbers, and operate on integers only.

3. bc, the precision calculator is an advanced utility for mathematical operations. It has a wide range of options. We can perform floating point operations and use advanced functions as follows:

```
echo "4 * 0.56" | bc
2.24
```

```
no=54;
result=`echo "$no * 1.5" | bc`
echo $result
81.0
```

Additional parameters can be passed to bc with prefixes to the operation with semicolon as delimiters through `stdin`.

❑ **Decimal places scale with bc**: In the following example the `scale=2` parameter sets the number of decimal places to 2. Hence, the output of bc will contain a number with two decimal places:

```
echo "scale=2;3/8" | bc
0.37
```

- **Base conversion with bc**: We can convert from one base number system to another one. Let us convert from decimal to binary, and binary to octal:

```
#!/bin/bash
Desc: Number conversion

no=100
echo "obase=2;$no" | bc
1100100
no=1100100
echo "obase=10;ibase=2;$no" | bc
100
```

- Calculating squares and square roots can be done as follows:

```
echo "sqrt(100)" | bc #Square root
echo "10^10" | bc #Square
```

Playing with file descriptors and redirection

File descriptors are integers that are associated with file input and output. They keep track of opened files. The best-known file descriptors are stdin, stdout, and stderr. We even can redirect the contents of one file descriptor to another. This recipe shows examples on how to manipulate and redirect with file descriptors.

Getting ready

While writing scripts we use standard input (stdin), standard output (stdout), and standard error (stderr) frequently. Redirection of an output to a file by filtering the contents is one of the essential things we need to perform. While a command outputs some text, it can be either an error or an output (nonerror) message. We cannot distinguish whether it is output text or an error text by just looking at it. However, we can handle them with file descriptors. We can extract text that is attached to a specific descriptor.

File descriptors are integers associated with an opened file or data stream. File descriptors 0, 1, and 2 are reserved as follows:

- 0: stdin (standard input)
- 1: stdout (standard output)
- 2: stderr (standard error)

How to do it...

1. Redirecting or saving output text to a file can be done as follows:

    ```
    $ echo "This is a sample text 1" > temp.txt
    ```

    This would store the echoed text in `temp.txt` by truncating the file, the contents will be emptied before writing.

2. To append text to a file, consider the following example:

    ```
    $ echo "This is sample text 2" >> temp.txt
    ```

3. You can view the contents of the file as follows:

    ```
    $ cat temp.txt
    This is sample text 1
    This is sample text 2
    ```

4. Let us see what a standard error is and how you can redirect it. `stderr` messages are printed when commands output an error message. Consider the following example:

    ```
    $ ls +
    ls: cannot access +: No such file or directory
    ```

    Here + is an invalid argument and hence an error is returned.

> **Successful and unsuccessful commands**
>
> When a command returns after an error, it returns a nonzero exit status. The command returns zero when it terminates after successful completion. The return status can be read from special variable $? (run `echo $?` immediately after the command execution statement to print the exit status).

The following command prints the `stderr` text to the screen rather than to a file (and because there is no `stdout` output, `out.txt` will be empty):

```
$ ls + > out.txt
ls: cannot access +: No such file or directory
```

In the following command, we redirect `stderr` to `out.txt`:

```
$ ls + 2> out.txt # works
```

You can redirect `stderr` exclusively to a file and `stdout` to another file as follows:

```
$ cmd 2>stderr.txt 1>stdout.txt
```

It is also possible to redirect `stderr` and `stdout` to a single file by converting `stderr` to `stdout` using this preferred method:

```
$ cmd 2>&1 output.txt
```

Or the alternate approach:

```
$ cmd &> output.txt
```

5. Sometimes, the output may contain unnecessary information (such as debug messages). If you don't want the output terminal burdened with the `stderr` details then you should redirect the `stderr` output to `/dev/null`, which removes it completely. For example, consider that we have three files a1, a2, and a3. However, a1 does not have the read-write-execute permission for the user. When you need to print the contents of files starting with a, we use the `cat` command. Set up the test files as follows:

```
$ echo a1 > a1
$ cp a1 a2 ; cp a2 a3;
$ chmod 000 a1   #Deny all permissions
```

While displaying contents of the files using wildcards (a*), it will show an error message for file a1 as it does not have the proper read permission:

```
$ cat a*
cat: a1: Permission denied
a1
a1
```

Here, `cat: a1: Permission denied` belongs to the `stderr` data. We can redirect the `stderr` data into a file, whereas `stdout` remains printed in the terminal. Consider the following code:

```
$ cat a* 2> err.txt #stderr is redirected to err.txt
a1
a1

$ cat err.txt
cat: a1: Permission denied
```

Take a look at the following code:

```
$ cmd 2>/dev/null
```

When redirection is performed for `stderr` or `stdout`, the redirected text flows into a file. As the text has already been redirected and has gone into the file, no text remains to flow to the next command through pipe (|), and it appears to the next set of command sequences through `stdin`.

6. However, there is a way to redirect data to a file, as well as provide a copy of redirected data as `stdin` for the next set of commands. This can be done using the `tee` command. For example, to print `stdout` in the terminal as well as redirect `stdout` into a file, the syntax for `tee` is as follows:

```
command | tee FILE1 FILE2
```

In the following code, the `stdin` data is received by the `tee` command. It writes a copy of `stdout` to the `out.txt` file and sends another copy as `stdin` for the next command. The `cat -n` command puts a line number for each line received from `stdin` and writes it into `stdout`:

```
$ cat a* | tee out.txt | cat -n
cat: a1: Permission denied
     1a1
     2a1
```

Examine the contents of `out.txt` as follows:

```
$ cat out.txt
a1
a1
```

Note that `cat: a1: Permission denied` does not appear because it belongs to `stderr`. The `tee` command can read from `stdin` only.

By default, the `tee` command overwrites the file, but it can be used with appended options by providing the `-a` option, for example, `$ cat a* | tee -a out.txt | cat -n`.

Commands appear with arguments in the format: `command FILE1 FILE2` ... or simply `command FILE`.

7. We can use `stdin` as a command argument. It can be done by using - as the filename argument for the command as follows:

```
$ cmd1 | cmd2 | cmd -
```

For example:

```
$ echo who is this | tee -
who is this
who is this
```

Alternately, we can use `/dev/stdin` as the output filename to use `stdin`.

Similarly, use `/dev/stderr` for standard error and `/dev/stdout` for standard output. These are special device files that correspond to `stdin`, `stderr`, and `stdout`.

How it works...

For output redirection, > and >> operators are different. Both of them redirect text to a file, but the first one empties the file and then writes to it, whereas the later one adds the output to the end of the existing file.

When we use a redirection operator, the output won't print in the terminal but it is directed to a file. When redirection operators are used, by default, they operate on standard output. To explicitly take a specific file descriptor, you must prefix the descriptor number to the operator.

> is equivalent to `1>` and similarly it applies for >> (equivalent to `1>>`).

When working with errors, the `stderr` output is dumped to the `/dev/null` file. `./dev/null` is a special device file where any data received by the file is discarded. The null device is often known as a **black hole** as all the data that goes into it is lost forever.

There's more...

A command that reads `stdin` for input can receive data in multiple ways. Also, it is possible to specify file descriptors of our own using `cat` and pipes, for example:

```
$ cat file | cmd
$ cmd1 | cmd
```

Redirection from a file to a command

By using redirection, we can read data from a file as `stdin` as follows:

```
$ cmd < file
```

Redirecting from a text block enclosed within a script

Sometimes we need to redirect a block of text (multiple lines of text) as standard input. Consider a particular case where the source text is placed within the shell script. A practical usage example is writing a logfile header data. It can be performed as follows:

```
#!/bin/bash
cat<<EOF>log.txt
LOG FILE HEADER
This is a test log file
Function: System statistics
EOF
```

The lines that appear between `cat <<EOF >log.txt` and the next `EOF` line will appear as the `stdin` data. Print the contents of `log.txt` as follows:

```
$ cat log.txt
LOG FILE HEADER
This is a test log file
Function: System statistics
```

Custom file descriptors

A file descriptor is an abstract indicator for accessing a file. Each file access is associated with a special number called a file descriptor. 0, 1, and 2 are reserved descriptor numbers for `stdin`, `stdout`, and `stderr`.

We can create our own custom file descriptors using the `exec` command. If you are already familiar with file programming with any other programming language, you might have noticed modes for opening files. Usually, the following three modes are used:

> ► Read mode
> ► Write with truncate mode
> ► Write with append mode

`<` is an operator used to read from the file to `stdin`. `>` is the operator used to write to a file with truncation (data is written to the target file after truncating the contents). `>>` is an operator used to write to a file by appending (data is appended to the existing file contents and the contents of the target file will not be lost). File descriptors can be created with one of the three modes.

Create a file descriptor for reading a file, as follows:

```
$ exec 3<input.txt # open for reading with descriptor number 3
```

We could use it in the following way:

```
$ echo this is a test line > input.txt
$ exec 3<input.txt
```

Now you can use file descriptor 3 with commands. For example, we will use `cat <&3` as follows:

```
$ cat<&3
this is a test line
```

If a second read is required, we cannot re-use the file descriptor 3. It is required that we reassign the file descriptor 3 for read using `exec` for making a second read.

Create a file descriptor for writing (truncate mode) as follows:

```
$ exec 4>output.txt # open for writing
```

For example:

```
$ exec 4>output.txt
$ echo newline >&4
$ cat output.txt
newline
```

Create a file descriptor for writing (append mode) as follows:

```
$ exec 5>>input.txt
```

For example:

```
$ exec 5>>input.txt
$ echo appended line >&5
$ cat input.txt
newline
appended line
```

Arrays and associative arrays

Arrays are a very important component for storing a collection of data as separate entities using indexes. Regular arrays can use only integers as their array index. On the other hand, Bash also supports associative arrays that can take a string as their array index. Associative arrays are very useful in many types of manipulations where having a string index makes more sense. In this recipe, we will see how to use both of these.

Getting ready

To use associate arrays, you must have Bash Version 4 or higher.

How to do it...

1. An array can be defined in many ways. Define an array using a list of values in a line as follows:

   ```
   array_var=(1 2 3 4 5 6)
   #Values will be stored in consecutive locations starting from
   index 0.
   ```

Alternately, define an array as a set of index-value pairs as follows:

```
array_var[0]="test1"
array_var[1]="test2"
array_var[2]="test3"
array_var[3]="test4"
array_var[4]="test5"
array_var[5]="test6"
```

2. Print the contents of an array at a given index using the following commands:

```
echo ${array_var[0]}
test1
index=5
echo ${array_var[$index]}
test6
```

3. Print all of the values in an array as a list using the following commands:

```
$ echo ${array_var[*]}
test1 test2 test3 test4 test5 test6
```

Alternately, you could use:

```
$ echo ${array_var[@]}
test1 test2 test3 test4 test5 test6
```

4. Print the length of an array (the number of elements in an array) as follows:

```
$ echo ${#array_var[*]}
6
```

There's more...

Associative arrays have been introduced to Bash from Version 4.0 and they are useful entities to solve many problems using the hashing technique. Let us go into more detail.

Defining associative arrays

In an associative array, we can use any text data as an array index. Initially, a declaration statement is required to declare a variable name as an associative array. This can be done as follows:

```
$ declare -A ass_array
```

After the declaration, elements can be added to the associative array using two methods as follows:

- ▶ By using inline index-value list method, we can provide a list of index-value pairs:

  ```
  $ ass_array=([index1]=val1 [index2]=val2)
  ```

- ▶ Alternately, you could use separate index-value assignments:

  ```
  $ ass_array[index1]=val1
  $ ass_array'index2]=val2
  ```

For example, consider the assignment of price for fruits using an associative array:

```
$ declare -A fruits_value
$ fruits_value=([apple]='100dollars' [orange]='150 dollars')
```

Display the content of an array as follows:

```
$ echo "Apple costs ${fruits_value[apple]}"
Apple costs 100 dollars
```

Listing of array indexes

Arrays have indexes for indexing each of the elements. Ordinary and associative arrays differ in terms of index type. We can obtain the list of indexes in an array as follows:

```
$ echo ${!array_var[*]}
```

Or, we can also use:

```
$ echo ${!array_var[@]
```

In the previous `fruits_value` array example, consider the following command:

```
$ echo ${!fruits_value[*]}
orange apple
```

This will work for ordinary arrays too.

Visiting aliases

An **alias** is basically a shortcut that takes the place of typing a long-command sequence. In this recipe, we will see how to create aliases using the `alias` command.

How to do it...

There are various operations you can perform on aliases, these are as follows:

1. An alias can be created as follows:

   ```
   $ alias new_command='command sequence'
   ```

   Giving a shortcut to the install command, `apt-get install`, can be done as follows:

   ```
   $ alias install='sudo apt-get install'
   ```

   Therefore, we can use `install pidgin` instead of `sudo apt-get install pidgin`.

2. The `alias` command is temporary; aliasing exists until we close the current terminal only. To keep these shortcuts permanent, add this statement to the `~/.bashrc` file. Commands in `~/.bashrc` are always executed when a new shell process is spawned:

   ```
   $ echo 'alias cmd="command seq"' >> ~/.bashrc
   ```

3. To remove an alias, remove its entry from `~/.bashrc` (if any) or use the `unalias` command. Alternatively, `alias example=` should unset the alias named `example`.

4. As an example, we can create an alias for `rm` so that it will delete the original and keep a copy in a backup directory:

   ```
   alias rm='cp $@ ~/backup && rm $@'
   ```

 When you create an alias, if the item being aliased already exists, it will be replaced by this newly aliased command for that user.

There's more...

There are situations when aliasing can also be a security breach. See how to identify them.

Escaping aliases

The `alias` command can be used to alias any important command, and you may not always want to run the command using the alias. We can ignore any aliases currently defined by escaping the command we want to run. For example:

```
$ \command
```

The \ character escapes the command, running it without any aliased changes. While running privileged commands on an untrusted environment, it is always good security practice to ignore aliases by prefixing the command with \. The attacker might have aliased the privileged command with his/her own custom command to steal the critical information that is provided by the user to the command.

Grabbing information about the terminal

While writing command-line shell scripts, we will often need to heavily manipulate information about the current terminal, such as the number of columns, rows, cursor positions, masked password fields, and so on. This recipe helps in collecting and manipulating terminal settings.

Getting ready

`tput` and `stty` are utilities that can be used for terminal manipulations. Let us see how to use them to perform different tasks.

How to do it...

There are specific information you can gather about the terminal as shown in the following list:

- Get the number of columns and rows in a terminal by using the following commands:

  ```
  tput cols
  tput lines
  ```

- To print the current terminal name, use the following command:

  ```
  tput longname
  ```

- To move the cursor to a 100,100 position, you can enter:

  ```
  tput cup 100 100
  ```

- Set the background color for the terminal using the following command:

  ```
  tputsetb n
  ```

  n can be a value in the range of 0 to 7.

- Set the foreground color for text by using the following command:

  ```
  tputsetf n
  ```

  n can be a value in the range of 0 to 7.

- To make text bold use this:

  ```
  tput bold
  ```

- To start and end underlining use this:

```
tput smul
tput rmul
```

- To delete from the cursor to the end of the line use the following command:

```
tputed
```

- While typing a password, we should not display the characters typed. In the following example, we will see how to do it using `stty`:

```
#!/bin/sh
#Filename: password.sh
echo -e "Enter password: "
stty -echo
read password
stty echo
echo
echo Password read.
```

 The -echo option in the preceding command disables the output to the terminal, whereas echo enables output.

Getting and setting dates and delays

Many applications require printing dates in different formats, setting date and time, and performing manipulations based on date and time. Delays are commonly used to provide a wait time (such as 1 second) during the program execution. Scripting contexts, such as monitoring a task every 5 seconds, demands the understanding of writing delays in a program. This recipe will show you how to work with dates and time delays.

Getting ready

Dates can be printed in variety of formats. We can also set dates from the command line. In Unix-like systems, dates are stored as an integer, which denotes the number of seconds since 1970-01-01 00:00:00 UTC. This is called **epoch** or **Unix time**. Let us see how to read dates and set them.

How to do it...

It is possible to read the dates in different formats and also to set the date. This can be accomplished with these steps:

1. You can read the date as follows:

   ```
   $ date
   ```
   ```
   Thu May 20 23:09:04 IST 2010
   ```

2. The epoch time can be printed as follows:

   ```
   $ date +%s
   ```
   ```
   1290047248
   ```

   We can find out epoch from a given formatted date string. You can use dates in multiple date formats as input. Usually, you don't need to bother about the date string format that you use if you are collecting the date from a system log or any standard application generated output. Convert the date string into epoch as follows:

   ```
   $ date --date "Thu Nov 18 08:07:21 IST 2010" +%s
   ```
   ```
   1290047841
   ```

   The --date option is used to provide a date string as input. However, we can use any date formatting options to print the output. Feeding the input date from a string can be used to find out the weekday, given the date.

   For example:

   ```
   $ date --date "Jan 20 2001" +%A
   ```
   ```
   Saturday
   ```

   The date format strings are listed in the table mentioned in the *How it works...* section:

3. Use a combination of format strings prefixed with + as an argument for the date command to print the date in the format of your choice. For example:

   ```
   $ date "+%d %B %Y"
   ```
   ```
   20 May 2010
   ```

4. We can set the date and time as follows:

   ```
   # date -s "Formatted date string"
   ```

   For example:

   ```
   # date -s "21 June 2009 11:01:22"
   ```

5. Sometimes we need to check the time taken by a set of commands. We can display it using the following code:

```
#!/bin/bash
#Filename: time_take.sh
start=$(date +%s)
commands;
statements;

end=$(date +%s)
difference=$(( end - start))
echo Time taken to execute commands is $difference seconds.
```

 An alternate method would be to use `time <scriptpath>` to get the time that it took to execute the script.

How it works...

While considering dates and time, epoch is defined as the number of seconds that have elapsed since midnight proleptic **Coordinated Universal Time (UTC)** of January 1, 1970, not counting leap seconds. Epoch time is very useful when you need to calculate the difference between two dates or time. You may find out the epoch times for two given timestamps and take the difference between the epoch values. Therefore, you can find out the total number of seconds between two dates.

To write a date format to get the output as required, use the following table:

Date component	Format
Weekday	%a (for example, Sat)
	%A (for example, Saturday)
Month	%b (for example, Nov)
	%B (for example, November)
Day	%d (for example, 31)
Date in format (mm/dd/yy)	%D (for example, 10/18/10)
Year	%y (for example, 10)
	%Y (for example, 2010)
Hour	%I or %H (For example, 08)
Minute	%M (for example, 33)
Second	%S (for example, 10)

Date component	Format
Nano second	%N (for example, 695208515)
Epoch Unix time in seconds	%s (for example, 1290049486)

There's more...

Producing time intervals is very essential when writing monitoring scripts that execute in a loop. Let us see how to generate time delays.

Producing delays in a script

To delay execution in a script for a particular period of time, use sleep:$ sleepno_of_ seconds. For example, the following script counts from 0 to 40 by using tput and sleep:

```bash
#!/bin/bash
#Filename: sleep.sh
echo -n Count:
tput sc

count=0;
while true;
do
    if [ $count -lt 40 ];
    then
        let count++;
        sleep 1;
        tput rc
        tput ed
        echo -n $count;
    else exit 0;
    fi
done
```

In the preceding example, a variable count is initialized to 0 and is incremented on every loop execution. The echo statement prints the text. We use tput sc to store the cursor position. On every loop execution we write the new count in the terminal by restoring the cursor position for the number. The cursor position is restored using tput rc. This clears text from the current cursor position to the end of the line, so that the older number can be cleared and the count can be written. A delay of 1 second is provided in the loop by using the sleep command.

Debugging the script

Debugging is one of the critical features that every programming language should implement to produce race-back information when something unexpected happens. Debugging information can be used to read and understand what caused the program to crash or to act in an unexpected fashion. Bash provides certain debugging options that every sysadmin should know. This recipe shows how to use these.

How to do it...

We can either use Bash's inbuilt debugging tools or write our scripts in such a manner that they become easy to debug, here's how:

1. Add the -x option to enable debug tracing of a shell script as follows:

    ```
    $ bash -x script.sh
    ```

    Running the script with the -x flag will print each source line with the current status. Note that you can also use sh -x script.

2. Debug only portions of the script using set -x and set +x. For example:

    ```
    #!/bin/bash
    #Filename: debug.sh
    for i in {1..6};
    do
        set -x
        echo $i
        set +x
    done
    echo "Script executed"
    ```

    In the preceding script, the debug information for echo $i will only be printed, as debugging is restricted to that section using -x and +x.

3. The aforementioned debugging methods are provided by Bash built-ins. But they always produce debugging information in a fixed format. In many cases, we need debugging information in our own format. We can set up such a debugging style by passing the _DEBUG environment variable.

    Look at the following example code:

    ```
    #!/bin/bash
    function DEBUG()
    {
        [ "$_DEBUG" == "on" ] && $@ || :
    }
    ```

```
for i in {1..10}
do
    DEBUG echo $i
done
```

We can run the above script with debugging set to "on" as follows:

```
$ _DEBUG=on ./script.sh
```

We prefix DEBUG before every statement where debug information is to be printed. If _DEBUG=on is not passed to the script, debug information will not be printed. In Bash, the command : tells the shell to do nothing.

How it works...

The -x flag outputs every line of script as it is executed to stdout. However, we may require only some portions of the source lines to be observed such that commands and arguments are to be printed at certain portions. In such conditions we can use set builtin to enable and disable debug printing within the script.

- ▶ set -x: This displays arguments and commands upon their execution
- ▶ set +x: This disables debugging
- ▶ set -v: This displays input when they are read
- ▶ set +v: This disables printing input

There's more...

We can also use other convenient ways to debug scripts. We can make use of shebang in a trickier way to debug scripts.

Shebang hack

The shebang can be changed from #!/bin/bash to #!/bin/bash -xv to enable debugging without any additional flags (-xv flags themselves).

Functions and arguments

Like any other scripting languages, Bash also supports functions. Let us see how to define and use functions.

How to do it...

We can create functions to perform tasks and we can also create functions that take parameters (also called arguments) as you can see in the following steps:

1. A function can be defined as follows:

```
function fname()
{
    statements;
}
Or alternately,
fname()
{
    statements;
}
```

2. A function can be invoked just by using its name:

```
$ fname ; # executes function
```

3. Arguments can be passed to functions and can be accessed by our script:

```
fname arg1 arg2 ; # passing args
```

Following is the definition of the function `fname`. In the `fname` function, we have included various ways of accessing the function arguments.

```
fname()
{
  echo $1, $2; #Accessing arg1 and arg2
  echo "$@"; # Printing all arguments as list at once
  echo "$*"; # Similar to $@, but arguments taken as single entity
  return 0; # Return value
}
```

Similarly, arguments can be passed to scripts and can be accessed by `script:$0` (the name of the script):

- ❏ $1 is the first argument
- ❏ $2 is the second argument
- ❏ $n is the *n*th argument
- ❏ "$@"expands as "$1" "$2" "$3" and so on
- ❏ "$*" expands as "$1c$2c$3", where c is the first character of IFS
- ❏ "$@" is used more often than "$*"since the former provides all arguments as a single string

There's more...

Let us explore through more tips on Bash functions.

The recursive function

Functions in Bash also support recursion (the function that can call itself). For example, `F ()
{ echo $1; F hello; sleep 1; }`.

Fork bomb

We can write a recursive function, which is basically a function that calls itself:

```
:(){ :|:& };:
```

It infinitely spawns processes and ends up in a denial-of-service attack. `&` is postfixed with the function call to bring the subprocess into the background. This is a dangerous code as it forks processes and, therefore, it is called a fork bomb.

You may find it difficult to interpret the preceding code. See the Wikipedia page `http://en.wikipedia.org/wiki/Fork_bomb` for more details and interpretation of the fork bomb.

It can be prevented by restricting the maximum number of processes that can be spawned from the `config` file at `/etc/security/limits.conf`.

Exporting functions

A function can be exported—like environment variables—using `export`, such that the scope of the function can be extended to subprocesses, as follows:

```
export -f fname
```

Reading the return value (status) of a command

We can get the return value of a command or function in the following way:

```
cmd;
```

```
echo $?;
```

`$?` will give the return value of the command `cmd`.

The return value is called **exit status**. It can be used to analyze whether a command completed its execution successfully or unsuccessfully. If the command exits successfully, the exit status will be zero, otherwise it will be a nonzero value.

We can check whether a command terminated successfully or not by using the following script:

```
#!/bin/bash
#Filename: success_test.sh
CMD="command" #Substitute with command for which you need to test the
exit status
$CMD
if [ $? -eq 0 ];
then
    echo "$CMD executed successfully"
else
    echo "$CMD terminated unsuccessfully"
fi
```

Passing arguments to commands

Arguments to commands can be passed in different formats. Suppose -p and -v are the options available and -k N is another option that takes a number. Also, the command takes a filename as argument. It can be executed in multiple ways as shown:

- ▸ $ command -p -v -k 1 file
- ▸ $ command -pv -k 1 file
- ▸ $ command -vpk 1 file
- ▸ $ command file -pvk 1

Reading the output of a sequence of commands in a variable

One of the best-designed features of shell scripting is the ease of combining many commands or utilities to produce output. The output of one command can appear as the input of another, which passes its output to another command, and so on. The output of this combination can be read in a variable. This recipe illustrates how to combine multiple commands and how its output can be read.

Getting ready

Input is usually fed into a command through stdin or arguments. Output appears as stderr or stdout. While we combine multiple commands, we usually use stdin to give input and stdout to provide an output.

In this context, the commands are called **filters**. We connect each filter using pipes, the piping operator being |. An example is as follows:

```
$ cmd1 | cmd2 | cmd3
```

Here we combine three commands. The output of cmd1 goes to cmd2 and output of cmd2 goes to cmd3 and the final output (which comes out of cmd3) will be printed, or it can be directed to a file.

How to do it...

We typically use pipes and use them with the subshell method for combining outputs of multiple files. Here's how:

1. Let us start with combining two commands:

   ```
   $ ls | cat -n > out.txt
   ```

   Here the output of ls (the listing of the current directory) is passed to cat -n, which in turn puts line numbers to the input received through stdin. Therefore, its output is redirected to the out.txt file.

2. We can read the output of a sequence of commands combined by pipes as follows:

   ```
   cmd_output=$(COMMANDS)
   ```

   This is called **subshell method**. For example:

   ```
   cmd_output=$(ls | cat -n)
   echo $cmd_output
   ```

   Another method, called **back quotes** (some people also refer to it as **back tick**) can also be used to store the command output as follows:

   ```
   cmd_output=`COMMANDS`
   ```

   For example:

   ```
   cmd_output=`ls | cat -n`
   echo $cmd_output
   ```

   Back quote is different from the single-quote character. It is the character on the ~ button in the keyboard.

There's more...

There are multiple ways of grouping commands. Let us go through a few of them.

Spawning a separate process with subshell

Subshells are separate processes. A subshell can be defined using the ( ) operators as follows:

```
pwd;
(cd /bin; ls);
pwd;
```

When some commands are executed in a subshell, none of the changes occur in the current shell; changes are restricted to the subshell. For example, when the current directory in a subshell is changed using the cd command, the directory change is not reflected in the main shell environment.

The pwd command prints the path of the working directory.

The cd command changes the current directory to the given directory path.

Subshell quoting to preserve spacing and the newline character

Suppose we are reading the output of a command to a variable using a subshell or the back quotes method. We always quote them in double quotes to preserve the spacing and newline character (\n). For example:

```
$ cat text.txt
1
2
3


$ out=$(cat text.txt)
$ echo $out
1 2 3 # Lost \n spacing in 1,2,3


$ out="$(cat tex.txt)"
$ echo$out
1
2
3
```

Reading n characters without pressing the return key

`read` is an important Bash command to read text from the keyboard or standard input. We can use `read` to interactively read an input from the user, but `read` is capable of much more. Most of the input libraries in any programming language read the input from the keyboard; but string input termination is done when *return* is pressed. There are certain critical situations when *return* cannot be pressed, but the termination is done based on a number of characters or a single character. For example, in a game, a ball is moved upward when + is pressed. Pressing + and then pressing *return* every time to acknowledge the + press is not efficient. In this recipe we will use the `read` command that provides a way to accomplish this task without having to press *return*.

How to do it...

You can use various options of the `read` command to obtain different results as shown in the following steps:

1. The following statement will read *n* characters from input into the `variable_name` variable:

   ```
   read -n number_of_chars variable_name
   ```

   For example:

   ```
   $ read -n 2 var
   $ echo $var
   ```

2. Read a password in the nonechoed mode as follows:

   ```
   read -s var
   ```

3. Display a message with `read` using:

   ```
   read -p "Enter input:"  var
   ```

4. Read the input after a timeout as follows:

   ```
   read -t timeout var
   ```

   For example:

   ```
   $ read -t 2 var
   #Read the string that is typed within 2 seconds into variable var.
   ```

5. Use a delimiter character to end the input line as follows:

```
read -d delim_char var
```

For example:

```
$ read -d ":" var
hello:#var is set to hello
```

Running a command until it succeeds

When using your shell for everyday tasks, there will be cases where a command might succeed only after some conditions are met, or the operation depends on an external event (such as a file being available to download). In such cases, one might want to run a command repeatedly until it succeeds.

How to do it...

Define a function in the following way:

```
repeat()
{
  while true
  do
    $@ && return
  done
}
```

Or, add this to your shell's `rc` file for ease of use:

```
repeat() { while true; do $@ && return; done }
```

How it works...

We create a function called `repeat` that has an infinite `while` loop, which attempts to run the command passed as a parameter (accessed by $@) to the function. It then returns if the command was successful, thereby exiting the loop.

There's more...

We saw a basic way to run commands until they succeed. Let us see what we can do to make things more efficient.

A faster approach

On most modern systems, true is implemented as a binary in /bin. This means that each time the aforementioned while loop runs, the shell has to spawn a process. To avoid this, we can use the : shell built-in, which always returns an exit code 0:

```
repeat() { while :; do $@ && return; done }
```

Though not as readable, this is certainly faster than the first approach.

Adding a delay

Let's say you are using repeat () to download a file from the Internet which is not available right now, but will be after some time. An example would be:

repeat wget -c http://www.example.com/software-0.1.tar.gz

In the current form, we will be sending too much traffic to the web server at www.example.com, which causes problems to the server (and maybe even to you, if say the server blacklists your IP for spam). To solve this, we can modify the function and add a small delay as follows:

```
repeat() { while :; do $@ && return; sleep 30; done }
```

This will cause the command to run every 30 seconds.

Field separators and iterators

The **internal field separator** (**IFS**) is an important concept in shell scripting. It is very useful while manipulating text data. We will now discuss delimiters that separate different data elements from single data stream. An internal field separator is a delimiter for a special purpose. An internal field separator is an environment variable that stores delimiting characters. It is the default delimiter string used by a running shell environment.

Consider the case where we need to iterate through words in a string or **comma separated values** (**CSV**). In the first case we will use IFS=" " and in the second, IFS=",". Let us see how to do it.

Getting ready

Consider the case of CSV data:

```
data="name,sex,rollno,location"
To read each of the item in a variable, we can use IFS.
oldIFS=$IFS
IFS=, now,
for item in $data;
do
```

```
        echo Item: $item
    done

    IFS=$oldIFS
```

The output is as follows:

Item: name

Item: sex

Item: rollno

Item: location

The default value of IFS is a space component (newline, tab, or a space character).

When IFS is set as , the shell interprets the comma as a delimiter character, therefore, the $item variable takes substrings separated by a comma as its value during the iteration.

If IFS is not set as , then it would print the entire data as a single string.

How to do it...

Let us go through another example usage of IFS by taking the /etc/passwd file into consideration. In the /etc/passwd file, every line contains items delimited by ":". Each line in the file corresponds to an attribute related to a user.

Consider the input: root:x:0:0:root:/root:/bin/bash. The last entry on each line specifies the default shell for the user. To print users and their default shells, we can use the IFS hack as follows:

```
#!/bin/bash
#Desc: Illustration of IFS
line="root:x:0:0:root:/root:/bin/bash"
oldIFS=$IFS;
IFS=":"
count=0
for item in $line;
do

    [ $count -eq 0 ]  && user=$item;
    [ $count -eq 6 ]  && shell=$item;
    let count++
done;
IFS=$oldIFS
echo $user\'s shell is $shell;
```

The output will be:

`root's shell is /bin/bash`

Loops are very useful in iterating through a sequence of values. Bash provides many types of loops. Let us see how to use them:

- Using a `for` loop:

```
for var in list;
do
    commands; # use $var
done
list can be a string, or a sequence.
```

  We can generate different sequences easily.

  `echo {1..50}` can generate a list of numbers from 1 to 50. `echo {a..z}` or `{A..Z}` or `{a..h}` can generate lists of alphabets. Also, by combining these we can concatenate data.

  In the following code, in each iteration, the variable `i` will hold a character in the range `a` to `z`:

```
for i in {a..z}; do actions; done;
```

  The `for` loop can also take the format of the `for` loop in C. For example:

```
for((i=0;i<10;i++))
{
    commands; # Use $i
}
```

- Using a `while` loop:

```
while condition
do
    commands;
done
```

  For an infinite loop, use `true` as the condition.

- Using a `until` loop:

  A special loop called `until` is available with Bash. This executes the loop until the given condition becomes true. For example:

```
x=0;
until [ $x -eq 9 ]; # [ $x -eq 9 ] is the condition
do
    let x++; echo $x;
done
```

Comparisons and tests

Flow control in a program is handled by comparison and test statements. Bash also comes with several options to perform tests that are compatible with the Unix system-level features. We can use `if`, `if else`, and logical operators to perform tests and certain comparison operators to compare data items. There is also a command called `test` available to perform tests. Let us see how to use these.

How to do it...

We will have a look at all the different methods used for comparisons and performing tests:

- Using an `if` condition:

```
if condition;
then
    commands;
fi
```

- Using `else if` and `else`:

```
if condition;
then
    commands;
else if condition; then
    commands;
else
    commands;
fi
```

Nesting is also possible with `if` and `else`. The `if` conditions can be lengthy, to make them shorter we can use logical operators as follows:

- `[ condition ] && action;` # `action` executes if the condition is true
- `[ condition ] || action;` # `action` executes if the condition is false

`&&` is the logical AND operation and `||` is the logical OR operation. This is a very helpful trick while writing Bash scripts.

- Performing mathematical comparisons: Usually conditions are enclosed in square brackets []. Note that there is a space between [or] and operands. It will show an error if no space is provided. An example is as follows:

```
[$var -eq 0 ] or [ $var -eq 0]
```

Performing mathematical conditions over variables or values can be done as follows:

```
[ $var -eq 0 ]  # It returns true when $var equal to 0.
[ $var -ne 0 ] # It returns true when $var is not equal to 0
```

Other important operators are as follows:

- -gt: Greater than
- -lt: Less than
- -ge: Greater than or equal to
- -le: Less than or equal to

Multiple test conditions can be combined as follows:

```
[ $var1 -ne 0 -a $var2 -gt 2 ]  # using and -a
[ $var1 -ne 0 -o var2 -gt 2 ] # OR -o
```

- Filesystem related tests: We can test different filesystem-related attributes using different condition flags as follows:

  - [-f $file_var]: This returns true if the given variable holds a regular file path or filename
  - [-x $var]: This returns true if the given variable holds a file path or filename that is executable
  - [-d $var]: This returns true if the given variable holds a directory path or directory name
  - [-e $var]: This returns true if the given variable holds an existing file
  - [-c $var]: This returns true if the given variable holds the path of a character device file
  - [-b $var]: This returns true if the given variable holds the path of a block device file
  - [-w $var]: This returns true if the given variable holds the path of a file that is writable
  - [-r $var]: This returns true if the given variable holds the path of a file that is readable
  - [-L $var]: This returns true if the given variable holds the path of a symlink

An example of the usage is as follows:

```
fpath="/etc/passwd"
if [ -e $fpath ]; then
    echo File exists;
else
    echo Does not exist;
fi
```

▶ String comparisons: While using string comparison, it is best to use double square brackets, since the use of single brackets can sometimes lead to errors.

Two strings can be compared to check whether they are the same in the following manner:

- ❏ `[[ $str1 = $str2 ]]`: This returns true when `str1` equals `str2`, that is, the text contents of `str1` and `str2` are the same

- ❏ `[[ $str1 == $str2 ]]`: It is an alternative method for string equality check

We can check whether two strings are not the same as follows:

- ❏ `[[ $str1 != $str2 ]]`: This returns true when `str1` and `str2` mismatch

We can find out the alphabetically smaller or larger string as follows:

- ❏ `[[ $str1 > $str2 ]]`: This returns true when `str1` is alphabetically greater than `str2`

- ❏ `[[ $str1 < $str2 ]]`: This returns true when `str1` is alphabetically lesser than `str2`

 Note that a space is provided after and before =, if it is not provided, it is not a comparison, but it becomes an assignment statement.

- ❏ `[[ -z $str1 ]]`: This returns true if `str1` holds an empty string

- ❏ `[[ -n $str1 ]]`: This returns true if `str1` holds a nonempty string

It is easier to combine multiple conditions using logical operators such as `&&` and `||` in the following code:

```
if [[ -n $str1 ]] && [[ -z $str2 ]] ;
then
    commands;
fi
```

For example:

```
str1="Not empty "
str2=""
if [[ -n $str1 ]] && [[ -z $str2 ]];
then
      echo str1 is nonempty and str2 is empty string.
fi
```

Output:

```
str1 is nonempty and str2 is empty string.
```

The test command can be used for performing condition checks. It helps to avoid usage of many braces. The same set of test conditions enclosed within [] can be used for the test command.

For example:

```
if   [ $var -eq 0 ]; then echo "True"; fi
can be written as
if   test $var -eq 0 ; then echo "True"; fi
```

2

Have a Good Command

In this chapter, we will cover:

- ▸ Concatenating with cat
- ▸ Recording and playingback of terminal sessions
- ▸ Finding files and file listing
- ▸ Playing with xargs
- ▸ Translating with tr
- ▸ Checksum and verification
- ▸ Cryptographic tools and hashes
- ▸ Sorting unique and duplicates
- ▸ Temporary file naming and random numbers
- ▸ Splitting files and data
- ▸ Slicing filenames based on extension
- ▸ Renaming and moving files in bulk
- ▸ Spell checking and dictionary manipulation
- ▸ Automating interactive input
- ▸ Making commands quicker by running parallel processes

Introduction

Unix-like systems have the privilege of having the best command-line tools. They help us achieve many tasks making our work easier. While each command has a specific focus, with practice you'll be able to solve complex problems by combining two or more commands. Some frequently used commands are grep, awk, sed, and find.

Mastering the Unix/Linux command line is an art; you will get better at using it as you practice and gain experience. This chapter will introduce you to some of the most interesting and useful commands.

Concatenating with cat

cat is one of the first commands that a command-line warrior must learn. It is usually used to read, display, or concatenate the contents of a file, but cat is capable of more than just that. We even scratch our heads when we need to combine standard input data, as well as data from a file using a single-line command. The regular way of combining the stdin data, as well as file data, is to redirect stdin to a file and then append two files. But we can use the cat command to do it easily in a single invocation. In this recipe we will see basic and advanced usages of cat.

How to do it...

The cat command is a very simple and frequently used command and it stands for concatenate.

The general syntax of cat for reading contents is:

```
$ cat file1 file2 file3 ...
```

This command concatenates data from the files specified as command-line arguments.

- To print contents of a single file:

  ```
  $ cat file.txt
  This is a line inside file.txt
  This is the second line inside file.txt
  ```

- To print contents of more than one file:

  ```
  $ cat one.txt two.txt
  This is line from one.txt
  This is line from two.txt
  ```

How it works...

cat can be used in a variety of ways, let's walk through some of these now.

The cat command can not only read from files and concatenate the data, but can also read the input from the standard input.

To read from the standard input, use a pipe operator as follows:

```
OUTPUT_FROM_SOME COMMANDS | cat
```

Similarly, we can concatenate content from input files along with standard input using `cat`. Combine `stdin` and data from another file, as follows:

```
$ echo 'Text through stdin' | cat - file.txt
```

In this example, - acts as the filename for the `stdin` text.

There's more...

The `cat` command has a few other options for viewing files. Let's go through them.

Getting rid of extra blank lines

Sometimes text files may contain two or more blank lines together. If you need to remove the extra blank lines, use the following syntax:

```
$ cat -s file
```

For example:

```
$ cat multi_blanks.txt
line 1



line2

line3



line4

$ cat -s multi_blanks.txt # Squeeze adjacent blank lines
line 1

line2

line3

line4
```

Alternately, we can remove all blank lines using `tr`, as discussed in the *Translating with tr* recipe in this chapter.

Displaying tabs as ^I

It is hard to distinguish tabs and repeated space characters. While writing programs in languages such as Python, tabs and spaces have different meanings for indentation purposes. Therefore, the use of tab instead of spaces causes problems in indentation. It may become difficult to track where the misplacement of the tab or space occurred by looking through a text editor. `cat` has a feature that can highlight tabs. This is very helpful in debugging indentation errors. Use the `-T` option with `cat` to highlight tab characters as `^I`. An example is as follows:

```
$ cat file.py
def function():
    var = 5
        next = 6
    third = 7


$ cat -T file.py
def function():
^Ivar = 5
        next = 6
^Ithird = 7^I
```

Line numbers

By using the `-n` flag for the `cat` command will output each line with a line number prefixed. It is to be noted that the `cat` command never changes a file; instead it produces an output on `stdout` with modifications to input according to the options provided. For example:

```
$ cat lines.txt
line
line
line


$ cat -n lines.txt
     1 line
     2 line
     3 line
```

-n will make the cat command output line numbers even for blank lines. If you want to skip numbering blank lines, use the -b option.

Recording and playing back of terminal sessions

When you need to show somebody how to do something in the terminal, or you need to prepare a tutorial on how to do something through the command line, you would normally type the commands manually and show them. Or, you could record a screencast and playback the video to them. There are other options for doing this. Using the commands script and scriptreplay, we can record the order and timing of the commands and save the data to text files. Using these files, others can replay and see the output of the commands on the terminal until the playback is complete.

Getting ready

The script and scriptreplay commands are available in most of the GNU/Linux distributions. Recording the terminal sessions to a file will be interesting. You can create tutorials of command-line hacks and tricks to achieve a task by recording the terminal sessions. You can also share the recorded files for others to playback and see how to perform a particular task using the command line.

How to do it...

We can start recording the terminal session using the following commands:

```
$ script -t 2> timing.log -a output.session
type commands;
...
..
exit
```

 Note that this recipe will not work with shells that do not support redirecting only stderr to a file, such as the csh shell.

Two configuration files are passed to the `script` command as arguments. One file is for storing timing information (`timing.log`) at which each of the commands is run, whereas the other file (`output.session`) is used for storing the command output. The `-t` flag is used to dump timing data to `stderr`. Here, you will see, `2>` is used to redirect `stderr` to `timing.log`.

By using the two files, `timing.log` (stores timing information) and `output.session` (stores command output information), we can replay the sequence of command execution as follows:

```
$ scriptreplay timing.log output.session
# Plays the sequence of commands and output
```

How it works...

Usually, we record desktop videos to prepare tutorials. However, videos require considerable amount of storage. On the other hand, a terminal script file is just a text file, usually only in the order of kilobytes.

You can share the `timing.log` and `output.session` files to anyone who wants to replay a terminal session in their terminal.

Finding files and file listing

`find` is one of the great utilities in the Unix/Linux command-line toolbox. It is a very useful command for shell scripts; however, many people do not use it to its fullest effectiveness. This recipe deals with most of the common ways to utilize `find` to locate files.

Getting ready

The `find` command uses the following strategy: `find` descends through a hierarchy of files, matches the files that meet specified criteria, and performs some actions. Let's go through different use cases of `find` and its basic usages.

How to do it...

To list all the files and folders from the current directory to the descending child directories, use the following syntax:

```
$ find base_path
```

`base_path` can be any location from which `find` should start descending (for example, `/home/slynux/`).

An example of this command is as follows:

```
$ find . -print
# Print lists of files and folders
```

`.` specifies current directory and `..` specifies the parent directory. This convention is followed throughout the Unix filesystem.

The `-print` argument specifies to print the names (path) of the matching files. When `-print` is used, `'\n'` will be the delimiting character for separating each file. Also, note that even if you omit `-print`, the `find` command will print the filenames by default.

The `-print0` argument specifies each matching filename printed with the delimiting character `'\0'`. This is useful when a filename contains a space character.

There's more...

In this recipe we have learned the usage of the most commonly-used `find` command with an example. The `find` command is a powerful command-line tool and it is armed with a variety of interesting options. Let us take a look at them.

Search based on filename or regular expression match

The `-name` argument specifies a matching string for the filename. We can pass wildcards as its argument text. The `*.txt` command matches all the filenames ending with `.txt` and prints them. The `-print` option prints the filenames or file paths in the terminal that matches the conditions (for example, `-name`) given as options to the `find` command.

```
$ find /home/slynux -name "*.txt" -print
```

The `find` command has an option `-iname` (ignore case), which is similar to `-name` but it matches filenames while ignoring the case.

For example:

```
$ ls
example.txt  EXAMPLE.txt  file.txt
$ find . -iname "example*" -print
./example.txt
./EXAMPLE.txt
```

If we want to match either of the multiple criteria, we can use OR conditions as shown in the following:

```
$ ls
new.txt   some.jpg   text.pdf
$ find . \( -name "*.txt" -o -name "*.pdf" \) -print
./text.pdf
./new.txt
```

The previous command will print all of the `.txt` and `.pdf` files, since the `find` command matches both `.txt` and `.pdf` files. `\(` and `\)` are used to treat `-name "*.txt" -o -name "*.pdf"` as a single unit.

The `-path` argument can be used to match the file path for files that match the wildcards. `-name` always matches using the given filename. However, `-path` matches the file path as a whole. For example:

```
$ find /home/users -path "*/slynux/*" -print
This will match files as following paths.
/home/users/list/slynux.txt
/home/users/slynux/eg.css
```

 The `-regex` argument is similar to `-path`, but `-regex` matches the file paths based on regular expressions.

Regular expressions are an advanced form of wildcard matching, which enables us to specify text with patterns. By using patterns, we can make matches to the text and print them. A typical example of text matching using regular expressions is: parsing all e-mail addresses from a given pool of text. An e-mail address takes the form `name@host.root`. So, it can be generalized as `[a-z0-9]+@[a-z0-9]+.[a-z0-9]+`. The + sign signifies that the previous class of characters can occur one or more times, repeatedly, in the characters that follow.

The following command matches the `.py` or `.sh` files:

```
$ ls
new.PY   next.jpg   test.py
$ find . -regex ".*\(\.py\|\.sh\)$"
./test.py
```

Similarly, using -iregex ignores the case for the regular expressions that are available.
For example:

```
$ find . -iregex ".*\(\.py\|\.sh\)$"
./test.py
./new.PY
```

 We will learn more about regular expressions in *Chapter 4,
Texting and Driving.

Negating arguments

find can also exclude things that match a pattern using !:

```
$ find . ! -name "*.txt" -print
```

This will match all the files whose names do not end in .txt. The following example shows
the result of the command:

```
$ ls
list.txt   new.PY   new.txt   next.jpg   test.py

$ find . ! -name "*.txt" -print
.
./next.jpg
./test.py
./new.PY
```

Search based on the directory depth

When the find command is used, it recursively walks through all the subdirectories as
much as possible, until it reaches the leaf of the subdirectory tree. We can restrict the
depth to which the find command traverses using some depth parameters given to
find. -maxdepth and -mindepth are the parameters.

In most of the cases, we need to search only in the current directory. It should not further
descend into the subdirectories from the current directory. In such cases, we can restrict the
depth to which the find command should descend using depth parameters. To restrict find
from descending into the subdirectories from the current directory, the depth can be set as 1.
When we need to descend to two levels, the depth is set as 2, and so on for the rest of
the levels.

For specifying the maximum depth we use the -maxdepth level parameter. Similarly, we can also specify the minimum level at which the descending should start. If we want to start searching from the second level onwards, we can set the minimum depth using the -mindepth level parameter. To restrict the find command to descend to a maximum depth of 1, use the following command:

```
$ find . -maxdepth 1 -name "f*" -print
```

This command lists all the files whose names begin with "f", but only from the current directory. If there are subdirectories they are not printed or traversed. Similarly, -maxdepth 2 traverses up to at most two descending levels of subdirectories.

-mindepth is similar to -maxdepth, but it sets the least depth level for the find traversal. It can be used to find and print the files that are located with a minimum level of depth from the base path. For example, to print all the files whose names begin with "f", and are at least two subdirectories distant from the current directory, use the following command:

```
$ find . -mindepth 2 -name "f*" -print
./dir1/dir2/file1
./dir3/dir4/f2
```

Even if there are files in the current directory or dir1 and dir3, it will not be printed.

> -maxdepth and -mindepth should be specified as the third argument to the find command. If they are specified as the fourth or further arguments, it may affect the efficiency of find as it has to do unnecessary checks (for example, if -maxdepth is specified as the fourth argument and -type as the third argument, the find command first finds out all the files having the specified -type and then finds all of the matched files having the specified depth. However, if the depth were specified as the third argument and -type as the fourth, find could collect all the files having at most the specified depth and then check for the file type, which is the most efficient way to search.

Search based on file type

Unix-like operating systems treat every object as a file. There are different kinds of files, such as regular file, directory, character devices, block devices, symlinks, hardlinks, sockets, FIFO, and so on.

The file search can be filtered out using the -type option. By using -type, we can specify to the find command that it should only match files having a specified type.

List only directories including descendants as follows:

```
$ find . -type d -print
```

It is hard to list directories and files separately. But find helps to do it. List only regular files as follows:

```
$ find . -type f -print
```

List only symbolic links as follows:

```
$ find . -type l -print
```

You can use the type arguments from the following table to properly match the required file type:

File type	Type argument
Regular file	f
Symbolic link	l
Directory	d
Character special device	c
Block device	b
Socket	s
FIFO	p

Search on file times

Unix/Linux filesystems have three types of timestamps on each file. They are as follows:

- **Access time** (-atime): It is the last timestamp of when the file was accessed by a user
- **Modification time** (-mtime): It is the last timestamp of when the file content was modified
- **Change time** (-ctime): It is the last timestamp of when the metadata for a file (such as permissions or ownership) was modified

 There is no such thing as creation time in Unix.

-atime, -mtime, and -ctime are the time parameter options available with find. They can be specified with integer values in "number of days". These integer values are often attached with - or + signs. The - sign implies less than, whereas the + sign implies greater than. For example:

- ▸ Print all the files that were accessed within the last seven days as follows:

  `$ find . -type f -atime -7 -print`

- ▸ Print all the files that are having access time exactly seven-days old as follows:

  `$ find . -type f -atime 7 -print`

- ▸ Print all the files that have an access time older than seven days as follows:

  `$ find . -type f -atime +7 -print`

Similarly, we can use the -mtime parameter for search files based on the modification time and -ctime for search based on the change time.

-atime, -mtime, and -ctime are time-based parameters that use the time metric in days. There are some other time-based parameters that use the time metric in minutes. These are as follows:

- ▸ -amin (access time)
- ▸ -mmin (modification time)
- ▸ -cmin (change time)

For example:

To print all the files that have an access time older than seven minutes, use the following command:

`$ find . -type f -amin +7 -print`

Another good feature available with find is the -newer parameter. By using -newer, we can specify a reference file to compare with the timestamp. We can find all the files that are newer (older modification time) than the specified file with the -newer parameter.

For example, find all the files that have a modification time greater than that of the modification time of a given file.txt file as follows:

`$ find . -type f -newer file.txt -print`

Timestamp manipulation flags for the find command are very useful for writing the system backup and maintenance scripts.

Search based on file size

Based on the file sizes of the files, a search can be performed as follows:

```
$ find . -type f -size +2k
# Files having size greater than 2 kilobytes
```

```
$ find . -type f -size -2k
# Files having size less than 2 kilobytes
```

```
$ find . -type f -size 2k
# Files having size 2 kilobytes
```

Instead of `k` we can use different size units such as the following:

- `b`: 512 byte blocks
- `c`: Bytes
- `w`: Two-byte words
- `k`: Kilobyte (1024 bytes)
- `M`: Megabyte (1024 kilobytes)
- `G`: Gigabyte (1024 megabytes)

Deleting based on the file matches

The `-delete` flag can be used to remove files that are matched by `find`.

Remove all the `.swp` files from the current directory as follows:

```
$ find . -type f -name "*.swp" -delete
```

Match based on the file permissions and ownership

It is possible to match files based on the file permissions. We can list out the files having specified file permissions as follows:

```
$ find . -type f -perm 644 -print
# Print files having permission 644
```

`-perm` specifies that `find` should only match files with their permission set to a particular value. Permissions are explained in more detail in the *File permissions, ownership, and the sticky bit* in *Chapter 3, File In, File Out*.

As an example usage case, we can consider the case of the Apache web server. The PHP files in the web server require proper permissions to execute. We can find out the PHP files that don't have proper execute permissions as follows:

```
$ find . -type f -name "*.php" ! -perm 644 -print
```

We can also search files based on ownership of the files. The files owned by a specific user can be found out using the `-user USER` option.

The `USER` argument can be a username or UID.

For example, to print the list of all files owned by the user `slynux`, you can use the following command:

```
$ find . -type f -user slynux -print
```

Executing commands or actions with find

The `find` command can be coupled with many of the other commands using the `-exec` option. It is one of the most powerful features that comes with `find`.

Consider the example in the previous section. We used `-perm` to find out the files that do not have proper permissions. Similarly, in the case where we need to change the ownership of all files owned by a certain user (for example, `root`) to another user (for example, `www-data`, the default Apache user in the web server), we can find all the files owned by root by using the `-user` option and using `-exec` to perform the ownership change operation.

 You must run the `find` command as root if you want to change ownership of files or directories.

Let's have a look at the following example:

```
# find . -type f -user root -exec chown slynux {} \;
```

In this command, { } is a special string used with the `-exec` option. For each file match, { } will be replaced with the filename for `-exec`. For example, if the `find` command finds two files `test1.txt` and `test2.txt` with owner `slynux`, the `find` command will perform:

```
chown slynux {}
```

This gets resolved to `chown slynux test1.txt` and `chown slynux test2.txt`.

 Sometimes we don't want to run the command for each file. Instead, we might want to run it a fewer times with a list of files as parameters. For this, we use + instead of ; in the `exec` syntax.

Another usage example is to concatenate all the C program files in a given directory and write it to a single file, say, `all_c_files.txt`. We can use `find` to match all the C files recursively and use the `cat` command with the `-exec` flag as follows:

```
$ find . -type f -name "*.c" -exec cat {} \;>all_c_files.txt
```

`-exec` is followed by any command. `{}` is a match. For every matched filename, `{}` is replaced with the filename.

To redirect the data from `find` to the `all_c_files.txt` file, we have used the `>` operator instead of `>>` (append) because the entire output from the `find` command is a single data stream (`stdin`). `>>` is necessary only when multiple data streams are to be appended to a single file.

For example, to copy all the `.txt` files that are older than 10 days to a directory `OLD`, use the following command:

```
$ find . -type f -mtime +10 -name "*.txt" -exec cp {} OLD  \;
```

Similarly, the `find` command can be coupled with many other commands.

> **-exec with multiple commands**
>
> We cannot use multiple commands along with the `-exec` parameter. It accepts only a single command, but we can use a trick. Write multiple commands in a shell script (for example, `commands.sh`) and use it with `-exec` as follows:
>
> `-exec ./commands.sh {} \;`

`-exec` can be coupled with `printf` to produce a very useful output. For example:

```
$ find . -type f -name "*.txt" -exec printf "Text file: %s\n" {} \;
```

Skipping specified directories when using the find command

Skipping certain subdirectories for performance improvement is sometimes required while doing a directory search and performing an action. For example, when programmers look for particular files on a development source tree, which is under the version control system such as Git, the source hierarchy will always contain the `.git` directory in each of the subdirectories (`.git` stores version-control-related information for every directory). Since version-control-related directories do not produce useful output, they should be excluded from the search. The technique of excluding files and directories from the search is known as **pruning**. It can be performed as follows:

```
$ find devel/source_path  \( -name ".git" -prune \) -o \( -type f -print
\)

# Instead of \( -type -print \), use required filter.
```

The preceding command prints the name (path) of all the files that are not from the `.git` directories.

Here, `\( -name ".git" -prune \)` is the exclude portion, which specifies that the `.git` directory should be excluded and `\( -type f -print \)` specifies the action to be performed. The actions to be performed are placed in the second block `-type f -print` (the action specified here is to print the names and path of all the files).

Playing with xargs

We use pipes to redirect `stdout` (standard output) of a command to `stdin` (standard input) of another command. For example:

```
cat foo.txt | grep "test"
```

Some of the commands accept data as command-line arguments rather than a data stream through `stdin` (standard input). In that case, we cannot use pipes to supply data through command-line arguments.

We should try alternate methods. `xargs` is a command that is very helpful in handling standard input data to the command-line argument conversions. It can manipulate `stdin` and convert to command-line arguments for the specified command. Also, `xargs` can convert any one-line or multiple-line text inputs into other formats, such as multiple lines (specified number of columns) or a single line and vice versa.

All Bash users love one-liner commands, which are command sequences that are joined by using the pipe operator, but do not use the semicolon terminator (`;`) between the commands used. Crafting one-line commands makes tasks more efficient and simpler to solve. It requires proper understanding and practice to formulate one-liners for solving text processing problems. `xargs` is one of the important components for building one-liner commands.

Getting ready

When using the pipe operator, the `xargs` command should always be the first thing to appear after the operator. `xargs` uses standard input as the primary data stream source. It uses `stdin` and executes another command by providing command-line arguments for that executing command using the `stdin` data source. For example:

```
command | xargs
```

How to do it...

The `xargs` command can supply arguments to a command by reformatting the data received through `stdin`.

xargs can act as a substitute that can perform similar actions as the -exec argument in the case of the find command. Let's see a variety of hacks that can be performed using the xargs command.

- ▸ **Converting multiple lines of input to a single-line output**: Multiple-line input can be converted simply by removing the newline character and replacing with the " " (space) character. '\n' is interpreted as a newline character, which is the delimiter for the lines. By using xargs, we can ignore all the newlines with space so that multiple lines can be converted into a single-line text as follows:

```
$ cat example.txt # Example file

1 2 3 4 5 6

7 8 9 10

11 12


$ cat example.txt | xargs

1 2 3 4 5 6 7 8 9 10 11 12
```

- ▸ **Converting single-line into multiple-line output**: Given a maximum number of arguments in a line = n, we can split any stdin (standard input) text into lines of n arguments each. An argument is a piece of a string delimited by " " (space). Space is the default delimiter. A single line can be split into multiple lines as follows:

```
$ cat example.txt | xargs -n 3

1 2 3

4 5 6

7 8 9

10 11 12
```

How it works...

The xargs command is appropriate to be applied to many problem scenarios with its many options. Let's see how these options can be used wisely to solve problems.

We can also use our own delimiter towards separating arguments. To specify a custom delimiter for input, use the -d option as follows:

```
$ echo "splitXsplitXsplitXsplit" | xargs -d X

split split split split
```

In the preceding code, stdin contains a string consisting of multiple X characters. We can use X as the input delimiter by using it with -d. Here, we have explicitly specified X as the input delimiter, whereas in the default case xargs takes the **internal field separator** (space) as the input delimiter.

By using -n along with the previous command, we can split the input into multiple lines having two words each as follows:

```
$ echo "splitXsplitXsplitXsplit" | xargs -d X -n 2
split split
split split
```

There's more...

We have learned how to format stdin to different output as arguments from the previous examples. Now, let's learn how to supply this formatted output as arguments to commands.

Passing formatted arguments to a command by reading stdin

Write a small custom echo script for better understanding of example usages with xargs to provide command arguments:

```
#!/bin/bash
#Filename: cecho.sh

echo $*'#'
```

When arguments are passed to the cecho.sh shell, it will print the arguments terminated by the # character. For example:

```
$ ./cecho.sh arg1 arg2
arg1 arg2 #
```

Let's have a look at a problem:

- I have a list of arguments in a file (one argument in each line) to be provided to a command (say, cecho.sh). I need to provide arguments in two methods. In the first method, I need to provide one argument each for the command as follows:

  ```
  ./cecho.sh arg1
  ./cecho.sh arg2
  ./cecho.sh arg3
  ```

  Or, alternately, I need to provide two or three arguments each for each execution of the command. For two arguments each, it would be similar to the following:

  ```
  ./cecho.sh arg1 arg2
  ./cecho.sh arg3
  ```

- In the second method, I need to provide all arguments at once to the command as follows:

  ```
  ./cecho.sh arg1 arg2 arg3
  ```

Run the preceding commands and note the output before going through the following section.

These problems can be solved using `xargs`. We have the list of arguments in a file called `args.txt`. The contents are as follows:

```
$ cat args.txt
arg1
arg2
arg3
```

For the first problem, we can execute the command multiple times with one argument per execution, therefore, use:

```
$ cat args.txt | xargs -n 1 ./cecho.sh
arg1 #
arg2 #
arg3 #
```

For executing a command with X arguments per each execution, use:

```
    INPUT | xargs -n X
```

For example:

```
$ cat args.txt | xargs -n 2 ./cecho.sh
arg1 arg2 #
arg3 #
```

For the second problem, in order to execute the command at once with all the arguments, use:

```
$ cat args.txt | xargs ./ccat.sh
arg1 arg2 arg3 #
```

In the preceding examples, we have supplied command-line arguments directly to a specific command (for example, `cecho.sh`). We could only supply the arguments from the `args.txt` file. However, in real time, we may also need to add a constant parameter with the command (for example, `cecho.sh`), along with the arguments taken from `args.txt`. Consider the following example with the format:

```
    ./cecho.sh -p arg1 -l
```

In the preceding command execution `arg1` is the only variable text. All others should remain constant. We should read arguments from a file (`args.txt`) and supply it as:

```
    ./cecho.sh -p arg1 -l
    ./cecho.sh -p arg2 -l
    ./cecho.sh -p arg3 -l
```

To provide a command execution sequence as shown, `xargs` has an option `-I`. By using `-I`, we can specify a replacement string that will be replaced while `xargs` expands. When `-I` is used with `xargs`, it will execute as one command execution per argument.

Let's do it as follows:

```
$ cat args.txt | xargs -I {} ./cecho.sh -p {} -1
-p arg1 -1 #
-p arg2 -1 #
-p arg3 -1 #
```

`-I {}` specifies the replacement string. For each of the arguments supplied for the command, the `{}` string will be replaced with arguments read through `stdin`.

When used with `-I`, the command is executed in a loop. When there are three arguments the command is executed three times along with the command `{}`. Each time `{}` is replaced with arguments one by one.

Using xargs with find

`xargs` and `find` are best friends. They can be combined to perform tasks easily. Usually, people combine them in the wrong way. For example:

```
$ find . -type f -name "*.txt"  -print | xargs rm -f
```

This is dangerous. It may sometimes cause removal of unnecessary files. Here, we cannot predict the delimiting character (whether it is `'\n'` or `' '`) for the output of the `find` command. Many of the filenames may contain a space character (`' '`) and hence, `xargs` may misinterpret it as a delimiter (for example, `"hell text.txt"` is misinterpreted by `xargs` as `"hell"` and `"text.txt"`).

Hence, we must use `-print0` along with `find` to produce an output with a delimited character null (`'\0'`) whenever we use the `find` output as the `xargs` input.

Let's use `find` to match and list of all the `.txt` files and remove them using `xargs`:

```
$ find . -type f -name "*.txt" -print0 | xargs -0 rm -f
```

This removes all `.txt` files. `xargs -0` interprets that the delimiting character is `\0`.

Counting the number of lines of C code in a source code directory

This is a task most programmers do, that is, counting all C program files for **Lines of Code** (**LOC**). The code for this task is as follows:

```
$ find source_code_dir_path -type f -name "*.c" -print0 | xargs -0 wc -1
```

If you want more statistics about your source code, there is a utility called **SLOCCount**, which is very useful. Modern GNU/Linux distributions usually have packages or you can get it from `http://www.dwheeler.com/sloccount/`.

While and subshell trick with stdin

`xargs` is restricted to providing arguments in limited ways to supply arguments. Also, `xargs` cannot supply arguments to multiple sets of commands. For executing commands with collected arguments from the standard input, we have a very flexible method. A subshell with a `while` loop can be used to read arguments and execute commands in a trickier way as follows:

```
$ cat files.txt  | ( while read arg; do cat $arg; done )
# Equivalent to cat files.txt | xargs -I {} cat {}
```

Here, by replacing `cat $arg` with any number of commands using a `while` loop, we can perform many command actions with the same arguments. We can also pass the output to other commands without using pipes. Subshell ( ) tricks can be used in a variety of problematic environments. When enclosed within subshell operators, it acts as a single unit with multiple commands inside, like so:

```
$ cmd0 | ( cmd1;cmd2;cmd3) | cmd4
```

If `cmd1` is `cd /`, within the subshell, the path of the working directory changes. However, this change resides inside the subshell only. `cmd4` will not see the directory change.

Translating with tr

`tr` is a small and beautiful command in the Unix command-warrior toolkit. It is one of the important commands frequently used to craft beautiful one-liner commands. It can be used to perform substitution of characters, deletion of the characters, and squeezing of repeated characters from the standard input. It is often called **translate**, since it can translate a set of characters to another set. In this recipe we will see how to use `tr` to perform basic translation between sets.

Getting ready

`tr` accepts input only through `stdin` (standard input) and cannot accept input through command-line arguments. It has the following invocation format:

```
tr [options] set1 set2
```

Input characters from `stdin` are mapped from `set1` to `set2` and the output is written to `stdout` (standard output). `set1` and `set2` are character classes or a set of characters. If the length of sets is unequal, `set2` is extended to the length of `set1` by repeating the last character, or else, if the length of `set2` is greater than that of `set1`, all the characters exceeding the length of `set1` are ignored from `set2`.

How to do it...

To perform translation of characters in the input from uppercase to lowercase, use the following command:

```
$ echo "HELLO WHO IS THIS" | tr 'A-Z' 'a-z'
```

`'A-Z'` and `'a-z'` are the sets. We can specify custom sets as needed by appending characters or character classes.

`'ABD-}'`, `'aA.,'`, `'a-ce-x'`, `'a-c0-9'`, and so on are valid sets. We can define sets easily. Instead of writing continuous character sequences, we can use the `'startchar-endchar'` format. It can also be combined with any other characters or character classes. If `startchar-endchar` is not a valid continuous character sequence, they are then taken as a set of three characters (for example, `startchar`, `-`, and `endchar`). You can also use special characters such as `'\t'`, `'\n'`, or any ASCII characters.

How it works...

By using `tr` with the concept of sets, we can map characters from one set to another set easily. Let's go through an example on how to use `tr` for encrypting and decrypting numeric characters:

```
$ echo 12345 | tr '0-9' '9876543210'
87654 #Encrypted
```

```
$ echo 87654 | tr '9876543210' '0-9'
12345 #Decrypted
```

Let's look at another interesting example.

ROT13 is a well-known encryption algorithm. In the ROT13 scheme, the same function is used to encrypt and decrypt text. The ROT13 scheme performs alphabetic rotation of characters for 13 characters. Let's perform ROT13 using `tr` as follows:

```
$ echo "tr came, tr saw, tr conquered." | tr 'a-zA-Z' 'n-za-mN-ZA-M'
```

The output will be:

```
ge pnzr, ge fnj, ge pbadhrerq.
```

By sending the encrypted text again to the same ROT13 function, we get:

```
$ echo ge pnzr, ge fnj, ge pbadhrerq. | tr 'a-zA-Z' 'n-za-mN-ZA-M'
```

The output will be:

```
tr came, tr saw, tr conquered.
```

`tr` can be used to convert tab characters into space as follows:

```
$ tr '\t' ' ' < file.txt
```

There's more...

We saw some basic translations using the `tr` command. Let's see what else can `tr` help us achieve.

Deleting characters using tr

`tr` has an option `-d` to delete a set of characters that appear on `stdin` by using the specified set of characters to be deleted as follows:

```
$ cat file.txt | tr -d '[set1]'
#Only set1 is used, not set2
```

For example:

```
$ echo "Hello 123 world 456" | tr -d '0-9'
Hello world
# Removes the numbers from stdin and print
```

Complementing character set

We can use a set to complement `set1` by using the `-c` flag. `set2` is optional in the following command:

```
tr -c [set1] [set2]
```

The complement of `set1` means that it is the set having all the characters except characters in `set1`.

The best usage example is to delete all the characters from the input text except the ones specified in the complement set. For example:

```
$ echo hello 1 char 2 next 4 | tr -d -c '0-9 \n'
 1  2  4
```

Here, the complement set is the set containing all numerals, space characters, and newline characters. All other characters are removed since `-d` is used with `tr`.

Squeezing characters with tr

The `tr` command is very helpful in many text-processing contexts. Repeated continuous characters should be squeezed to a single character in many circumstances. Squeezing of whitespace is a frequently occurring task.

`tr` provides the `-s` option to squeeze repeating characters from the input. It can be performed as follows:

```
$ echo "GNU is        not        UNIX. Recursive    right ?" | tr -s ' '
GNU is not UNIX. Recursive right ?
# tr -s '[set]'
```

Let's use `tr` in a tricky way to add a given list of numbers from a file as follows:

```
$ cat sum.txt
1
2
3
4
5


$ cat sum.txt | echo $[ $(tr '\n' '+' ) 0 ]
15
```

How does this hack work?

Here, the `tr` command is used to replace `'\n'` with the `'+'` character, hence we form the string `"1+2+3+..5+"`, but at the end of the string we have an extra + operator. In order to nullify the effect of the + operator, 0 is appended.

`$[ operation ]` performs a numeric operation. Hence, it forms the string as follows:

```
echo $[ 1+2+3+4+5+0 ]
```

If we use a loop to perform the addition by reading numbers from a file, it would take a few lines of code. Here a one-liner does the trick.

`tr` can also be used in this way to get rid of extra newlines as follows:

```
$ cat multi_blanks.txt | tr -s '\n'
line 1
line2
line3
line4
```

In the preceding usage of `tr`, it removes the extra `'\n'` characters into a single `'\n'` (newline character).

Character classes

`tr` can use different character classes as sets. The different classes are as follows:

- `alnum`: Alphanumeric characters
- `alpha`: Alphabetic characters
- `cntrl`: Control (nonprinting) characters
- `digit`: Numeric characters
- `graph`: Graphic characters
- `lower`: Lowercase alphabetic characters
- `print`: Printable characters
- `punct`: Punctuation characters
- `space`: Whitespace characters
- `upper`: Uppercase characters
- `xdigit`: Hexadecimal characters

We can select the required classes and use them as follows:

```
tr [:class:] [:class:]
```

For example:

```
tr '[:lower:]' '[:upper:]'
```

Checksum and verification

Checksum programs are used to generate checksum key strings from the files and verify the integrity of the files later by using that checksum string. A file might be distributed over the network or any storage media to different destinations. Due to many reasons, there are chances of the file being corrupted due to a few bits missing during the data transfer by different reasons. These errors happen most often while downloading the files from the Internet, transferring through a network, CD-ROM damage, and so on.

Hence, we need to know whether the received file is the correct one or not by applying some kind of test. The special key string that is used for this file integrity test is known as a **checksum**.

We calculate the checksum for the original file as well as the received file. By comparing both of the checksums, we can verify whether the received file is the correct one or not. If the checksums (calculated from the original file at the source location and the one calculated from the destination) are equal, it means that we have received the correct file without causing any erroneous data loss during the data transfer. Otherwise, the user has to repeat the data transfer and try the checksum comparison again.

Checksums are crucial while writing backup scripts or maintenance scripts that transfer files through the network. By using checksum verification, files corrupted during the data transfer over the network can be identified and those files can be resent again from the source to the destination.

In this recipe we will see how to compute checksums to verify integrity of data.

Getting ready

The most famous and widely used checksum techniques are **md5sum** and **SHA-1**. They generate checksum strings by applying the corresponding algorithm to the file content. Let's see how we can generate a checksum from a file and verify the integrity of that file.

How to do it...

To compute the md5sum, use the following command:

```
$ md5sum filename
68b329da9893e34099c7d8ad5cb9c940 filename
```

md5sum is a 32-character hexadecimal string as given.

We redirect the checksum output into a file and use that MD5 file for verification as follows:

```
$ md5sum filename > file_sum.md5
```

How it works...

The syntax for the md5sum checksum calculation is as follows:

```
$ md5sum file1 file2 file3 ..
```

When multiple files are used, the output will contain a checksum for each of the files having one checksum string per line, as follows:

```
[checksum1]    file1
[checksum1]    file2
[checksum1]    file3
```

The integrity of a file can be verified by using the generated file as follows:

```
$ md5sum -c file_sum.md5
# It will output a message whether checksum matches or not
```

Or, alternately, if we need to check all the files using all `.md5` information available, use:

```
$ md5sum -c *.md5
```

SHA-1 is another commonly used checksum algorithm like md5sum. It generates a 40-character hex code from a given input file. The command used for calculating an SHA-1 string is `sha1sum`. Its usage is very similar to that of `md5sum`. Simply replace `md5sum` with `sha1sum` in all the commands previously mentioned. Instead of `file_sum.md5`, change the output filename to `file_sum.sha1`.

Checksum verification is very useful to verify the integrity of files that we download from the Internet. For example, ISO images are very susceptible to erroneous bits. A few wrong bits in the wrong location and the ISO may not be useable. Therefore, to check whether we received the file correctly, checksums are widely used. For the same file data the checksum program will always produce the same checksum string:

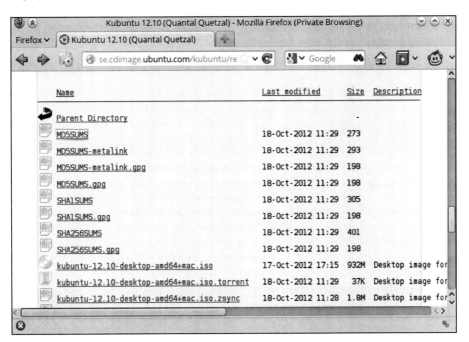

This is the md5sum checksum that is created:

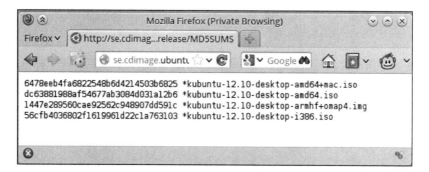

Checksums are also useful when used with a number of files. Let us see how to apply checksums to a collection of files and verify correctness.

Checksum for directories

Checksums are calculated for files. Calculating the checksum for a directory would mean that we would need to calculate the checksums for all the files in the directory, recursively.

It can be achieved by the `md5deep` or `sha1deep` command. Install the `md5deep` package to make these commands available. An example of this command is as follows:

```
$ md5deep -rl directory_path > directory.md5
# -r to enable recursive traversal
# -l for using relative path. By default it writes absolute file path in
output
```

Alternately, use a combination of `find` to calculate checksums recursively:

```
$ find directory_path -type f -print0 | xargs -0 md5sum >> directory.md5
```

To verify, use the following command:

```
$ md5sum -c directory.md5
```

Cryptographic tools and hashes

Encryption techniques are used mainly to protect data from unauthorized access. There are many algorithms available and we have discussed the most commonly used ones. There are a few tools available in a Linux environment for performing encryption and decryption. Sometimes we use encryption algorithm hashes for verifying data integrity. This section will introduce a few commonly used cryptographic tools and a general set of algorithms that these tools can handle.

How to do it...

Let us see how to use tools such as `crypt`, `gpg`, `base64`, `md5sum`, `sha1sum`, and `openssl`:

- ► The `crypt` command is a simple and relatively insecure cryptographic utility that takes a file from `stdin` and a passphrase as input and output encrypted data into `stdout` (and, hence, we use redirection for the input and output files):

    ```
    $ crypt <input_file >output_file
    Enter passphrase:
    ```

    It will interactively ask for a passphrase. We can also provide a passphrase through command-line arguments:

    ```
    $ crypt PASSPHRASE <input_file >encrypted_file
    ```

    In order to decrypt the file, use:

    ```
    $ crypt PASSPHRASE -d <encrypted_file >output_file
    ```

- ► `gpg` (GNU privacy guard) is a widely used tool for protecting files with encryption that ensures that data is not read until it reaches its intended destination. Here we discuss how to encrypt and decrypt a file.

 gpg signatures are also widely used in e-mail communications to "sign" e-mail messages, proving the authenticity of the sender.

    In order to encrypt a file with `gpg` use:

    ```
    $ gpg -c filename
    ```

    This command reads the passphrase interactively and generates `filename.gpg`. In order to decrypt a `gpg` file use:

    ```
    $ gpg filename.gpg
    ```

    This command reads a passphrase and decrypts the file.

 We don't cover gpg in much detail in this book. If you're interested in more information, please see `http://en.wikipedia.org/wiki/GNU_Privacy_Guard`.

- Base64 is a group of similar encoding schemes that represents binary data in an ASCII string format by translating it into a radix-64 representation. The `base64` command can be used to encode and decode the Base64 string. In order to encode a binary file into the Base64 format, use:

```
$ base64 filename > outputfile
```

Or:

```
$ cat file | base64 > outputfile
```

It can read from `stdin`.

Decode Base64 data as follows:

```
$ base64 -d file > outputfile
```

Or:

```
$ cat base64_file | base64 -d > outputfile
```

- **md5sum** and **SHA-1** are unidirectional hash algorithms, which cannot be reversed to form the original data. These are usually used to verify the integrity of data or for generating a unique key from a given data:

```
$ md5sum file
8503063d5488c3080d4800ff50850dc9  file
```

```
$ sha1sum file
1ba02b66e2e557fede8f61b7df282cd0a27b816b  file
```

These types of hashes are commonly used for storing passwords. Passwords are stored as their hashes and when a user wants to authenticate, the password is read and converted to the hash. Then, this hash is compared to the one that is stored already. If they are the same, the password is authenticated and access is provided, otherwise it is denied. Storing plain text password strings is risky and poses a security risk.

Although commonly used, md5sum and SHA-1 are no longer considered secure. This is because of the rise of computing power in recent times that makes it easier to crack them. It is recommended to use tools such as bcrypt or sha512sum instead. Read more about this at `http://codahale.com/how-to-safely-store-a-password/`.

► **Shadow-like hash (salted hash)**

Let us see how to generate a shadow-like salted hash for passwords. The user passwords in Linux are stored as their hashes in the `/etc/shadow` file. A typical line in `/etc/shadow` will look like this:

```
test:$6$fG4eWdUi$ohTKOlEUzNk77.4S8MrYe07NTRV4M3LrJnZP9p.qc1bR5c.
EcOruzPXfEu1uloBFUa18ENRH7F70zhodas3cR.:14790:0:99999:7:::
```

`6fG4eWdUi$ohTKOlEUzNk77.4S8MrYe07NTRV4M3LrJnZP9p.qc1bR5c.
EcOruzPXfEu1uloBFUa18ENRH7F70zhodas3cR` is the shadow hash corresponding to its password.

In some situations, we may need to write critical administration scripts that may need to edit passwords or add users manually using a shell script. In that case we have to generate a shadow password string and write a similar line as the preceding one to the shadow file. Let's see how to generate a shadow password using `openssl`.

Shadow passwords are usually salted passwords. SALT is an extra string used to obfuscate and make the encryption stronger. The salt consists of random bits that are used as one of the inputs to a key derivation function that generates the salted hash for the password.

For more details on salt, see the Wikipedia page `http://en.wikipedia.org/wiki/Salt_(cryptography)`.

```
$ opensslpasswd -1 -salt SALT_STRING PASSWORD
$1$SALT_STRING$323VkWkSLHuhbt1zkSsUG.
```

Replace `SALT_STRING` with a random string and `PASSWORD` with the password you want to use.

Sorting unique and duplicates

Sorting is a common task that we can encounter with text files. The `sort` command helps us to perform sort operations over text files and `stdin`. Most often, it can also be coupled with many other commands to produce the required output. `uniq` is another command that is often used along with a `sort` command. It helps to extract unique (or duplicate) lines from a text or `stdin`. This recipe illustrates most of the use cases with `sort` and `uniq` commands.

Getting ready

The `sort` command accepts input as filenames, as well as from `stdin` (standard input) and outputs the result by writing into `stdout`. The same applies to the `uniq` command.

How to do it...

1. We can easily sort a given set of files (for example, `file1.txt` and `file2.txt`) as follows:

   ```
   $ sort file1.txt file2.txt > sorted.txt
   ```

   Or:

   ```
   $ sort file1.txt file2.txt -o sorted.txt
   ```

2. For a numerical sort, we can use:

   ```
   $ sort -n file.txt
   ```

3. To sort in the reverse order, we can use:

   ```
   $ sort -r file.txt
   ```

4. For sorting by months (in the order Jan, Feb, March,...), use:

   ```
   $ sort -M months.txt
   ```

5. To merge two already sorted files, use:

   ```
   $ sort -m sorted1 sorted2
   ```

6. To find the unique lines from a sorted file, use:

   ```
   $ sort file1.txt file2.txt | uniq
   ```

7. To check if a file has already been sorted, use:

   ```
   #!/bin/bash
   #Desc: Sort
   sort -C filename ;
   if [ $? -eq 0 ]; then
      echo Sorted;
   else
      echo Unsorted;
   fi
   ```

   Replace `filename` with the file you want to check and run the script.

How it works...

As shown in the examples, `sort` takes numerous parameters that can be used to sort the data in files in different ways. Furthermore, it is useful when using the `uniq` command, which expects its input to be sorted.

There are numerous scenarios where the `sort` and `uniq` commands can be used. Let's go through the various options and usage techniques.

For checking if a file is already sorted or not, we exploit the fact that `sort` returns an exit code (`$?`) of 0 if the file is sorted and nonzero otherwise.

There's more...

These were some basic usages of the `sort` command. Let us see some ways of using it to accomplish complex tasks:

Sorting according to the keys or columns

We can use a column with sort if we need to sort a text as follows:

```
$ cat data.txt
1   mac     2000
2   winxp     4000
3   bsd     1000
4   linux     1000
```

We can sort this in many ways; currently it is numeric, sorted by the serial number (the first column). We can also sort by the second column and the third column.

`-k` specifies the key by which the sort is to be performed. Key is the column number by which sort is to be done. `-r` specifies the sort command to sort in the reverse order. For example:

```
# Sort reverse by column1
$ sort -nrk 1  data.txt
4   linux     1000
3   bsd     1000
2   winxp     4000
1   mac     2000
# -nr means numeric and reverse

# Sort by column 2
$ sort -k 2  data.txt
```

```
3   bsd     1000
4   linux   1000
1   mac     2000
2   winxp   4000
```

 Always be careful about the -n option for numeric sort. The `sort` command treats alphabetical sort and numeric sort differently. Hence, in order to specify numeric sort the -n option should be provided.

Usually, by default, keys are columns in the text file. Columns are separated by space characters. But, in certain circumstances, we may need to specify keys as a group of characters in the given character number range (for example, `key1 = character4-character8`). In such cases where keys are to be specified explicitly as a range of characters, we can specify the key as ranges with the character position at key starts and key ends as follows:

```
$ cat data.txt
1010hellothis
2189ababbba
7464dfddfdfd
$ sort -nk 2,3 data.txt
```

The highlighted characters are to be used as numeric keys. To extract, use their positions in the lines as the key format (in the previous example, they're 2 and 3).

To use the first character as the key, use:

```
$ sort -nk 1,1 data.txt
```

To make the sort's output `xargs` compatible with the `\0` terminator, use the following command:

```
$ sort -z data.txt | xargs -0
#Zero terminator is used to make safe use with xargs
```

Sometimes, the text may contain unnecessary extraneous characters such as spaces. To sort them in dictionary order, by ignoring punctuations and folds, use:

```
$ sort -bd unsorted.txt
```

The -b option is used to ignore leading blank lines from the file and the -d option is used to specify sort in the dictionary order.

uniq

uniq is a command used to find out the unique lines from the given input (stdin or from a filename as command argument) by eliminating the duplicates. It can also be used to find out the duplicate lines from the input.

uniq can be applied only for sorted data input. Hence, uniq is to be used always along with the sort command using pipe or using a sorted file as input.

Produce the unique lines (all lines in the input are printed and even the duplicate lines are printed only once) from the given input data as follows:

```
$ cat sorted.txt
bash
foss
hack
hack

$ uniq sorted.txt
bash
foss
hack
```

Or:

```
$ sort unsorted.txt | uniq
```

Display only unique lines (the lines which are not repeated or duplicated in the input file) as follows:

```
$ uniq -u sorted.txt
bash
foss
```

Or:

```
$ sort unsorted.txt | uniq -u
```

To count how many times each of the lines appears in the file, use the following command:

```
$ sort unsorted.txt | uniq -c
      1 bash
      1 foss
      2 hack
```

To find duplicate lines in the file:

```
$ sort unsorted.txt   | uniq -d
hack
```

To specify keys, we can use the combination of the -s and -w arguments.

► -s specifies the number for the first *N* characters to be skipped

► -w specifies the maximum number of characters to be compared

This comparison key is used as the index for the uniq operation as follows:

```
$ cat data.txt
u:01:gnu
d:04:linux
u:01:bash
u:01:hack
```

We need to use the highlighted characters as the unique key. This is used to ignore the first two characters (-s 2) and the maximum number of comparison characters is specified using the -w option (-w 2):

```
$ sort data.txt | uniq -s 2 -w 2
d:04:linux
u:01:bash
```

While we use output from one command as input to the xargs command, it is always preferable to use a zero-byte terminator for each of the lines of the output, which act as the source for xargs. While using the uniq commands output as the source for xargs, we should use a zero terminated output. If a zero-byte terminator is not used, by default the space characters are used as the delimiter to split the arguments in the xargs command. For example, a line with text "this is a line" from stdin will be taken as four separate arguments by the xargs command. Actually, it is a single line. When a zero-byte terminator is used, \0 is used as the delimiter character and, hence, a single line including a space is interpreted as a single argument.

Zero-byte-terminated output can be generated from the uniq command as follows:

```
$ uniq -z file.txt
```

The following command removes all the files, with filenames read from files.txt:

```
$ uniq -z file.txt | xargs -0 rm
```

If multiple-line entries of filenames exist in the file, the uniq command writes the filename only once to stdout.

Temporary file naming and random numbers

While writing shell scripts, we often need to store temporary data. The most suitable location to store temporary data is /tmp (which will be cleaned out by the system on reboot). We can use two methods to generate standard filenames for temporary data.

How to do it...

Perform the following steps to create a temporary file and perform different naming operations on it:

1. Create a temporary file as follows:

   ```
   $ filename=`mktemp`
   $ echo $filename
   /tmp/tmp.8xvhkjF5fH
   ```

   This will create a temporary file and print its filename which we store in $filename in this example.

2. To create a temporary directory, use the following commands:

   ```
   $ dirname=`mktemp -d`
   $ echo $dirname
   tmp.NI8xzW7VRX
   ```

   This will create a temporary directory and print its filename which we store in $dirname in this example.

3. To just generate a filename without actually creating a file or directory, use this:

   ```
   $ tmpfile=`mktemp -u`
   $ echo $tmpfile
   /tmp/tmp.RsGmilRpcT
   ```

   Here, the filename will be stored in $tmpfile, but the file won't be created.

4. To create the temporary filename according to a template, use:

   ```
   $mktemp test.XXX
   test.2tc
   ```

How it works...

The `mktemp` command is very straightforward. It generates a random file and returns its filename (or directory names, in case of directories).

When providing custom templates, `X` will be replaced by a random alphanumeric character. Also note that there must be at least three `X` characters in the template for `mktemp` to work.

Splitting files and data

Splitting of files into many smaller pieces becomes essential in certain situations. Earlier, when memory was limited with devices such as floppy disks, it was crucial to split files into smaller file sizes to split files across many disks. However, nowadays we split files for other purposes, such as readability, for generating logs, sending files over e-mail, and so on. In this recipe we will see various ways of splitting files in different chunks.

How to do it...

Let's say we have a test file called `data.file`, which has a size of 100 KB. You can split this file into smaller files of 10k each by specifying the split size as follows:

```
$ split -b 10k data.file
$ ls
data.file  xaa  xab  xac  xad  xae  xaf  xag  xah  xai  xaj
```

It will split `data.file` into many files, each of a 10k chunk. The chunks will be named the manner `xab`, `xac`, `xad`, and so on. This means it will have alphabetic suffixes. To use the numeric suffixes, use an additional `-d` argument. It is also possible to specify a suffix length using `-a length`:

```
$ split -b 10k data.file -d -a 4
```

Instead of the k (kilobyte) suffix we can use M for MB, G for GB, c for byte, w for word, and so on.

```
$ ls
data.file x0009  x0019  x0029  x0039  x0049  x0059  x0069  x0079
```

There's more...

The `split` command has more options. Let's go through them.

Specifying a filename prefix for the split files

The previous split files have a filename prefix x. We can also use our own filename prefix by providing a prefix filename. The last command argument for the split command is PREFIX. It is in the format:

```
$ split [COMMAND_ARGS] PREFIX
```

Let's run the previous command with the prefix filename for split files:

```
$ split -b 10k data.file -d -a 4 split_file
$ ls
data.file        split_file0002  split_file0005  split_file0008  strtok.c
split_file0000   split_file0003  split_file0006  split_file0009
split_file0001   split_file0004  split_file0007
```

To split files based on the number of lines in each split rather than chunk size, use -l no_of_lines as follows:

```
$ split -l 10 data.file
# Splits into files of 10 lines each.
```

There is another interesting utility called csplit. It can be used to split logfile-based specified conditions and string match options. Let's see how to work with it.

csplit is a variant of the split utility. The split utility can only split files based on chunk size or based on the number of lines. csplit makes the split based on context based split. It can be used to split files based on the existence of a certain word or text content.

Look at the following example log:

```
$ cat server.log
SERVER-1
[connection] 192.168.0.1 success
[connection] 192.168.0.2 failed
[disconnect] 192.168.0.3 pending
[connection] 192.168.0.4 success
SERVER-2
[connection] 192.168.0.1 failed
[connection] 192.168.0.2 failed
[disconnect] 192.168.0.3 success
[connection] 192.168.0.4 failed
SERVER-3
[connection] 192.168.0.1 pending
```

```
[connection] 192.168.0.2 pending
[disconnect] 192.168.0.3 pending
[connection] 192.168.0.4 failed
```

We may need to split the files into `server1.log`, `server2.log`, and `server3.log` from the contents for each `SERVER` in each file. This can be done as follows:

```
$ csplit server.log /SERVER/ -n 2 -s {*}  -f server -b "%02d.log"  ; rm
server00.log
```

```
$ ls
```

```
server01.log   server02.log   server03.log   server.log
```

The details of the command are as follows:

▸ `/SERVER/` is the line used to match a line by which a split is to be carried out.

▸ `/[REGEX]/` is the format. It copies from the current line (first line) up to the matching line that contains `"SERVER"` excluding the match line.

▸ `{*}` is used to specify to repeat a split based on the match up to the end of the file. By using `{integer}`, we can specify the number of times it is to be continued.

▸ `-s` is the flag to make the command silent rather than printing other messages.

▸ `-n` is used to specify the number of digits to be used as suffix. 01, 02, 03, and so on.

▸ `-f` is used for specifying the filename prefix for split files (`server` is the prefix in the previous example).

▸ `-b` is used to specify the suffix format. `"%02d.log"` is similar to the `printf` argument format in C. Here, the filename = prefix + suffix, that is, `"server"` + `"%02d.log"`.

We remove `server00.log` since the first split file is an empty file (the match word is the first line of the file).

Slicing filenames based on extension

Several shell scripts perform manipulations based on filenames. We may need to perform actions such as renaming the files by preserving the extension, converting files from one format to another (change the extension by preserving the name), extracting a portion of the filename, and so on. The shell comes with inbuilt features for slicing filenames based on different conditions. Let us see how to do it.

How to do it...

The name from `name.extension` can be easily extracted using the `%` operator. You can extract the name from `"sample.jpg"` as follows:

```
file_jpg="sample.jpg"
name=${file_jpg%.*}
echo File name is: $name
```

The output is:

File name is: sample

The next task is to extract the extension of a file from its filename. The extension can be extracted using the `#` operator as follows:

Extract `.jpg` from the filename stored in the variable `file_jpg` as follows:

```
extension=${file_jpg#*.}
echo Extension is: jpg
```

The output is:

Extension is: jpg

How it works...

In the first task, in order to extract the name from the filename in the format `name.extension` we have used the `%` operator.

`${VAR%.*}` can be interpreted as:

▶   Remove the string match from the `$VAR` for the wildcard pattern that appears to the right-hand side of `%` (`.*` in the previous example). Evaluating from the right to left direction should make the wildcard match.

▶   Let's store the filename as `VAR=sample.jpg`. Therefore, the wildcard match for `.*` from right to left is `.jpg`. Thus, it is removed from the `$VAR` string and the output will be `sample`.

`%` is a nongreedy operation. It finds the minimal match for the wildcard from right to left. There is an operator `%%`, which is similar to `%`. But it is greedy in nature. This means, it finds the maximal match of the string for the wildcard. For example, we have:

VAR=hack.fun.book.txt

Using the % operator, we have:

```
$ echo ${VAR%.*}
```

The output will be: `hack.fun.book.`

The % operator performs a nongreedy match for `.*` from right to left (`.txt`).

Using the %% operator, we have:

```
$ echo ${VAR%%.*}
```

The output will be: `hack`

The %% operator performs a greedy match for `.*` going right to left (`.fun.book.txt`).

In the second task, we have used the # operator to extract the extension from the filename. It is similar to %. But it evaluates from left to right.

`${VAR#*.}` can be interpreted as:

▶ Remove the string match from `$VARIABLE` for the wildcard pattern match appears to the right-hand side of the # (`*.` in the previous example). Evaluating from the left to right direction should make the wildcard match.

Similarly, as in the case of %%, we have another greedy operator for #, which is ##.

It makes greedy matches by evaluating from left to right and removes the match string from the specified variable.

Let's use this example:

VAR=hack.fun.book.txt

By using the # operator, we have:

```
$ echo ${VAR#*.}
```

The output will be: `fun.book.txt.`

The # operator performs a nongreedy match for `*.` from left to right (`hack.`).

By using the ## operator, we have:

```
$ echo ${VAR##*.}
```

The output will be: `txt.`

The ## operator matches a greedy match for `*.` from left to right (`txt`).

The ## operator is preferred over the # operator to extract the extension from a filename since the filename may contain multiple "." characters. Since ## makes a greedy match, it always extracts extensions only.

Here is practical example that can be used to extract different portions of a domain name, given a URL="www.google.com":

```
$ echo ${URL%.*} # Remove rightmost .*
www.google
```

```
$ echo ${URL%%.*} # Remove right to leftmost  .* (Greedy operator)
www
```

```
$ echo ${URL#*.} # Remove leftmost  part before *.
google.com
```

```
$ echo ${URL##*.} # Remove left to rightmost  part before *. (Greedy operator)
com
```

Renaming and moving files in bulk

Renaming a number of files is one of the tasks we frequently come across. A simple example is when you download photos from your digital camera to your computer you may delete unnecessary files and it causes discontinuous numbering of image files. Sometimes, you may need to rename them with a custom prefix and continuous numbering for filenames. We sometimes use third-party tools for performing rename operations. We can use Bash commands to perform a rename operation in a couple of seconds.

Moving all the files having a particular substring in their filenames (for example, the same prefix for filenames) or with a specific file type to a given directory is another use case we frequently perform. Let's see how to write scripts to perform these kinds of operations.

Getting ready

The `rename` command helps to change filenames using Perl regular expressions.
By combining the commands `find`, `rename`, and `mv`, we can perform a lot of things.

How to do it...

The easiest way of renaming image files in the current directory to our own filename, with a specific format, is by using the following script:

```
#!/bin/bash
#Filename: rename.sh
#Desc: Rename jpg and png files

count=1;
for img in `find . -iname '*.png' -o -iname '*.jpg' -type f -maxdepth 1`
do
  new=image-$count.${img##*.}

  echo "Renaming $img to $new"
  mv "$img" "$new"
  let count++

done
```

The output is as follows:

```
$ ./rename.sh
Renaming hack.jpg to image-1.jpg
Renaming new.jpg to image-2.jpg
Renaming next.png to image-3.png
```

The script renames all the `.jpg` and `.png` files in the current directory and its subdirectories to new filenames in the format `image-1.jpg`, `image-2.jpg`, `image-3.png`, `image-4.png`, and so on.

How it works...

In the previous script, we have used a `for` loop to iterate through the names of all files ending with a `.jpg` or `.png` extension. We use the `find` command to perform this search, where the `-o` option is used to specify multiple `-iname` options, which perform a case-insensitive match. By using `-maxdepth 1`, we make sure that `$img` will contain a filename only from the current directories, not its subdirectories.

We have initialized a variable `count=1` in order to keep track of the image number. The next step is to rename the file using the `mv` command. The new name of the file should be formulated for renaming. `${img##*.}` in the script parses the extension of the filename currently in the loop (see the *Slicing filenames based on extension* recipe for interpretation of `${img##*.}`).

`let count++` is used to increment the file number for each execution of the loop.

There are a variety of other ways to perform rename operations. Let us walk through a few of them:

- Renaming `*.JPG` to `*.jpg`:

  ```
  $ rename *.JPG *.jpg
  ```

- To replace space in the filenames with the "_" character:

  ```
  $ rename 's/ /_/g' *
  ```

  ```
  # 's/ /_/g' is the replacement part in the filename and * is the wildcard for the
  ```
  target files. It can be `*.txt` or any other wildcard pattern.

- To convert any filename of files from uppercase to lowercase and vice versa:

  ```
  $ rename 'y/A-Z/a-z/' *
  $ rename 'y/a-z/A-Z/' *
  ```

- To recursively move all the `.mp3` files to a given directory:

  ```
  $ find path -type f -name "*.mp3" -exec mv {} target_dir \;
  ```

- To recursively rename all the files by replacing space with the "_" character:

  ```
  $ find path -type f -exec rename 's/ /_/g' {} \;
  ```

Spell checking and dictionary manipulation

Most of the Linux distributions come with a dictionary file along with them. However, I find very few people to be aware of the dictionary file and hence, few make use of them. There is a command-line utility called `aspell` that functions as a spell checker. Let's go through a few scripts that make use of the dictionary file and the spell checker.

How to do it...

The `/usr/share/dict/` directory contains some of the dictionary files. Dictionary files are text files that contain a list of dictionary words. We can use this list to check whether a word is a dictionary word or not.

```
$ ls /usr/share/dict/
american-english  british-english
```

To check whether the given word is a dictionary word, use the following script:

```bash
#!/bin/bash
#Filename: checkword.sh
word=$1
grep "^$1$" /usr/share/dict/british-english -q
if [ $? -eq 0 ]; then
   echo $word is a dictionary word;
else
   echo $word is not a dictionary word;
fi
```

The usage is as follows:

```
$ ./checkword.sh ful
ful is not a dictionary word
```

```
$ ./checkword.sh fool
fool is a dictionary word
```

How it works...

In `grep`, `^` is the word-start-marker character and the `$` character is the word-end marker.

`-q` is used to suppress any output and to be silent.

Or, alternatively, we can use the spell check, `aspell`, to check whether a word is in a dictionary or not, as follows:

```bash
#!/bin/bash
#Filename: aspellcheck.sh
word=$1

output=`echo \"$word\" | aspell list`

if [ -z $output ]; then
        echo $word is a dictionary word;
else
        echo $word is not a dictionary word;
fi
```

The `aspell list` command returns output text when the given input is not a dictionary word, and does not output anything when the input is a dictionary word. A `-z` command checks whether $output is an empty string or not.

List all words in a file starting with a given word as follows:

```
$ look word filepath
```

Or alternately, use:

```
$ grep "^word" filepath
```

By default, if the filename argument is not given to the `look` command, it looks up into the default dictionary (`/usr/share/dict/words`) and returns an output:

```
$look word
# When used like this it takes default dictionary as file
```

For example:

```
$ look android
android
android's
androids
```

Automating interactive input

Automating interactive input for command-line utilities are extremely useful for writing automation tools or testing tools. There will be many situations when we deal with commands that read input interactively. An example of executing a command and supplying the interactive input is as follows:

```
$ command
Enter a number: 1
Enter name : hello
You have entered 1,hello
```

Getting ready

Creating utilities that can automate the acceptance of input are useful to supply input to local commands, as well as for remote applications. Let us see how to automate them.

How to do it...

Think about the sequence of an interactive input. From the previous code, we can formulate the steps of the sequence as follows:

```
1 [Return] hello [Return]
```

Converting the preceding steps 1, Return, hello, and Return by observing the characters that are actually typed in the keyboard, we can formulate the following string:

```
"1\nhello\n"
```

The \n character is sent when we press *return*. By appending the return (\n) characters, we get the actual string that is passed to stdin (standard input).

Hence, by sending the equivalent string for the characters typed by the user, we can automate the passing of input in the interactive processes.

How it works...

Let's write a script that reads input interactively and uses this script for automation examples:

```
#!/bin/bash
#Filename: interactive.sh
read -p "Enter number:" no ;
read -p "Enter name:" name
echo You have entered $no, $name;
```

Let's automate the sending of input to the command as follows:

```
$ echo -e "1\nhello\n" | ./interactive.sh
You have entered 1, hello
```

Thus crafting input with \n works.

We have used echo -e to produce the input sequence where -e signals to echo to interpret escape sequences. If the input is large we can use an input file and redirection operator to supply input:

```
$ echo -e "1\nhello\n" > input.data
$ cat input.data
1
hello
```

You can also manually craft the input file without the echo commands by hand typing. For example:

```
$ ./interactive.sh < input.data
```

This redirects interactive input data from a file.

If you are a reverse engineer, you may have played with buffer overflow exploits. To exploit them we need to redirect a shellcode such as `"\xeb\x1a\x5e\x31\xc0\x88\x46"`, which is written in hex. These characters cannot be typed directly through the keyboard as keys for these characters are not present in the keyboard. Therefore, we should use:

```
echo -e \xeb\x1a\x5e\x31\xc0\x88\x46"
```

This will redirect the shellcode to a vulnerable executable.

We have described a method to automate interactive input programs by redirecting expected input text through `stdin` (standard input). We are sending the input without checking the input the program asks for. We are also expecting the program to ask for input in a specific (static) order. If the program asks for input randomly or in a changing order, or sometimes certain inputs are never asked for, the aforementioned method fails. It will send the wrong inputs to different input prompts by the program. In order to handle a dynamic input supply and provide input by checking the input requirements by the program on runtime, we have a great utility called `expect`. The `expect` command supplies the correct input for the correct input prompt by the program.

There's more...

Trailing from the previous section, let's see how to use `expect`. Automation of interactive input can also be done using other methods. Expect scripting is another method for automation. Let's go through it.

Automating with expect

`expect` does not come by default with most of the common Linux distributions. You have to install the expect package manually using your package manager.

`expect` expects for a particular input prompt and sends data by checking messages in the input prompt:

```
#!/usr/bin/expect
#Filename: automate_expect.sh
spawn ./interactive .sh
expect "Enter number:"
send "1\n"
expect "Enter name:"
send "hello\n"
expect eof
```

Run it as follows:

```
$ ./automate_expect.sh
```

The #spawn parameter specifies which commands are to be automated.

The #expect parameter provides the expected message.

#send is the message to be sent. # expect eof defines the end of the command interaction.

Making commands quicker by running parallel processes

Computing power has increased a lot over the last couple of years. However, this is not just because of having processors with higher clock cycles; the thing that makes modern processors faster is multiple cores. What this means to the user is in a single hardware processor there are multiple logical processors.

However, the multiple cores are useless unless the software makes use of them. For example, if you have a program that does huge calculations, it will only run on one of the cores, the others will sit idle. The software has to be aware and take advantage of the multiple cores if we want it to be faster.

In this recipe we will see how we can make our commands run faster.

How to do it...

Let us take an example of the md5sum command that we discussed in the previous recipes. This command is CPU-intensive as it has to perform the calculation. Now, if we have more than one file that we want to generate a checksum of, we can run multiple instances of md5sum using a script like this:

```
#/bin/bash
#filename: generate_checksums.sh
PIDARRAY=()
for file in File1.iso File2.iso
do
   md5sum $file &
   PIDARRAY+=("$!")
done
wait ${PIDARRAY[@]}
```

When we run this, we get the following output:

```
$ ./generate_checksums.sh
330dcb53f253acdf76431cecca0fefe7  File1.iso
bd1694a6fe6df12c3b8141dcffaf06e6  File2.iso
```

The output will be the same as running the following command:

```
md5sum File1.iso File2.iso
```

However, as the md5sum commands ran simultaneously, you'll get the results quicker if you have a multi-core processor (you can verify this using the time command).

How it works...

We exploit the Bash operand &, which instructs the shell to send the command to the background and continue with the script. However, this means that our script will exit as soon as the loop completes while the md5sum processes are still running in the background. To prevent this, we get the PIDs of the processes using $!, which in Bash holds the PID of the last background process. We append these PIDs to an array and then use the wait command to wait for these processes to finish.

3
File In, File Out

In this chapter, we will cover:

- ▶ Generating files of any size
- ▶ The intersection and set difference (A-B) on text files
- ▶ Finding and deleting duplicate files
- ▶ Working with file permissions, ownership, and the sticky bit
- ▶ Making files immutable
- ▶ Generating blank files in bulk
- ▶ Finding symbolic links and their targets
- ▶ Enumerating file type statistics
- ▶ Using loopback files
- ▶ Creating ISO files and hybrid ISO
- ▶ Finding the difference between files, patching
- ▶ Using head and tail for printing the last or first 10 lines
- ▶ Listing only directories – alternative methods
- ▶ Fast command-line navigation using pushd and popd
- ▶ Counting the number of lines, words, and characters in a file
- ▶ Printing the directory tree

Introduction

Unix treats every object in the operating system as a file. We can find the files associated with every action performed and can make use of them for different system or process-related manipulations. For example, the command terminal that we use is associated with a device file. We can write to the terminal by writing to the corresponding device file for that specific terminal. Files take different forms such as directories, regular files, block devices, character-special devices, symbolic links, sockets, named pipes, and so on. Filename, size, file type, modification time, access time, change time, inode, links associated, and the filesystem the file is on are all attributes and properties that files can have. This chapter deals with recipes that handle operations or properties related to files.

Generating files of any size

For various reasons, you may need to generate a file filled with random data. It may be for creating a test file to perform tests, such as an application efficiency test that uses a large file as input, or to test the splitting of files into many parts, or to create loopback filesystems (**loopback files** are files that can contain a filesystem itself and these files can be mounted similarly to a physical device using the mount command). It takes effort to create such files by writing specific programs. So we use general utilities.

How to do it...

The easiest way to create a large-size file with the given size is to use the dd command. The dd command clones the given input and writes an exact copy to the output. Input can be stdin, a device file, a regular file, or so on. Output can be stdout, a device file, a regular file, or so on. An example of the dd command is as follows:

```
$ dd if=/dev/zero of=junk.data bs=1M count=1
1+0 records in
1+0 records out
1048576 bytes (1.0 MB) copied, 0.00767266 s, 137 MB/s
```

The preceding command will create a file called junk.data that is exactly 1 MB in size. Let's go through the parameters: if stands for the - input file, of stands for the - output file, bs stands for bytes for a block, and count stands for the number of blocks of bs specified to be copied.

Be careful while using the dd command, it operates on a very low level with the devices. If you make a mistake, you might end up wiping your disk or corrupting data otherwise. So, always double check your dd command syntax, especially your of= parameter for correctness.

In the previous example, we are only creating a file, which is 1 MB in size, by specifying bs as 1 MB with a count of 1. If bs was set to 2M and count to 2, the total file size would be 4 MB.

We can use various units for **block size (BS)** as follows. Append any of the following characters to the number to specify the size in bytes:

Unit size	Code
Byte (1 B)	c
Word (2 B)	w
Block (512 B)	b
Kilobyte (1024 B)	k
Megabyte (1024 KB)	M
Gigabyte (1024 MB)	G

We can generate a file of any size using this. Instead of MB we can use any other unit notations, such as the ones mentioned in the previous table.

/dev/zero is a character special device, which infinitely returns the zero byte (\0).

If the input parameter (if) is not specified, it will read the input from stdin by default. Similarly, if the output parameter (of) is not specified, it will use stdout as the default output sink.

The dd command can also be used to measure the speed of memory operations by transferring a large quantity of data and checking the command output (for example, 1048576 bytes (1.0 MB) copied, 0.00767266 s, 137 MB/s as seen in the previous example).

The intersection and set difference (A-B) on text files

Intersection and set difference operations are commonly used in mathematical classes on set theory. However, similar operations on strings are also very helpful in some scenarios.

Getting ready

The comm command is a utility to perform a comparison between the two files. It has many good options to arrange the output in such a way that we can perform intersection, difference, and set difference operations.

- ▶ **Intersection**: The intersection operation will print the lines that the specified files have in common with one another

- ▸ **Difference:** The difference operation will print the lines that the specified files contain and that are not the same in all of those files
- ▸ **Set difference:** The set difference operation will print the lines in file "A" that do not match those in all of the set of files specified ("B" plus "C" for example)

How to do it...

Note that comm takes only sorted files as input. Take a look at the following example:

```
$ cat A.txt
apple
orange
gold
silver
steel
iron

$ cat B.txt
orange
gold
cookies
carrot

$ sort A.txt -o A.txt ; sort B.txt -o B.txt
```

1. First, execute comm without any options:

```
$ comm A.txt B.txt
apple
        carrot
        cookies
                gold
iron
                orange
silver
steel
```

The first column of the output contains lines that are only in A.txt. The second column contains lines that are only in B.txt. The third column contains the common lines from A.txt and B.txt. Each of the columns are delimited using the tab (\t) character.

2. In order to print the intersection of two files, we need to remove the first and second columns and print the third column only as follows:

```
$ comm A.txt B.txt -1 -2
gold
orange
```

3. Print lines that are uncommon in two files as follows:

```
$ comm A.txt B.txt   -3
apple
        carrot
        cookies
iron
silver
steel
```

In this output, columns have their fields blank for each of the unique lines. Hence, both columns will not have the content on the same line. In order to make it more usable, we need to remove the blank fields and make two columns into a single-column output as follows:

```
apple
carrot
cookies
iron
silver
steel
```

4. In order to produce a unified output, use the following command line:

```
$ comm A.txt B.txt   -3 | sed 's/^\t//'
apple
carrot
cookies
iron
silver
steel
```

5. By removing the unnecessary columns, we can produce the set difference for A.txt and B.txt as follows:

    ❏   Set difference for A.txt:

        $ comm A.txt B.txt -2 -3

        `-2` `-3` removes the second and third columns.

    ❏   Set difference for B.txt:

        $ comm A.txt B.txt -1 -3

        `-2` `-3` removes the second and third columns.

How it works...

The command-line options for comm format the output as per our requirement. These are:

▶   `-1` – removes the first column from the output

▶   `-2` – removes the second column

▶   `-3` – removes the third column

While creating a unified output, the sed command is piped to the comm output. The sed removes the \t character at the beginning of the lines. s in the sed script stands for substitute. /^\t/ matches the \t character at the beginning of the lines (^ is the start of the line marker). // (no character) is the replacement string for every \t character at the beginning of the line. Hence, every \t at the start of the line gets removed.

The set difference operation enables you to compare two files and print all the lines that are in the file A.txt or B.txt excluding the common lines in A.txt and B.txt. When A.txt and B.txt are given as arguments to the comm command, the output will contain column-1 with the set difference for A.txt with regard to B.txt and column-2 will contain the set difference for B.txt with regard to A.txt.

Finding and deleting duplicate files

Duplicate files are copies of the same files. In some circumstances, we may need to remove duplicate files and keep a single copy of them. Identification of duplicate files by looking at the file content is an interesting task. It can be done using a combination of shell utilities. This recipe deals with finding duplicate files and performing operations based on the result.

Getting ready

We can identify the duplicate files by comparing file content. Checksums are ideal for this task, since files with exactly the same content will produce the same checksum values. We can use this fact to remove duplicate files.

How to do it...

1. Generate some test files as follows:

   ```
   $ echo "hello" > test ; cp test test_copy1 ; cp test test_copy2;
   $ echo "next" > other;
   # test_copy1 and test_copy2 are copy of test
   ```

2. The code for the script to remove the duplicate files is as follows:

   ```bash
   #!/bin/bash
   #Filename: remove_duplicates.sh
   #Description:  Find and remove duplicate files and keep one sample
   of each file.

   ls -lS --time-style=long-iso | awk 'BEGIN {
     getline; getline;
     name1=$8; size=$5
   }
   {
     name2=$8;
     if (size==$5)
     {
       "md5sum "name1 | getline; csum1=$1;
       "md5sum "name2 | getline; csum2=$1;
       if ( csum1==csum2 )
       {
         print name1; print name2
       }
     };

     size=$5; name1=name2;
   }' | sort -u > duplicate_files


   cat duplicate_files | xargs -I {} md5sum {} | sort | uniq -w 32 |
   awk '{ print "^"$2"$" }' | sort -u >  duplicate_sample

   echo Removing..
   ```

```
comm duplicate_files duplicate_sample  -2 -3 | tee /dev/stderr |
xargs rm
echo Removed duplicates files successfully.
```

3. Run it as:

```
$ ./remove_duplicates.sh
```

How it works...

The preceding commands will find the copies of the same file in a directory and remove all except one copy of the file. Let us go through the code and see how it works.

`ls -1S` will list the details of the files sorted by file size in the current directory. `--time-style=long-iso` tells `ls` to print dates in the ISO format. `awk` will read the output of `ls -1S` and perform comparisons on columns and rows of the input text to find out the duplicate files.

The logic behind the code is as follows:

▶ We list the files sorted by size so that the similarly sized files will be grouped together. The files having the same file size are identified as a first step to finding files that are the same. Next, we calculate the checksum of the files. If the checksums match, the files are duplicates and one set of the duplicates are removed.

▶ The `BEGIN{}` block of `awk` is executed first before the lines are read from the file. Reading lines takes place in the `{}` block and after the end of reading and processing all lines, the `END{}` block statements are executed. The output of `ls -1S` is:

```
total 16

-rw-r--r-- 1 slynux slynux 5 2010-06-29 11:50 other

-rw-r--r-- 1 slynux slynux 6 2010-06-29 11:50 test

-rw-r--r-- 1 slynux slynux 6 2010-06-29 11:50 test_copy1

-rw-r--r-- 1 slynux slynux 6 2010-06-29 11:50 test_copy2
```

▶ The output of the first line tells us the total number of files, which in this case is not useful. We use `getline` to read the first line and then dump it. We need to compare each of the lines and the next line for sizes. For that, we read the first line explicitly using `getline` and store the name and size (which are the eighth and fifth columns). Hence, a line is read ahead using `getline`. Now, when `awk` enters the `{}` block (in which the rest of the lines are read), that block is executed for every read of a line. It compares the size obtained from the current line and the previously stored size kept in the `size` variable. If they are equal, it means two files are duplicates by size. Hence, they are to be further checked by `md5sum`.

We have played some tricks on the way to the solution.

The external command output can be read inside `awk` as:

```
"cmd"| getline
```

Then, we receive the output in line `$0` and each column output can be received in `$1`, `$2`, ... ,`$n`, and so on. Here, we read the md5sum checksum of files in the `csum1` and `csum2` variables. Variables `name1` and `name2` are used to store consecutive filenames. If the checksums of two files are the same, they are confirmed to be duplicates and are printed.

We need to find a file from each group of duplicates so that we can remove all other duplicates. We calculate the `md5sum` value of the duplicates and print one file from each group of duplicates by finding unique lines, comparing `md5sum` only from each line using `-w 32` (the first 32 characters in the `md5sum` output; usually, the `md5sum` output consists of a 32-character hash followed by the filename). Therefore, one sample from each group of duplicates is written in `duplicate_sample`.

Now, we need to remove all the files listed in `duplicate_files`, excluding the files listed in `duplicate_sample`. The `comm` command prints files in `duplicate_files` but not in `duplicate_sample`.

For that, we use a set difference operation (refer to the recipes on intersection, difference, and set difference).

`comm` always accepts files that are sorted. Therefore, `sort -u` is used as a filter before redirecting to `duplicate_files` and `duplicate_sample`.

Here the `tee` command is used to perform a trick so that it can pass filenames to the `rm` command as well as `print`. The `tee` command writes lines that appear as `stdin` to a file and sends them to `stdout`. We can also print text to the terminal by redirecting to `stderr`. `/dev/stderr` is the device corresponding to `stderr` (standard error). By redirecting to a `stderr` device file, text that appears through `stdin` will be printed in the terminal as standard error.

Working with file permissions, ownership, and the sticky bit

File permissions and ownership are one of the distinguishing features of the Unix/Linux filesystems such as **extfs (extended FS)**. In many circumstances while working on Unix/Linux platforms, we come across issues related to permissions and ownership. This recipe is a walk through the different use cases of these.

In Linux systems, each file is associated with many types of permissions. Out of these permissions, three sets of permissions (user, group, and others) are commonly manipulated.

The **user** is the owner of the file. The **group** is the collection of users (as defined by the system administrator) that are permitted some access to the file. **Others** are any entities other than the user or group owner of the file.

Permissions of a file can be listed by using the `ls -l` command:

```
-rw-r--r-- 1 slynux slynux  2497  2010-02-28 11:22 bot.py
drwxr-xr-x 2 slynux slynux  4096  2010-05-27 14:31 a.py
-rw-r--r-- 1 slynux slynux  539   2010-02-10 09:11 cl.pl
```

The first column of the output specifies the following, with the first letter corresponding to:

- ▶ – – if it is a regular file
- ▶ d – if it is a directory
- ▶ c – for a character device
- ▶ b – for a block device
- ▶ l – if it is a symbolic link
- ▶ s – for a socket
- ▶ p – for a pipe

The rest can be divided into three groups of three letters each (— — —). The first — three characters correspond to the permissions of the user (owner), the second set of three characters correspond to the permissions of the group, and the third set of three characters correspond to the permissions of others. Each character in the nine-character sequence (nine permissions) specifies whether permission is set or unset. If the permission is set, a character appears in the corresponding position, otherwise a - character appears in that position, which means that the corresponding permission is unset (unavailable).

Let's take a look at what each of these three character sets mean for the user, group, and others:

- ▶ **User** (permission string: `rwx------`): The first letter in the three letters specifies whether the user has read permission for the file. If the read permission is set for the user, the character `r` will appear as the first character. Similarly, the second character specifies write (modify) permission (w) and the third character specifies whether the user has execute (x) permission (the permission to run the file). The execute permission is usually set for executable files. The user has one more special permission called **setuid** (S), which appears in the position of execute (x). The setuid permission enables an executable file to be executed effectively as its owner, even when the executable is run by another user.

  An example for a file with setuid permission set is `-rwS------`.

The read, write, and execute permissions are also applied to the directories. However, the meanings of read, write, and execute permissions are slightly different in the context of directories as follows:

- ❏ The read permission (r) for the directories enables reading the list of files and subdirectories in the directory
- ❏ The write permission (w) for a directory enables creating or removing files and directories from a directory
- ❏ The execute permission (x) specifies whether the access to the files and directories in a directory is possible or not

▸ **Group** (permission string: ---rwx---): The second set of three characters specifies the group permissions. The interpretation of permissions rwx is the same as the permissions for the user. Instead of setuid, the group has a **setgid** (S) bit. This enables the item to run an executable file with an effective group as the owner group. But the group, which initiates the command, may be different.

An example of group permission is ----rwS---.

▸ **Others** (permission string: ------rwx): Other permissions appear as the last three character set in the permission string. Others have the same read, write, and execute permissions as the user and group. But it does not have permission S (such as setuid or setgid).

Directories have a special permission called a **sticky bit**. When a sticky bit is set for a directory, only the user who created the directory can delete the files in the directory, even if the group and others have write permissions. The sticky bit appears in the position of execute character (x) in the others permission set. It is represented as character t or T. The t character appears in the position of x if the execute permission is unset and the sticky bit is set. If the sticky bit and the execute permission are set, the character T appears in the position of x. For example:

```
------rwt , ------rwT
```

A typical example of a directory with sticky bit turned on is /tmp.

In each of the ls -l output lines, the string slynux slynux corresponds to the owned user and owned group. Here, the first slynux is the user and the second slynux is the group owner.

How to do it...

In order to set permissions for files, we use the chmod command.

Assume that we need to set permission: rwx rw- r—.

This could be set using chmod as follows:

```
$ chmod u=rwx g=rw o=r filename
```

Here:

- u – specifies user permissions
- g – specifies group permissions
- o – specifies others permissions

Use + to add permission to a user, group, or others and use - to remove the permissions.

Add the executable permission to a file, which is already having the permission rwx rw- r— as follows:

```
$ chmod o+x filename
```

This command adds the x permission for others.

Add the executable permission to all permission categories, that is, for user, group, and others as follows:

```
$ chmod a+x filename
```

Here a means all.

In order to remove a permission, use -. For example:

```
$ chmod a-x filename
```

Alternatively, permissions can also be denoted by three-digit octal numbers in which each of the digits corresponds to user, group, and other in that order.

Read, write, and execute permissions have unique octal numbers as follows:

- r-- = 4
- -w- = 2
- --x = 1

We can get the required combination of permissions by adding the octal values for the required permission sets. For example:

- rw- = 4 + 2 = 6
- r-x = 4 + 1 = 5

The permission `rwx rw- r--` in the numeric method is as follows:

- ▶ `rwx` = 4 + 2 + 1 = 7
- ▶ `rw-` = 4 + 2 = 6
- ▶ `r--` = 4

Therefore, `rwx rw- r--` is equal to 764, and the command for setting the permissions using octal values is:

`$ chmod 764 filename`

There's more...

Let's go through some additional tasks that can be performed for files and directories.

Changing ownership

In order to change ownership of files, use the `chown` command as follows:

`$ chown user.group filename`

For example:

`$ chown slynux.slynux test.sh`

Here, `slynux` is the user, as well as the group.

Setting sticky bit

The sticky bit is an interesting type of permission applied to directories. By setting the sticky bit, it restricts only the user owning it to delete the files even though group and others may have sufficient permissions.

In order to set the sticky bit, `+t` is applied on a directory with `chmod` as follows:

`$ chmod a+t directory_name`

Applying permissions recursively to files

Sometimes it may be required to recursively change the permissions of all the files and directories inside the current directory. This can be done as follows:

`$ chmod 777 . -R`

The `-R` option specifies to apply change to a permission recursively.

We have used . to specify the path as the current working directory. It is equivalent to:

```
$ chmod 777 "$(pwd)" -R.
```

Applying ownership recursively

We can apply the ownership recursively by using the -R flag with the `chown` command as follows:

```
$ chown user.group . -R
```

Running an executable as a different user (setuid)

Some executables need to be executed as a different user (other than the current user that initiates the execution of the file), effectively, whenever they are executed, by using the file path, such as ./executable_name. A special permission attribute for files called the setuid permission enables effective execution as the file owner when any other user runs the program.

First, change the ownership to the user that needs to execute it and then log in as the user. Then, run the following command:

```
$ chmod +s executable_file

# chown root.root executable_file
# chmod +s executable_file
$ ./executable_file
```

Now it executes effectively as the root user every time.

setuid is restricted such that setuid won't work for scripts, but only for Linux ELF binaries. This is a fix for ensuring security.

Making files immutable

Files on extended type filesystems, which are common in Linux (for example, **ext2, ext3, ext4**, and so on) can be made immutable using a certain type of file attributes. When a file is made immutable, any user or super user cannot remove the file until the immutable attribute is removed from the file. We can easily find out the filesystem type of any mounted partition by looking at the /etc/mtab file. The first column of the file specifies the partition device path (for example, /dev/sda5) and the third column specifies the file system type (for example, ext3).

Making a file immutable is one of the methods for securing files from modification. An example would be to use it for the /etc/resolv.conf file which stores a list of DNS servers. A DNS server is used to convert domain names (such as packtpub.com) to IP addresses. Usually, the DNS server will be set to your ISP's DNS server. However, some people prefer to use a third-party server and they can modify /etc/resolv.conf to point to that DNS. However, the next time you get connected to your ISP, /etc/resolv.conf will revert back to point to ISP's DNS. To prevent this, we can make it immutable.

In this recipe we will see how to make files immutable and make then mutable when required.

Getting ready

The chattr command can be used to make files immutable. In addition to this, chattr has other useful options as well.

How to do it...

1. A file can be made immutable using the following command:

   ```
   # chattr +i file
   ```

2. The file is, therefore, made immutable. Now try the following command:

   ```
   rm file

   rm: cannot remove `file': Operation not permitted
   ```

3. In order to make it writable, remove the immutable attribute as follows:

   ```
   chattr -i file
   ```

Generating blank files in bulk

Sometimes we may need to generate test cases to test programs that operate on thousands of files. Let's discuss how to generate such files in this recipe.

Getting ready

touch is a command that can create blank files or modify the timestamp of files if they already exist. Let's take a look at how to use them.

How to do it...

1. A blank file with the name filename will be created using the following command:

   ```
   $ touch filename
   ```

2. Generate bulk files with a different name pattern as follows:

```
for name in {1..100}.txt
do
    touch $name
done
```

In the preceding code {1..100} will be expanded as a string "1, 2, 3, 4, 5, 6, 7...100". Instead of {1..100}.txt, we can use various shorthand patterns such as test{1..200}.c, test{a..z}.txt, and so on.

If a file already exists, the touch command changes all timestamps associated with the file to the current time. However, if we want to specify that only certain stamps are to be modified, we use the following options:

- ❏ touch -a modifies only the access time
- ❏ touch -m modifies only the modification time

3. Instead of using the current time for the timestamp, we can specify the time and date with which to stamp the file as follows:

```
$ touch -d "Fri Jun 25 20:50:14 IST 1999" filename
```

The date string that is used with -d need not always be in the same format. It will accept any simple date formats. We can omit time from the string and provide handy date formats such as "Jan 20 2010".

Finding symbolic links and their targets

Symbolic links are very common in Unix-like systems. There are various reasons you want to use them, ranging from convenient access to maintaining different versions of the same library or program. This recipe will discuss the basic techniques of handling symbolic links.

Symbolic links are just pointers to other files, they are similar in function to aliases in Mac OS X or shortcuts in Windows. When symbolic links are removed, they will not cause any harm to the original file.

How to do it...

The following steps will help you handle symbolic links:

1. We can create a symbolic link as follows:

```
$ ln -s target symbolic_link_name
```

For example:

```
$ ln -l -s /var/www/ ~/web
```

This creates a symbolic link (called **web**) in the current user's home directory, which points to `/var/www/`.

2. To verify that the link was created, run the following command:

```
$ ls -l web
lrwxrwxrwx 1 slynux slynux 8 2010-06-25 21:34 web -> /var/www
```

`web -> /var/www` specifies that `web` points to `/var/www`.

3. In order to print symbolic links in the current directory, use the following command:

```
$ ls -l | grep "^l"
```

4. Use `find` to print all symbolic links from the current directory and subdirectories:

```
$ find . -type l -print
```

5. To read the target path for a given symbolic link, use the `readlink` command:

```
$ readlink web
/var/www
```

How it works...

When looking for symbolic links in the current directory, `grep` will filter the lines from the `ls -l` output such that it displays only lines starting with `l` using `^`, which is the start marker for the string. This utilizes the fact that for every symbolic link, the permission notation block (`lrwxrwxrwx`) starts with letter `l`.

While using `find`, we use the argument `type` with `l`, which will instruct the command to search only for symbolic link files. The `-print` option is used to print the list of symbolic links to the standard output (`stdout`). The path from which the file search should begin is given as `.` which means it is the current directory.

Enumerating file type statistics

There are many file types. It will be an interesting exercise to write a script that can enumerate through all the files inside a directory, its descendants, print a report that provides details on types of files (files with different file types), and the count of each file type present. This recipe is an exercise on how to write scripts that can enumerate through many files and collect details.

Getting ready

The file command can be used to find out the type of the file by looking at the contents of the file. In Unix/Linux systems, file types are not determined based on the extension of the file (like the Microsoft Windows platform does). This recipe aims at collecting file type statistics of a number of files. For storing the count of files of the same type, we can use an associative array and the `file` command can be used to fetch the file type details from each of the files.

How to do it...

1. To print the type of a file use the following command:

   ```
   $ file filename
   ```

   ```
   $ file /etc/passwd
   /etc/passwd: ASCII text
   ```

2. Print the file type only by excluding the filename as follows:

   ```
   $ file -b filename
   ASCII text
   ```

3. The script for file statistics is as follows:

   ```bash
   #!/bin/bash
   # Filename: filestat.sh

   if [ $# -ne 1 ];
   then
     echo "Usage is $0 basepath";
     exit
   fi
   path=$1

   declare -A statarray;

   while read line;
   do
     ftype=`file -b "$line" | cut -d, -f1`
     let statarray["$ftype"]++;

   done < <(find $path -type f -print)

   echo ============ File types and counts =============
   for ftype in "${!statarray[@]}";
   do
     echo $ftype :  ${statarray["$ftype"]}
   done
   ```

4. The usage is as follows:

```
$ ./filestat.sh /home/slynux/temp
```

A sample output is shown as follows:

```
$ ./filetype.sh /home/slynux/programs
============ File types and counts =============
Vim swap file : 1
ELF 32-bit LSB executable : 6
ASCII text : 2
ASCII C program text : 10
```

How it works...

Here, an associative array named `statarray` is declared so that it can take the file type as file indices and store the count of each file type in the array. `let` is used to increment the count each time a file type is encountered. The `find` command is used to get the list of file paths recursively. A `while` loop is used to iterate line by line through the `find` command's output. The input line `ftype=`file -b "$line"` in the previous script is used to find out the file type using the `file` command. The `-b` option specifies the file command to print only the file type (without the filename in the output). The file type output consists of more details, such as image encoding used and resolution (in the case of an image file). But, we are not interested in all of the details; we need only the basic information. Details are comma-separated, as in the following example:

```
$ file a.out -b
ELF 32-bit LSB executable, Intel 80386, version 1 (SYSV), dynamically
linked (uses shared libs), for GNU/Linux 2.6.15, not stripped
```

We need to extract only `ELF 32-bit LSB executable` from the previous details. Hence, we use `cut -d, -f1`, which specifies to use , as the delimiter and print only the first field.

`done < <(find $path -type f -print);` is an important bit of code. The logic is as follows:

```
while read line;
do something
done < filename
```

Instead of the filename we used the output of `find`.

`<(find $path -type f -print)` is equivalent to a filename. But it substitutes filename with a subprocess output. Note that the first < is for input redirection and the second < is for converting the subprocess output to a filename. Also, there is a space between these two so that the shell won't interpret it as the << operator.

In Bash 3.x and higher we have a new operator <<< that lets us use a string output as an input file. Using this we can write the done line of the loop as follows:

```
done <<< "`find $path -type f -print`"
```

`${!statarray[@]}` is used to return the list of array indexes.

Using loopback files

Loopback filesystems are very interesting components of Linux-like systems. We usually create filesystems on devices (for example, disk drive partitions). These storage devices are available as device files such as `/dev/device_name`. In order to use the storage device filesystem, we mount it at a directory called a **mount point**. On the other hand, loopback filesystems are those that we create in files rather than a physical device. We can then mount those files as filesystems at a mount point. This essentially lets you create logical "disks" inside a file on your physical disk!

How to do it...

Let us see how to create an ext4 filesystem on a file of size 1 GB:

1. The following command will create a file that is 1 GB in size:

   ```
   $ dd if=/dev/zero of=loobackfile.img bs=1G count=1
   1024+0 records in
   1024+0 records out
   1073741824 bytes (1.1 GB) copied, 37.3155 s, 28.8 MB/s
   ```

   You can see that the size of the created file exceeds 1 GB. This is because the hard disk is a block device and, hence, storage must be allocated by integral multiples of blocks size.

2. Now format the 1 GB file to ext4 using the `mkfs` command as follows:

   ```
   $ mkfs.ext4 loopbackfile.img
   ```

3. Check the file type using the following command:

   ```
   $ file loobackfile.img
   loobackfile.img: Linux rev 1.0 ext4 filesystem data,
   UUID=c9d56c42-f8e6-4cbd-aeab-369d5056660a (extents) (large files)
   (huge files)
   ```

4. Now you can mount the loopback file as follows:

    ```
    # mkdir /mnt/loopback
    # mount -o loop loopbackfile.img /mnt/loopback
    ```

    The `-o loop` additional option is used to mount loopback filesystems.

    This is actually a short method where we don't have to manually attach it to any devices. But, internally it attaches to a device called `/dev/loop1` or `loop2`.

5. We can do it manually as follows:

    ```
    # losetup /dev/loop1 loopbackfile.img
    # mount /dev/loop1 /mnt/loopback
    ```

6. To umount (`unmount`), use the following syntax:

    ```
    # umount mount_point
    ```

    For example:

    ```
    # umount /mnt/loopback
    ```

7. Or, alternately, we can use the device file path as an argument to the `umount` command as:

    ```
    # umount /dev/loop1
    ```

 Note that the `mount` and `umount` commands should be executed as a root user since it is a privileged command.

How it works...

First we had to create a file that will act as a loopback file. For this we used dd, which is a generic command for copying raw data. It starts copying data from the file specified in its `if` parameter to the file specified in its `of` parameter. Additionally, we instruct dd to copy data in blocks of size 1 GB and copy one such block, hence creating a file of size 1 GB. The `/dev/zero` file is a special file, which will always contain 0 if you read from it.

We then used the `mkfts.ext4` command to create an ext4 filesystem in the file. A filesystem is needed because it provides a way of storing files on a disk/loopback file.

Finally, we used the `mount` command to mount the loopback file to a **mountpoint** (`/mnt/loopback` in this case). A mountpoint makes it possible for users to access the files stored on a filesystem. Before executing the `mount` command, the mountpoint should be created using the `mkdir` command. We pass the option `-o loop` to mount to tell it that what we are passing to it is a loopback file.

When `mount` knows that it is operating on a loopback file, it automatically sets up a device in `/dev` corresponding to the loopback file and then mounts it. If we wish to do it manually, we use the `losetup` command to set up the device and then the `mount` command to mount it.

There's more...

Let's explore some more possibilities with loopback files and mounting.

Creating partitions inside loopback images

Suppose we want to create a loopback file, want to partition it, and finally mount a subpartition. In this case, we cannot use `mount -o loop`. We have to manually set up the device and mount the partitions in it. Partition a file with zeros dumped in it as follows:

```
# losetup /dev/loop1 loopback.img
# fdisk /dev/loop1
```

> `fdisk` is a standard partitioning tool on Linux systems, a very concise tutorial on creating partitions using `fdisk` is available at `http://www.tldp.org/HOWTO/Partition/fdisk_partitioning.html` (make sure to use `/dev/loop1` instead of `/dev/hdb` in the aforementioned tutorial).

Create partitions in `loopback.img` and mount the first partition as follows:

```
# losetup -o 32256 /dev/loop2 loopback.img
```

Here, `/dev/loop2` will represent the first partition, `-o` is the offset flag, `32256` bytes are for a DOS partition scheme. The first partition starts after an offset of 32256 bytes from the start of the hard disk.

We can set up the second partition by specifying the required offset. After mounting, we can perform all regular operations as we can on physical devices.

Quicker way to mount loopback disk images with partitions

As we saw, we can manually pass partition offsets to `losetup` when we want to mount partitions inside a loopback disk image. However, there is a quicker way to mount all the partitions inside such an image using `kpartx`. This utility is usually not installed by default, so you will have to install it using your package manager:

```
# kpartx -v -a diskimage.img
add map loop0p1 (252:0): 0 114688 linear /dev/loop0 8192
add map loop0p2 (252:1): 0 15628288 linear /dev/loop0 122880
```

This creates mappings from the partitions in the disk image to devices in `/dev/mapper` which you can then mount. For example, to mount the first partition, use the following command:

```
# mount /dev/mapper/loop0p1 /mnt/disk1
```

When you're done with the devices (and unmounting any mounted partitions using `umount`), remove the mappings by:

```
# kpartx -d diskimage.img
loop deleted : /dev/loop0
```

Mounting ISO files as loopback

An ISO file is an archive of an optical media. We can mount ISO files in the same way that we mount physical disks by using loopback mounting.

We can even use a nonempty directory as the mount path. Then, the mount path will contain data from the devices rather than the original contents until the device is unmounted. For example:

```
# mkdir /mnt/iso
# mount -o loop linux.iso /mnt/iso
```

Now perform operations using files from `/mnt/iso`. ISO is a read-only filesystem.

Flush changing immediately with sync

While making changes on a mounted device, they are not immediately written to the physical devices. They are only written when the buffer is full. But, we can force writing of changes immediately by using the `sync` command as follows:

```
$ sync
```

Creating ISO files and hybrid ISO

An ISO image is an archive format that stores the exact storage images of optical disks such as CD-ROM, DVD-ROM, and so on. ISO files are commonly used to store content to be burned to optical media. We will now see how to create an ISO image from an optical disk. Many people rely on third-party utilities to do this, but using the command line, it's even simpler.

We also need to distinguish between bootable and non-bootable optical disks. Bootable disks are capable of booting from themselves and also running an operating system or another product. Non-bootable ISOs cannot do that. The important thing to note here is that just copying files from a bootable CD-ROM to another one is not sufficient to make the new one bootable. To preserve the bootable nature of a CD-ROM, it should be copied as a disk image using an ISO file.

Nowadays, most people use devices such as flash drives or hard disks as a replacement for optical disks. When we write a bootable ISO to a flash drive, it will no longer be bootable unless we use a special hybrid ISO image designed specifically for the purpose.

This recipe will give you an insight on ISO images and manipulations.

Getting ready

As we described many times in this book, Unix handles everything as files. Every device is a file. Hence, what if we want to copy an exact image of a device? We need to read all data from it and write to another file, right?

As we know, the `cat` command can be used to read any data and redirection can be used to write to a file.

How to do it...

In order to create an ISO image from `/dev/cdrom`, use the following command:

```
# cat /dev/cdrom > image.iso
```

Though this will work, the preferred way to create an ISO image is to use `dd`:

```
# dd if=/dev/cdrom of=image.iso
```

`mkisofs` is a command used to create an ISO system. The output file of `mkisofs` can be written to CD-ROM or DVD-ROM using utilities such as `cdrecord`. We can use `mkisofs` to create an ISO file using a directory containing all the required files that should appear as contents of an ISO file as follows:

```
$ mkisofs -V "Label" -o image.iso source_dir/
```

The `-o` option in the `mkisofs` command specifies the ISO file path. The `source_dir` command is the path of the directory that should be used as source content for the ISO and the `-V` option specifies the label that should be used for the ISO file.

There's more...

Let's learn more commands and techniques related to ISO files.

Hybrid ISO that boots off a flash drive or hard disk

Usually, bootable ISO files cannot be transferred or written to a USB storage device and booted the OS from the USB key. But, special type of ISO files called hybrid ISOs can be flashed and they are capable of booting from such devices.

We can convert standard ISO files into hybrid ISOs with the `isohybrid` command. The `isohybrid` command is a new utility and most Linux distros don't include this by default. If this is a case for your distro, you can download the syslinux package from `http://www.syslinux.org`.

Have a look at the following command:

```
# isohybrid image.iso
```

Using this command, we will have a hybrid ISO with the filename `image.iso` and it can be written to USB storage devices.

To write the ISO to a USB storage device, use the following command:

```
# dd if=image.iso of=/dev/sdb1
```

Use the appropriate device instead of `/dev/sdb1`, or, you can use `cat` as follows:

```
# cat image.iso >> /dev/sdb1
```

Burning an ISO from the command line

The `cdrecord` command is used to burn an ISO file into a CD-ROM or DVD-ROM. It can be used to burn the image to the CD-ROM as follows:

```
# cdrecord -v dev=/dev/cdrom image.iso
```

Some extra options are as follows:

▸ We can specify the burning speed with the `-speed` option as follows:

```
-speed SPEED
```

For example:

```
# cdrecord -v dev=/dev/cdrom image.iso -speed 8
```

Here, `8` is the speed specified as 8x.

▸ A CD-ROM can be burned in multisessions such that we can burn data multiple times on a disk. Multisession burning can be performed using the `-multi` option as follows:

```
# cdrecord -v dev=/dev/cdrom image.iso -multi
```

Playing with the CD-ROM tray

If you are on a desktop computer, try the following commands and have fun:

```
$ eject
```

This command is used to eject the tray.

```
$ eject -t
```

This command is used to close the tray.

For extra points, write a loop that opens and closes the tray a number of times.

Finding the difference between files, patching

When multiple versions of a file are available, it is very useful when we can find the differences between files being highlighted rather than comparing two files manually. If the files are large, it is very difficult and time consuming to compare them by hand. This recipe illustrates how to generate differences between files highlighted with line numbers. When working on large files by multiple developers, when one of them has made changes and these changes need to be shown to the other, sending the entire source code to other developers manually is time consuming. Sending a difference file instead is very helpful as it consists of only lines which are changed, or added or removed and line numbers are attached with it. This difference file is called a **patch file**. We can add the changes specified in the patch file to the original source code by using the patch command. We can also revert the changes by patching again. Let us see how to do this.

How to do it...

The diff command utility is used to generate difference files.

1. To generate difference information, create the following files:

   ❑ File 1: version1.txt

      ```
      this is the original text
      line2
      line3
      line4
      happy hacking !
      ```

   ❑ File 2: version2.txt

      ```
      this is the original text
      line2
      line4
      happy hacking !
      GNU is not UNIX
      ```

2. Nonunified `diff` output (without the `-u` flag) will be as follows:

```
$ diff version1.txt version2.txt
3d2
<line3
6c5
> GNU is not UNIX
```

3. The unified `diff` output will be as follows:

```
$ diff -u version1.txt version2.txt
--- version1.txt   2010-06-27 10:26:54.384884455 +0530
+++ version2.txt   2010-06-27 10:27:28.782140889 +0530
@@ -1,5 +1,5 @@
this is the original text
line2
-line3
line4
happy hacking !
-
+GNU is not UNIX
```

The `-u` option is used to produce a unified output. Everyone prefers unified output, as the unified output is more readable and because it is easier to interpret the difference that is being made between two files.

In unified `diff`, the lines starting with + are the newly-added lines and the lines starting with - are the removed lines.

4. A patch file can be generated by redirecting the `diff` output to a file, as follows:

```
$ diff -u version1.txt version2.txt > version.patch
```

Now, using the `patch` command we can apply changes to any of the two files. When applied to `version1.txt`, we get the `version2.txt` file. When applied to `version2.txt`, we receive `version1.txt`.

5. To apply the patch, use the following command:

```
$ patch -p1 version1.txt < version.patch
patching file version1.txt
```

We now have `version1.txt` with the same contents as that of `version2.txt`.

6. To revert the changes back, use the following command:

```
$ patch -p1 version1.txt < version.patch
patching file version1.txt
Reversed (or previously applied) patch detected!   Assume -R? [n] y
#Changes are reverted.
```

As shown, patching an already patched file reverts back the changes. To avoid prompting the user with y/n, we can use the -R option along with the patch command.

There's more...

Let's go through additional features available with diff.

Generating difference against directories

The diff command can also act recursively against directories. It will generate a difference output for all the descendant files in the directories. Use the following command:

```
$ diff -Naur directory1 directory2
```

The interpretation of each of the previous options is as follows:

- -N is for treating absent files as empty
- -a is to consider all files as text files
- -u is to produce unified output
- -r is to recursively traverse through the files in the directories

Using head and tail for printing the last or first 10 lines

When looking into a large file, which consists of thousands of lines, we will not use a command such as cat to print the entire file contents. Instead we look for a sample (for example, the first 10 lines of the file or the last 10 lines of the file). We may need to print the first *n* lines or last *n* lines and even print all the lines except the last *n* lines or all lines except first *n* lines.

Another use case is to print lines from *m*th to *n*th lines.

The commands head and tail can help us do this.

How to do it...

The head command always reads the header portion of the input file.

1. Print the first 10 lines as follows:

   ```
   $ head file
   ```

2. Read the data from stdin as follows:

   ```
   $ cat text | head
   ```

3. Specify the number of first lines to be printed as follows:

   ```
   $ head -n 4 file
   ```

   This command prints four lines.

4. Print all lines excluding the last M lines as follows:

   ```
   $ head -n -M file
   ```

   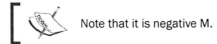 Note that it is negative M.

   For example, to print all the lines except the last five lines, use the following command line:

   ```
   $ seq 11 | head -n -5
   1
   2
   3
   4
   5
   6
   ```

   The following command will, however, print from 1 to 5:

   ```
   $ seq 100 | head -n 5
   ```

5. Printing by excluding the last lines is a very important usage of head. Now, let us see how to print, last few lines. Print the last 10 lines of a file as follows:

   ```
   $ tail file
   ```

6. In order to read from stdin, you can use the following command line:

   ```
   $ cat text | tail
   ```

7. Print the last five lines as follows:

```
$ tail -n 5 file
```

8. In order to print all lines excluding the first M lines, use the following code:

```
$ tail -n +(M+1)
```

For example, to print all lines except the first five lines, M + 1 = 6, therefore the command will be as follows:

```
$ seq 100 | tail -n +6
```

This will print from 6 to 100.

One of the important usages of `tail` is to read a constantly growing file. Since new lines are constantly appended to the end of the file, `tail` can be used to display all new lines as they are written to the file. When we run `tail` without specifying any options, it will read the last 10 lines and exit. However, by that time, new lines would have been appended to the file by a process. To constantly monitor the growth of file, `tail` has a special option -f or --follow, which enables `tail` to follow the appended lines and keep being updated as data is added:

```
$ tail -f growing_file
```

You will probably want to use this on logfiles. The command to monitor the growth of the files would be:

```
# tail -f /var/log/messages
```

Or:

```
$ dmesg | tail -f
```

We frequently run `dmesg` to look at kernel ring buffer messages either to debug the USB devices or to look at `sdX` (`X` is the minor number for the `sd` device corresponding to a SCSI disk). The `-f` tail can also add a sleep interval `-s`, so that we can set the interval during which the file updates are monitored.

`tail` has the interesting property that allows it to terminate after a given process ID dies.

Suppose we are reading a growing file, and a process `Foo` is appending data to the file, the `-f` tail should be executed until the process `Foo` dies.

```
$ PID=$(pidof Foo)
$ tail -f file --pid $PID
```

When the process `Foo` terminates, `tail` also terminates.

Let us work on an example.

1. Create a new file `file.txt` and open the file in gedit (you can use any text editor).

2. Add new lines to the file and make frequent file saves in the gedit.

3. Now run the following commands:

```
$ PID=$(pidof gedit)
$ tail -f file.txt --pid $PID
```

When you make frequent changes to the file, it will be written to the terminal by the `tail` command. When you close the gedit, the `tail` command will get terminated.

Listing only directories – alternative methods

Listing only directories via scripting can be deceptively difficult. This recipe is worth knowing since it introduces multiple ways of listing only directories with various useful techniques.

Getting ready

There are multiple ways of listing directories only. When you ask people about these techniques, the first answer that they would probably give is `dir`. However, the `dir` command is just another command like `ls`, but with fewer options. Let us see how to list directories.

How to do it...

There are several ways in which directories in the current path can be displayed:

1. Using `ls` with `-l` to print directories:

```
$ ls -d */
```

2. Using `ls` `-F` with `grep`:

```
$ ls -F | grep "/$"
```

3. Using `ls` `-l` with `grep`:

```
$ ls -l | grep "^d"
```

4. Using `find` to print directories:

```
$ find . -type d -maxdepth 1 -print
```

How it works...

When the -F parameter is used with ls, all entries are appended with some type of file characters such as @, *, |, and so on. For directories, entries are appended with the / character. We use grep to filter only entries ending with the /$ end-of-line indicator.

The first character of any line in the ls -d output is the type of file character. For a directory, the type of file character is "d". Hence, we use grep to filter lines starting with "d". ^ is a start-of-line indicator.

The find command can take the parameter type as directory and maxdepth is set to 1 since we don't want it to search inside the subdirectories.

Fast command-line navigation using pushd and popd

When dealing with multiple locations on a terminal or shell prompt, our common practice is to copy and paste the paths. However, this is ineffective when there is only command-line access without a GUI. For example, if we are dealing with locations /var/www, /home/slynux, and /usr/src, when we need to navigate to these locations one by one, it is really difficult to type the path every time when we need to switch between the paths. Hence, the **command-line interface (CLI)** based navigation techniques such as pushd and popd are used. Let us see how to use them in this recipe.

Getting ready

pushd and popd are used to switch between multiple directories without the copying and pasting of directory paths. pushd and popd operate on a stack. We know that a stack is a **last in first out (LIFO)** data structure. It will store the directory paths in a stack and switch between them using the push and pop operations.

How to do it...

We omit the use of the cd command while using pushd and popd:

1. To push and change a directory to a path, use the following command:

   ```
   ~ $ pushd /var/www
   ```

   Now the stack contains /var/www ~ and the current directory is changed to /var/www.

2. Now, again push the next directory path as follows:

   ```
   /var/www $ pushd /usr/src
   ```

Now the stack contains `/usr/src` `/var/www` `~` and the current directory is `/usr/src`.

You can similarly push as many directory paths as needed.

3. To view the stack contents, use the following command:

    ```
    $ dirs
    /usr/src /var/www ~ /usr/share /etc
    0        1          2 3          4
    ```

4. Now when you want to switch to any path in the list, number each path from 0 to n, then use the path number for which we need to switch, for example:

    ```
    $ pushd +3
    ```

    Now it will rotate the stack and switch to the `/usr/share` directory.

    `pushd` will always add paths to the stack, to remove paths from the stack use `popd`.

5. To remove a last pushed path and change directory to the next directory, use the following command:

    ```
    $ popd
    ```

    Suppose the stack is `/usr/src` `/var/www` `~` `/usr/share` `/etc` such that the current directory is `/usr/src`, then `popd` will change the stack to `/var/www` `~` `/usr/share` `/etc` and change the directory to `/var/www`.

6. To remove a specific path from the list, use `popd +num`:

    `num` is counted as 0 to n from left to right.

There's more...

Let's go through the essential directory navigation practices.

Most frequently used directory switching

`pushd` and `popd` can be used when there are more than three directory paths used. But when you use only two locations, there is an alternative and easier way. That is `cd -`.

The current path is `/var/www`.

```
/var/www $  cd /usr/src
/usr/src $ # do something
```

Now, to switch back to `/var/www`; you don't have to type again, but just execute:

```
/usr/src $ cd -
```

Now, again to switch to `/usr/src` as follows:

`/var/www $ cd -`

Counting the number of lines, words, and characters in a file

Counting the number of lines, words, and characters from a text file are very useful for text manipulations. In several cases, these counts are used in indirect ways to perform some hacks in order to produce the required output patterns and results. This book includes some tricky examples in other chapters. **Counting LOC (Lines of Code)** is a very important application for developers. We may need to count special types of files excluding unnecessary files. A combination of wc with other commands help to perform that.

wc is the utility used for counting. It stands for **word count**. Let us see how to use wc to count lines, words, and characters.

How to do it...

We can use various options for wc to count the number of lines, words, and characters:

1. Count the number of lines in the following manner:

   `$ wc -l file`

2. To use `stdin` as input, use the following command:

   `$ cat file | wc -l`

3. Count the number of words as follows:

   `$ wc -w file`

   `$ cat file | wc -w`

4. In order to count the number of characters, use the following commands:

   `$ wc -c file`

   `$ cat file | wc -c`

   For example, we can count the characters in a text as follows:

   `echo -n 1234 | wc -c`

   `4`

   `-n` is used to avoid an extra newline character.

5. To print the number of lines, words, and characters, execute `wc` without any options:

```
$ wc file
    1435    15763   112200
```

Those are the number of lines, words, and characters respectively.

6. Print the length of the longest line in a file using the `-L` option:

```
$ wc file -L
205
```

Printing the directory tree

Graphically representing directories and filesystems as a tree hierarchy is quite useful when preparing tutorials and documents. Also, they are sometimes useful in writing certain monitoring scripts that help to look at the filesystem using easy-to-read tree representations. Let us see how to do it.

Getting ready

The `tree` command is the hero that helps us to print graphical trees of files and directories. Usually, `tree` does not come with preinstalled Linux distributions. You have to install it using the package manager.

How to do it...

The following is a sample Unix filesystem tree to show an example:

```
$ tree ~/unixfs
unixfs/
|-- bin
|   |-- cat
|   `-- ls
|-- etc
|   `-- passwd
|-- home
|   |-- pactpub
|   |   |-- automate.sh
|   |   `-- schedule
|   `-- slynux
|-- opt
```

```
|-- tmp
`-- usr

8 directories, 5 files
```

The `tree` command comes with many interesting options, let us look at a few of them:

- To highlight only files matched by the pattern, use the following syntax:

  ```
  $ tree path -P PATTERN # Pattern should be wildcard
  ```

  For example:

  ```
  $ tree PATH -P "*.sh" # Replace PATH with a directory path
  |-- home
  |    |-- packtpub
  |    |    `-- automate.sh
  ```

- To highlight only files excluding the match pattern:

  ```
  $ tree path -I PATTERN
  ```

- To print the size along with files and directories, use the -h option:

  ```
  $ tree -h
  ```

There's more...

Let's see an interesting option that is available with the `tree` command.

HTML output for tree

It is possible to generate an HTML output from the `tree` command. For example, use the following command to create an HTML file with the tree output:

```
$ tree PATH -H http://localhost -o out.html
```

Replace `http://localhost` with the URL where you are planning to host the file. Replace PATH with a real path for the base directory. For the current directory use . as PATH.

The web page generated from the directory listing will look as follows:

```
Directory Tree

http://localhost
 |-- bin
 |-- etc
 |-- home
 |    |-- pactpub
 |    |    `-- automate.sh
 |    `-- slynux
 |-- opt
 |-- tmp
 `-- usr


8 directories, 1 file
```

tree v1.5.3 (c) 1996 - 2009 by Steve Baker and Thomas Moore
HTML output hacked and copyleft (c) 1998 by Francesc Rocher
Charsets / OS/2 support (c) 2001 by Kyosuke Tokoro

4
Texting and Driving

In this chapter, we will cover the following recipes:

- ▸ Using regular expressions
- ▸ Searching and mining text inside a file with grep
- ▸ Cutting a file column-wise with cut
- ▸ Using sed to perform text replacement
- ▸ Using awk for advanced text processing
- ▸ Finding frequency of words used in a given file
- ▸ Compressing or decompressing JavaScript
- ▸ Merging multiple files as columns
- ▸ Printing the nth word or column in a file or line
- ▸ Printing text between line numbers or patterns
- ▸ Printing lines in the reverse order
- ▸ Parsing e-mail address and URLs from text
- ▸ Removing a sentence in a file containing a word
- ▸ Replacing a pattern with text in all files in a directory
- ▸ Text slicing and parameter operations

Introduction

The shell scripting language is packed with all the essential problem-solving components for Unix/Linux systems. Text processing is one of the key areas where shell scripting is used, and there are beautiful utilities such as `sed`, `awk`, `grep`, and `cut`, which can be combined to solve problems related to text processing.

Various utilities help to process a file in fine detail of a character, line, word, column, row, and so on, allowing us to manipulate a text file in many ways. Regular expressions are the core of pattern-matching techniques, and most of the text-processing utilities come with support for it. By using suitable regular expression strings, we can produce the desired output, such as filtering, stripping, replacing, and searching.

This chapter includes a collection of recipes, which walk through many contexts of problems based on text processing that will be helpful in writing real scripts.

Using regular expressions

Regular expressions are the heart of text-processing techniques based on pattern matching. For fluency in writing text-processing tools, one must have a basic understanding of regular expressions. Using wild card techniques, the scope of matching text with patterns is very limited. Regular expressions are a form of tiny, highly-specialized programming language used to match text. A typical regular expression for matching an e-mail address might look like `[a-z0-9_]+@[a-z0-9]+\.[a-z]+`.

If this looks weird, don't worry, it is really simple once you understand the concepts through this recipe.

How to do it...

Regular expressions are composed of text fragments and symbols, which have special meanings. Using these, we can construct any suitable regular expression string to match any text according to the context. As **regex** is a generic language to match texts, we are not introducing any tools in this recipe. However, it follows in the other recipes in this chapter.

Let's see a few examples of text matching:

- To match all words in a given text, we can write the regex as follows:

  `( ?[a-zA-Z]+ ?)`

  `?` is the notation for zero or one occurrence of the previous expression, which in this case is the space character. The `[a-zA-Z]+` notation represents one or more alphabet characters (a-z and A-Z).

- To match an IP address, we can write the regex as follows:

  `[0-9]{1,3}\.[0-9]{1,3}\.[0-9]{1,3}\.[0-9]{1,3}`

  Or:

  `[[:digit:]]{1,3}\.[[:digit:]]{1,3}\.[[:digit:]]{1,3}\.[[:digit:]]{1,3}`

We know that an IP address is in the form `192.168.0.2`. It is in the form of four integers (each from 0 to 255), separated by dots (for example, `192.168.0.2`).

`[0-9]` or `[:digit:]` represents a match for digits from 0 to 9. `{1,3}` matches one to three digits and `\.` matches the dot character (`.`).

This regex will match an IP address in the text being processed. However, it doesn't check for the validity of the address. For example, an IP address of the form `123.300.1.1` will be matched by the regex despite being an invalid IP. This is because when parsing text streams, usually the aim is to only detect IPs.

How it works...

Let's first go through the basic components of regular expressions (regex):

regex	Description	Example
^	This specifies the start of the line marker.	`^tux` matches a line that starts with `tux`.
$	This specifies the end of the line marker.	`tux$` matches a line that ends with `tux`.
.	This matches any one character.	`Hack.` matches `Hack1`, `Hacki`, but not `Hack12` or `Hackil`; only one additional character matches.
[]	This matches any one of the characters enclosed in `[chars]`.	`coo[kl]` matches `cook` or `cool`.
[^]	This matches any one of the characters except those that are enclosed in `[^chars]`.	`9[^01]` matches `92` and `93`, but not `91` and `90`.
[-]	This matches any character within the range specified in `[]`.	`[1-5]` matches any digits from 1 to 5.
?	This means that the preceding item must match one or zero times.	`colou?r` matches `color` or `colour`, but not `colouur`.
+	This means that the preceding item must match one or more times.	`Rollno-9+` matches `Rollno-99` and `Rollno-9`, but not `Rollno-`.
*	This means that the preceding item must match zero or more times.	`co*l` matches `cl`, `col`, and `coool`.

regex	Description	Example
()	This treats the terms enclosed as one entity	`ma(tri)?x` matches `max` or `matrix`.
{n}	This means that the preceding item must match n times.	`[0-9]{3}` matches any three-digit number. `[0-9]{3}` can be expanded as `[0-9][0-9][0-9]`.
{n,}	This specifies the minimum number of times the preceding item should match.	`[0-9]{2,}` matches any number that is two digits or longer.
{n, m}	This specifies the minimum and maximum number of times the preceding item should match.	`[0-9]{2,5}` matches any number that has two digits to five digits.
|	This specifies the alternation—one of the items on either of side of | should match.	`Oct (1st | 2nd)` matches `Oct 1st` or `Oct 2nd`.
\	This is the escape character for escaping any of the special characters mentioned previously.	`a\.b` matches `a.b`, but not `ajb`. It ignores the special meaning of `.` because of `\`.

For more details on the regular expression components available, you can refer to the following URL:

`http://www.linuxforu.com/2011/04/sed-explained-part-1/`

There's more...

Let's see how the special meanings of certain characters are specified in the regular expressions.

Treatment of special characters

Regular expressions use some characters, such as $, ^, ., *, +, {, and }, as special characters. But, what if we want to use these characters as normal text characters? Let's see an example of a regex, `a.txt`.

This will match the character a, followed by any character (due to the '.' character), which is then followed by the string `txt`. However, we want '.' to match a literal '.' instead of any character. In order to achieve this, we precede the character with a backward slash \ (doing this is called escaping the character). This indicates that the regex wants to match the literal character rather than its special meaning. Hence, the final regex becomes `a\.txt`.

Visualizing regular expressions

Regular expressions can be tough to understand at times, but for people who are good at understanding things with diagrams, there are utilities available to help in visualizing regex. Here is one such tool that you can use by browsing to `http://www.regexper.com`; it basically lets you enter a regular expression and creates a nice graph to help understand it. Here is a screenshot showing the regular expression we saw in the previous section:

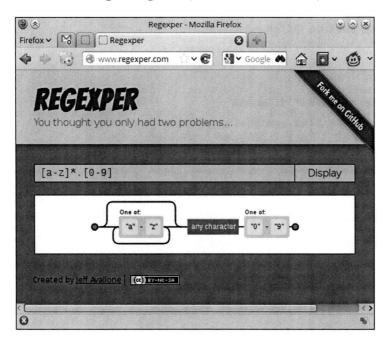

Searching and mining a text inside a file with grep

Searching inside a file is an important use case in text processing. We may need to search through thousands of lines in a file to find out some required data, by using certain specifications. This recipe will help you learn how to locate data items of a given specification from a pool of data.

How to do it...

The `grep` command is the magic Unix utility for searching in text. It accepts regular expressions, and can produce output in various formats. Additionally, it has numerous interesting options. Let's see how to use them:

1. To search for lines of text that contain the given pattern:

    ```
    $ grep pattern filename
    this is the line containing pattern
    ```

    Or:

    ```
    $ grep "pattern" filename
    this is the line containing pattern
    ```

2. We can also read from `stdin` as follows:

    ```
    $ echo -e "this is a word\nnext line" | grep word
    this is a word
    ```

3. Perform a search in multiple files by using a single `grep` invocation, as follows:

    ```
    $ grep "match_text" file1 file2 file3 ...
    ```

4. We can highlight the word in the line by using the `--color` option as follows:

    ```
    $ grep word filename --color=auto
    this is the line containing word
    ```

5. Usually, the `grep` command only interprets some of the special characters in `match_text`. To use the full set of regular expressions as input arguments, the `-E` option should be added, which means an extended regular expression. Or, we can use an extended regular expression enabled `grep` command, `egrep`. For example:

    ```
    $ grep -E "[a-z]+" filename
    ```

    Or:

    ```
    $ egrep "[a-z]+" filename
    ```

6. In order to output only the matching portion of a text in a file, use the `-o` option as follows:

    ```
    $ echo this is a line. | egrep -o "[a-z]+\."
    line.
    ```

7. In order to print all of the lines, except the line containing `match_pattern`, use:

    ```
    $ grep -v match_pattern file
    ```

    The `-v` option added to `grep` inverts the match results.

8. Count the number of lines in which a matching string or regex match appears in a file or text, as follows:

```
$ grep -c "text" filename
10
```

It should be noted that -c counts only the number of matching lines, not the number of times a match is made. For example:

```
$ echo -e "1 2 3 4\nhello\n5 6" | egrep  -c "[0-9]"
2
```

Even though there are six matching items, it prints 2, since there are only two matching lines. Multiple matches in a single line are counted only once.

9. To count the number of matching items in a file, use the following trick:

```
$ echo -e "1 2 3 4\nhello\n5 6" | egrep -o "[0-9]" | wc -1
6
```

10. Print the line number of the match string as follows:

```
$ cat sample1.txt
gnu is not unix
linux is fun
bash is art
$ cat sample2.txt
planetlinux

$ grep linux -n sample1.txt
2:linux is fun
```

or

```
$ cat sample1.txt | grep linux -n
```

If multiple files are used, it will also print the filename with the result as follows:

```
$ grep linux -n sample1.txt sample2.txt
sample1.txt:2:linux is fun
sample2.txt:2:planetlinux
```

11. Print the character or byte offset at which a pattern matches, as follows:

```
$ echo gnu is not unix | grep -b -o "not"
7:not
```

The character offset for a string in a line is a counter from 0, starting with the first character. In the preceding example, not is at the seventh offset position (that is, not starts from the seventh character in the line; that is, gnu is not unix).

The -b option is always used with -o.

12. To search over multiple files, and list which files contain the pattern, we use the following:

```
$ grep -l linux sample1.txt sample2.txt
sample1.txt
sample2.txt
```

The inverse of the -l argument is -L. The -L argument returns a list of non-matching files.

There's more...

We have seen the basic usages of the grep command, but that's not it; the grep command comes with even more features. Let's go through those.

Recursively search many files

To recursively search for a text over many directories of descendants, use the following command:

```
$ grep "text" . -R -n
```

In this command, "." specifies the current directory.

 The options -R and -r mean the same thing when used with grep.

For example:

```
$ cd src_dir
$ grep "test_function()" . -R -n
./miscutils/test.c:16:test_function();
```

test_function() exists in line number 16 of miscutils/test.c.

 This is one of the most frequently used commands by developers. It is used to find files in the source code where a certain text exists.

Ignoring case of pattern

The `-i` argument helps match patterns to be evaluated, without considering the uppercase or lowercase. For example:

```
$ echo hello world | grep -i "HELLO"
hello
```

grep by matching multiple patterns

Usually, we specify single patterns for matching. However, we can use an argument `-e` to specify multiple patterns for matching, as follows:

```
$ grep -e "pattern1" -e "pattern"
```

This will print the lines that contain either of the patterns and output one line for each match. For example:

```
$ echo this is a line of text | grep -e "this" -e "line" -o
this
line
```

There is also another way to specify multiple patterns. We can use a pattern file for reading patterns. Write patterns to match line-by-line, and execute `grep` with a `-f` argument as follows:

```
$ grep -f pattern_filesource_filename
```

For example:

```
$ cat pat_file
hello
cool


$ echo hello this is cool | grep -f pat_file
hello this is cool
```

Including and excluding files in a grep search

`grep` can include or exclude files in which to search. We can specify `include` files or `exclude` files by using wild card patterns.

To search only for `.c` and `.cpp` files recursively in a directory by excluding all other file types, use the following command:

```
$ grep "main()" . -r  --include *.{c,cpp}
```

Note, that `some{string1,string2,string3}` expands as `somestring1 somestring2 somestring3`.

Exclude all `README` files in the search, as follows:

```
$ grep "main()" . -r --exclude "README"
```

To exclude directories, use the `--exclude-dir` option.

To read a list of files to exclude from a file, use `--exclude-from FILE`.

Using grep with xargs with zero-byte suffix

The `xargs` command is often used to provide a list of file names as a command-line argument to another command. When filenames are used as command-line arguments, it is recommended to use a zero-byte terminator for the filenames instead of a space terminator. Some of the filenames can contain a space character, and it will be misinterpreted as a terminator, and a single filename may be broken into two file names (for example, `New file.txt` can be interpreted as two filenames `New` and `file.txt`). This problem can be avoided by using a zero-byte suffix. We use `xargs` so as to accept a `stdin` text from commands such as `grep` and `find`. Such commands can output text to `stdout` with a zero-byte suffix. In order to specify that the input terminator for filenames is zero byte (`\0`), we should use `-0` with `xargs`.

Create some test files as follows:

```
$ echo "test" > file1
$ echo "cool" > file2
$ echo "test" > file3
```

In the following command sequence, `grep` outputs filenames with a zero-byte terminator (`\0`), because of the `-Z` option with `grep`. `xargs -0` reads the input and separates filenames with a zero-byte terminator:

```
$ grep "test" file* -lZ | xargs -0 rm
```

Usually, `-Z` is used along with `-l`.

Silent output for grep

Sometimes, instead of actually looking at the matched strings, we are only interested in whether there was a match or not. For this, we can use the quiet option (`-q`), where the `grep` command does not write any output to the standard output. Instead, it runs the command and returns an exit status based on success or failure.

We know that a command returns 0 on success, and non-zero on failure.

Let's go through a script that makes use of grep in a quiet mode, for testing whether a match text appears in a file or not.

```
#!/bin/bash
#Filename: silent_grep.sh
#Desc: Testing whether a file contain a text or not

if [ $# -ne 2 ]; then
  echo "Usage: $0 match_text filename"
  exit 1
fi

match_text=$1
filename=$2
grep -q "$match_text" $filename

if [ $? -eq 0 ]; then
  echo "The text exists in the file"
else
  echo "Text does not exist in the file"
fi
```

The silent_grep.sh script can be run as follows, by providing a match word (Student) and a file name (student_data.txt) as the command argument:

```
$ ./silent_grep.sh Student student_data.txt
The text exists in the file
```

Printing lines before and after text matches

Context-based printing is one of the nice features of grep. Suppose a matching line for a given match text is found, grep usually prints only the matching lines. But, we may need "n" lines after the matching line, or "n" lines before the matching line, or both. This can be performed by using context-line control in grep. Let's see how to do it.

In order to print three lines after a match, use the -A option:

```
$ seq 10 | grep 5 -A 3
5
6
7
8
```

In order to print three lines before the match, use the `-B` option:

```
$ seq 10 | grep 5 -B 3
2
3
4
5
```

Print three lines after and before the match, and use the `-C` option as follows:

```
$ seq 10 | grep 5 -C 3
2
3
4
5
6
7
8
```

If there are multiple matches, then each section is delimited by a line "`--`":

```
$ echo -e "a\nb\nc\na\nb\nc" | grep a -A 1
a
b
--
a
b
```

Cutting a file column-wise with cut

We may need to cut the text by a column rather than a row. Let's assume that we have a text file containing student reports with columns, such as `Roll`, `Name`, `Mark`, and `Percentage`. We need to extract only the name of the students to another file or any nth column in the file, or extract two or more columns. This recipe will illustrate how to perform this task.

How to do it...

`cut` is a small utility that often comes to our help for cutting in column fashion. It can also specify the delimiter that separates each column. In `cut` terminology, each column is known as a **field**.

1. To extract particular fields or columns, use the following syntax:

```
cut -f FIELD_LIST filename
```

FIELD_LIST is a list of columns that are to be displayed. The list consists of column numbers delimited by commas. For example:

```
$ cut -f 2,3 filename
```

Here, the second and the third columns are displayed.

2. cut can also read input text from stdin.

   Tab is the default delimiter for fields or columns. If lines without delimiters are found, they are also printed. To avoid printing lines that do not have delimiter characters, attach the -s option along with cut. An example of using the cut command for columns is as follows:

```
$ cat student_data.txt
No   Name   Mark   Percent
1    Sarath   45   90
2    Alex   49   98
3    Anu   45   90


$ cut -f1 student_data.txt
No
1
2
3
```

3. Extract multiple fields as follows:

```
$ cut -f2,4 student_data.txt
Name        Percent
Sarath      90
Alex        98
Anu           90
```

4. To print multiple columns, provide a list of column numbers separated by commas as arguments to -f.

5. We can also complement the extracted fields by using the `--complement` option. Suppose you have many fields and you want to print all the columns except the third column, then use the following command:

```
$ cut -f3 --complement student_data.txt
No   Name     Percent
1    Sarath   90
2    Alex     98
3    Anu      90
```

6. To specify the delimiter character for the fields, use the `-d` option as follows:

```
$ cat delimited_data.txt
No;Name;Mark;Percent
1;Sarath;45;90
2;Alex;49;98
3;Anu;45;90


$ cut -f2 -d";" delimited_data.txt
Name
Sarath
Alex
Anu
```

There's more

The `cut` command has more options to specify the character sequences to be displayed as columns. Let's go through the additional options available with `cut`.

Specifying the range of characters or bytes as fields

Suppose that we don't rely on delimiters, but we need to extract fields in such a way that we need to define a range of characters (counting from 0 as the start of line) as a field. Such extractions are possible with cut.

Let's see what notations are possible:

N-	from the Nth byte, character, or field, to the end of the line
N-M	from the Nth to Mth (included) byte, character, or field
-M	from the first to Mth (included) byte, character, or field

We use the preceding notations to specify fields as a range of bytes or characters with the following options:

- ▸ -b for bytes
- ▸ -c for characters
- ▸ -f for defining fields

For example:

```
$ cat range_fields.txt
abcdefghijklmnopqrstuvwxyz
abcdefghijklmnopqrstuvwxyz
abcdefghijklmnopqrstuvwxyz
abcdefghijklmnopqrstuvwxy
```

You can print the first to fifth characters as follows:

```
$ cut -c1-5 range_fields.txt
abcde
abcde
abcde
abcde
```

The first two characters can be printed as follows:

```
$ cut range_fields.txt -c -2
ab
ab
ab
ab
```

Replace -c with -b to count in bytes.

We can specify the output delimiter while using with -c, -f, and -b, as follows:

```
--output-delimiter "delimiter string"
```

When multiple fields are extracted with -b or -c, the --output-delimiter is a must. Otherwise, you cannot distinguish between fields if it is not provided. For example:

```
$ cut range_fields.txt -c1-3,6-9 --output-delimiter ","
abc,fghi
abc,fghi
abc,fghi
abc,fghi
```

Using sed to perform text replacement

sed stands for **stream editor**. It is a very essential tool for text processing, and a marvelous utility to play around with regular expressions. A well-known usage of the sed command is for text replacement. This recipe will cover most of the frequently-used sed techniques.

How to do it...

sed can be used to replace occurrences of a string with another string in a given text.

1. It can be matched using regular expressions.

   ```
   $ sed 's/pattern/replace_string/' file
   ```

   Or:

   ```
   $ cat file | sed 's/pattern/replace_string/'
   ```

   This command reads from stdin.

    If you use the vi editor, you will notice that the command to replace the text is very similar to the one discussed here.

2. By default, sed only prints the substituted text. To save the changes along with the substitutions to the same file, use the -i option. Most of the users follow multiple redirections to save the file after making a replacement as follows:

   ```
   $ sed 's/text/replace/' file >newfile
   $ mv newfile file
   ```

   However, it can be done in just one line; for example:

   ```
   $ sed -i 's/text/replace/' file
   ```

3. These usages of the sed command will replace the first occurrence of the pattern in each line. If we want to replace every occurrence, we need to add the g parameter at the end, as follows:

   ```
   $ sed 's/pattern/replace_string/g' file
   ```

   The /g suffix means that it will substitute every occurrence. However, we sometimes need to replace only the Nth occurrence onwards. For this, we can use the /Ng form of the option.

Have a look at the following commands:

```
$ echo thisthisthisthis | sed 's/this/THIS/2g'
thisTHISTHISTHIS
```

```
$ echo thisthisthisthis | sed 's/this/THIS/3g'
thisthisTHISTHIS
```

```
$ echo thisthisthisthis | sed 's/this/THIS/4g'
thisthisthisTHIS
```

We have used / in `sed` as a delimiter character. We can use any delimiter characters as follows:

```
sed 's:text:replace:g'
sed 's|text|replace|g'
```

When the delimiter character appears inside the pattern, we have to escape it using the \ prefix, as follows:

```
sed 's|te\|xt|replace|g'
```

\| is a delimiter appearing in the pattern replaced with escape.

There's more...

The `sed` command comes with numerous options for text manipulation. By combining the options available with `sed` in logical sequences, many complex problems can be solved in one line. Let's see the different options available with `sed`.

Removing blank lines

Removing blank lines is a simple technique by using `sed` to remove blank lines. Blanks can be matched with regular expression ^$:

```
$ sed '/^$/d' file
```

/`pattern`/d will remove lines matching the pattern.

For blank lines, the line end marker appears next to the line start marker.

Performing replacement directly in the file

When a filename is passed to `sed`, it usually prints its output to `stdout`. Instead, if we want it to actually modify the contents of the file, we use the `-i` option, as follows:

```
$ sed 's/PATTERN/replacement/' -i filename
```

For example, replace all three-digit numbers with another specified number in a file, as follows:

```
$ cat sed_data.txt
11 abc 111 this 9 file contains 111 11 88 numbers 0000

$ sed -i 's/\b[0-9]\{3\}\b/NUMBER/g' sed_data.txt
$ cat sed_data.txt
11 abc NUMBER this 9 file contains NUMBER 11 88 numbers 0000
```

The preceding one-liner replaces three-digit numbers only. \b[0-9]\{3\}\b is the regular expression used to match three-digit numbers. [0-9] is the range of digits; that is, from 0 to 9. {3} is used for matching the preceding character thrice. \ in \{3\} is used to give a special meaning for { and }. \b is the word boundary marker.

It's a useful practice to first try the sed command without -i to make sure your regex is correct, and once you are satisfied with the result, add the -i option to actually make changes to the file. Alternatively, you can use the following form of sed:

```
sed -i .bak 's/abc/def/' file
```

In this case, sed will not only perform the replacement on the file, but it will also create a file called file.bak, which will contain the original contents.

Matched string notation (&)

In sed, we can use & as the matched string for the substitution pattern, in such a way that we can use the matched string in the replacement string.

For example:

```
$ echo this is an example | sed 's/\w\+/[&]/g'
[this] [is] [an] [example]
```

Here, regex \w\+ matches every word. Then, we replace it with [&]. & corresponds to the word that is matched.

Substring match notation (\1)

& corresponds to the matched string for the given pattern. We can also match the substrings of the given pattern. Let's see how to do it.

```
$ echo this is digit 7 in a number | sed 's/digit \([0-9]\)/\1/'
this is 7 in a number
```

The preceding command replaces `digit` 7 with 7. The substring matched is 7. `\(pattern\)` is used to match the substring. The pattern is enclosed in `()`, and is escaped with slashes. For the first substring match, the corresponding notation is `\1`; for the second, it is `\2`, and so on. Go through the following example with multiple matches:

```
$ echo seven EIGHT | sed 's/\([a-z]\+\) \([A-Z]\+\)/\2 \1/'
EIGHT seven
```

`([a-z]\+\)` matches the first word, and `\([A-Z]\+\)` matches the second word. `\1` and `\2` are used for referencing them. This type of referencing is called **back referencing**. In the replacement part, their order is changed as `\2 \1` and, hence, it appears in reverse order.

Combination of multiple expressions

The combination of multiple `sed` using a pipe can be replaced as follows:

```
sed 'expression' | sed 'expression'
```

The preceding command is equivalent to the following:

```
$ sed 'expression; expression'
```

Or:

```
$ sed -e 'expression' -e expression'
```

For example,

```
$ echo abc | sed 's/a/A/' | sed 's/c/C/'
AbC
$ echo abc | sed 's/a/A/;s/c/C/'
AbC
$ echo abc | sed -e 's/a/A/' -e 's/c/C/'
AbC
```

Quoting

Usually, it is seen that the `sed` expression is quoted by using single quotes. But, double quotes can also be used. Double quotes expand the expression by evaluating it. Using double quotes are useful when we want to use a variable string in a `sed` expression.

For example:

```
$ text=hello
$ echo hello world | sed "s/$text/HELLO/"
HELLO world
```

`$text` is evaluated as `hello`.

Using awk for advanced text processing

awk is a tool designed to work with data streams. It is very interesting, as it can operate on columns and rows. It supports many built-in functionalities, such as arrays and functions, in the C programming language. Its biggest advantage is its flexibility.

Getting ready...

The structure of an awk script is as follows:

```
awk ' BEGIN{  print "start" } pattern { commands } END{ print "end" }
file
```

The awk command can read from stdin also.

An awk script usually consists of three parts—BEGIN, END, and a common statements block with the pattern match option. The three of them are optional and any of them can be absent in the script.

How to do it...

Let's write a simple awk script enclosed in single quotes or double quotes, as follows:

```
awk 'BEGIN { statements } { statements } END { end statements }'
```

Or, alternately, use the following command:

```
awk "BEGIN { statements } { statements } END { end statements }"
```

For example:

```
$ awk 'BEGIN { i=0 } { i++ } END{ print i}' filename
```

Or:

```
$ awk "BEGIN { i=0 } { i++ } END{ print i }" filename
```

How it works...

The awk command works in the following manner:

1. Execute the statements in the BEGIN { commands } block.
2. Read one line from the file or stdin, and execute pattern { commands }. Repeat this step until the end of the file is reached.
3. When the end of the input stream is reached, execute the END { commands } block.

The BEGIN block is executed before awk starts reading lines from the input stream. It is an optional block. The statements, such as variable initialization and printing the output header for an output table, are common statements that are written in the BEGIN block.

The END block is similar to the BEGIN block. It gets executed when awk completes reading all the lines from the input stream. The statements, such as printing results after analyzing all the values calculated for all the lines or printing the conclusion are the commonly-used statements in the END block (for example, after comparing all the lines, print the maximum number from a file). This is an optional block.

The most important block is of the common commands with the pattern block. This block is also optional. If this block is not provided, by default { print } gets executed so as to print each of the lines read. This block gets executed for each line read by awk. It is like a while loop for lines read, with statements provided inside the body of the loop.

When a line is read, it checks whether the provided pattern matches the line. The pattern can be a regular expression match, conditions, range of lines match, and so on. If the current read line matches with the pattern, it executes the statements enclosed in { }.

The pattern is optional. If it is not used, all the lines are matched and the statements inside { } are executed.

Let's go through the following example:

```
$ echo -e "line1\nline2" | awk 'BEGIN{ print "Start" } { print } END{
print "End" } '
Start
line1
line2
End
```

When print is used without an argument, it will print the current line. There are two important things to be kept in mind about it. When the arguments of the print are separated by commas, they are printed with a space delimiter. Double quotes are used as the concatenation operator in the context of print in awk.

For example:

```
$ echo | awk '{ var1="v1"; var2="v2"; var3="v3"; \
print var1,var2,var3 ; }'
```

The preceding statement will print the values of the variables as follows:

```
v1 v2 v3
```

The `echo` command writes a single line into the standard output. Hence, the statements in the { } block of `awk` are executed once. If the standard input to `awk` contains multiple lines, the commands in `awk` will be executed multiple times.

Concatenation can be used as follows:

```
$ echo | awk '{ var1="v1"; var2="v2"; var3="v3"; \
print var1 "-" var2 "-" var3 ; }'
```

The output will be as follows:

```
v1-v2-v3
```

{ } is like a block in a loop, iterating through each line of a file.

 Usually, we place initial variable assignments, such as `var=0`; and `like` statements, print the file header in the `BEGIN` block. In the `END{ }` block, we place statements such as printing results.

There's more...

The `awk` command comes with a lot of rich features. In order to master the art of `awk` programming, you should be familiar with the important `awk` options and functionalities. Let's go through the essential functionalities of `awk`.

Special variables

Some special variables that can be used with `awk` are as follows:

- `NR`: It stands for the current record number, which corresponds to the current line number when it uses lines as records
- `NF`: It stands for the number of fields, and corresponds to the number of fields in the current record under execution (fields are delimited by space)
- `$0`: It is a variable that contains the text content of the current line under execution
- `$1`: It is a variable that holds the text of the first field
- `$2`: It is the variable that holds the text of the second field

For example:

```
$ echo -e "line1 f2 f3\nline2 f4 f5\nline3 f6 f7" | \

awk '{
```

```
print "Line no:"NR",No of fields:"NF, "$0="$0, "$1="$1,"$2="$2,"$3="$3
}'
Line no:1,No of fields:3 $0=line1 f2 f3 $1=line1 $2=f2 $3=f3
Line no:2,No of fields:3 $0=line2 f4 f5 $1=line2 $2=f4 $3=f5
Line no:3,No of fields:3 $0=line3 f6 f7 $1=line3 $2=f6 $3=f7
```

We can print the last field of a line as `print $NF`, last but the second as `$(NF-1)`, and so on.

`awk` also provides the `printf()` function with the same syntax as in C. We can also use that instead of print.

Let's see some basic `awk` usage examples. Print the second and third field of every line as follows:

```
$awk '{ print $3,$2 }'   file
```

In order to count the number of lines in a file, use the following command:

```
$ awk 'END{ print NR }' file
```

Here, we only use the `END` block. `NR` will be updated on entering each line by `awk` with its line number. When it reaches the end of the line, it will have the value of the last line number. Hence, in the `END` block `NR` will have the value of the last line number.

You can sum up all the numbers from each line of `field 1` as follows:

```
$ seq 5 | awk 'BEGIN{ sum=0; print "Summation:" }
{ print $1"+"; sum+=$1 } END { print "=="; print sum }'
Summation:
1+
2+
3+
4+
5+
==
15
```

Passing an external variable to awk

By using the `-v` argument, we can pass external values other than `stdin` to `awk`, as follows:

```
$ VAR=10000
$ echo | awk -v VARIABLE=$VAR '{ print VARIABLE }'
10000
```

There is a flexible alternate method to pass many variable values from outside `awk`. For example:

```
$ var1="Variable1" ; var2="Variable2"
$ echo | awk '{ print v1,v2 }' v1=$var1 v2=$var2
Variable1 Variable2
```

When an input is given through a file rather than standard input, use the following command:

```
$ awk '{ print v1,v2 }' v1=$var1 v2=$var2 filename
```

In the preceding method, variables are specified as key-value pairs, separated by a space and (v1=$var1 v2=$var2) as command arguments to `awk` soon after the BEGIN, { }, and END blocks.

Reading a line explicitly using getline

Usually, `awk` reads all the lines in a file by default. If you want to read one specific line, you can use the `getline` function. Sometimes, you may need to read the first line from the BEGIN block.

The syntax is `getline var`. The variable `var` will contain the content for the line. If `getline` is called without an argument, we can access the content of the line by using $0, $1, and $2.

For example:

```
$ seq 5 | awk 'BEGIN { getline; print "Read ahead first line", $0 } {
print $0 }'
Read ahead first line 1
2
3
4
5
```

Filtering lines processed by awk with filter patterns

We can specify some conditions for lines to be processed. For example:

```
$ awk 'NR < 5' # first four lines
$ awk 'NR==1,NR==4' #First four lines
$ awk '/linux/' # Lines containing the pattern linux (we can specify regex)
$ awk '!/linux/' # Lines not containing the pattern linux
```

Setting delimiter for fields

By default, the delimiter for fields is a space. We can explicitly specify a delimiter by using -F "delimiter":

```
$ awk -F: '{ print $NF }' /etc/passwd
```

Or:

```
awk 'BEGIN { FS=":" } { print $NF }' /etc/passwd
```

We can set the output fields separator by setting OFS="delimiter" in the BEGIN block.

Reading the command output from awk

In the following code, echo will produce a single blank line. The cmdout variable will contain the output of the command grep root /etc/passwd, and it will print the line containing the root:

The syntax for reading out the command in a variable output is as follows:

```
"command" | getline output ;
```

For example:

```
$ echo | awk '{ "grep root /etc/passwd" | getline cmdout ; print cmdout }'
root:x:0:0:root:/root:/bin/bash
```

By using getline, we can read the output of external shell commands in a variable called cmdout.

awk supports associative arrays, which can use the text as the index.

Using loop inside awk

A for loop is available in awk. It has the following format:

```
for(i=0;i<10;i++) { print $i ; }
```

Or:

```
for(i in array) { print array[i]; }
```

String manipulation functions in awk

awk comes with many built-in string manipulation functions. Let's have a look at a few of them:

- ▶ length(string): This returns the string length.
- ▶ index(string, search_string): This returns the position at which search_string is found in the string.
- ▶ split(string, array, delimiter): This stores the list of strings generated by using the delimiter in the array.
- ▶ substr(string, start-position, end-position): This returns the substring created from the string by using the start and end character offsets.
- ▶ sub(regex, replacement_str, string): This replaces the first occurring regular expression match from the string with replacment_str.
- ▶ gsub(regex, replacment_str, string): This is similar to sub(), but it replaces every regular expression match.
- ▶ match(regex, string): This returns the result of whether a regular expression (regex) match is found in the string or not. It returns a non-zero output if a match is found, otherwise it returns zero. Two special variables are associated with match(). They are RSTART and RLENGTH. The RSTART variable contains the position at which the regular expression match starts. The RLENGTH variable contains the length of the string matched by the regular expression.

Finding the frequency of words used in a given file

Finding the frequency of words used in a file is an interesting exercise to apply the text-processing skills. It can be done in many different ways. Let's see how to do it.

Getting ready

We can use associative arrays, awk, sed, grep, and so on, to solve this problem in different ways. **Words** are alphabetic characters, delimited by space or a period. First, we should parse all the words in a given file and then the count of each word needs to be found. Words can be parsed by using regex with any of the tools, such as sed, awk, or grep.

How to do it...

We just saw the logic and ideas about the solution; now let's create the shell script as follows:

```bash
#!/bin/bash
#Name: word_freq.sh
#Desc: Find out frequency of words in a file

if [ $# -ne 1 ];
then
   echo "Usage: $0 filename";
   exit -1
fi

filename=$1

egrep -o "\b[[:alpha:]]+\b" $filename | \

awk '{ count[$0]++ }
END{ printf("%-14s%s\n","Word","Count") ;
for(ind in count)
{  printf("%-14s%d\n",ind,count[ind]);   }

}'
```

A sample output is as follows:

```
$ ./word_freq.sh words.txt
Word          Count
used          1
this              2
counting   1
```

How it works...

`egrep -o "\b[[:alpha:]]+\b" $filename` is used to output only words. The `-o` option will print the matching character sequence, delimited by a newline character. Hence, we receive words in each line.

`\b` is the word boundary character. `[:alpha:]` is a character class for alphabets. The `awk` command is used to avoid the iteration through each word. Since `awk`, by default, executes the statements in the `{ }` block for each row, we don't need a specific loop for doing that. Hence, the count is incremented as `count[$0]++` by using the associative array. Finally, in the `END{ }` block, we print the words and their count by iterating through the words.

See also

▶ The *Using awk for advanced text processing* recipe in this chapter explains the awk command

▶ The *Arrays and associative arrays* recipe in *Chapter 1, Shell Something Out*, explains the arrays in Bash

Compressing or decompressing JavaScript

JavaScript is widely used for designing websites. While writing the JavaScript code, we use several white spaces, comments, and tabs for readability and maintenance of the code. This causes the file size to increase, and as the file size increases, so does the time taken to load the page. Hence, most of the professional websites use compressed JavaScript for fast loading. This compression (also known as **minified JS**) is mostly squeezing white spaces and newline characters. Once JavaScript is compressed, it can be decompressed by adding enough white space and newline characters, which makes it readable. This recipe is an attempt to produce similar capabilities in the shell.

Getting ready

We are going to write a JavaScript compressor or obfuscation tool as well as a decompressing tool. Let's consider the following sample JavaScript:

```
$ cat sample.js
function sign_out()
{

  $("#loading").show();
  $.get("log_in",{logout:"True"},

  function(){
    window.location="";
  });
}
```

Following are the tasks that we need to perform for compressing this JavaScript:

1. Remove newline and tab characters.

2. Squeeze spaces.

3. Replace comments that look like /* content */.

To decompress or to make the JavaScript more readable, we can use the following tasks:

- ▸ Replace ; with ;\n
- ▸ Replace { with {\n, and } with \n}

How to do it...

Using the steps that we now have in mind, we can use the following command chain:

```
$ cat sample.js |  \
tr -d '\n\t' |  tr -s ' ' \
| sed 's:/\*.*\*/::g' \
| sed 's/ \?\([{}();,:]\) \?/\1/g'
```

The output is as follows:

```
function sign_out(){$("#loading").show();$.get("log_
in",{logout:"True"},function(){window.location="";});}
```

We can write a decompression script for making the obfuscated code readable, as follows:

```
$ cat obfuscated.txt | sed 's/;/;\n/g; s/{/{\n\n/g; s/}/\n\n}/g'
```

Or:

```
$ cat obfuscated.txt | sed 's/;/;\n/g' | sed 's/{/{\n\n/g' | sed 's/}/\n\
n}/g'
```

There is a limitation in the script that it even gets rid of extra spaces where it is intended. For example, if you have a line like the following:

```
var a = "hello world"
```

The two spaces will be converted into one space. Things like these are possible to fix by using the pattern-matching tools we have discussed. Also, when dealing with mission-critical JavaScript code, it is advised to use well-established tools to do this.

How it works...

The compression command performs the following tasks:

- ▸ Removes the \n and \t characters:

  ```
  tr -d '\n\t'
  ```

▸ Removes extra spaces:

```
tr -s ' ' or sed 's/[ ]\+/ /g'
```

▸ Removes comments:

```
sed 's:/\*.*\*/::g'
```

: is used as a `sed` delimiter to avoid the need of escaping / since we need to use /* and */.

in sed, * is escaped as *.

.* is used to match all the text in between /* and */.

▸ Removes all the spaces preceding and suffixing the {, }, (,), ;, :, and ,.

```
sed 's/ \?\([{}();,:]\) \?/\1/g'
```

The preceding `sed` statement works as follows:

❑ / \?\([{}();,:]\) \?/ in the `sed` code is the match part, and /\1 /g is the replacement part.

❑ \([{}();,:]\) is used to match any one character in the set [{ } ( ) ; , :] (inserted spaces for readability). \(and \) are group operators used to memorize the match and back reference in the replacement part. (and) are escaped to give them a special meaning as a group operator. \? precedes and follows the group operators. It is to match the space character that may precede or follow any of the characters in the set.

❑ In the replacement part, the match string (that is, the combination of :, a space (optional), a character from the set, and again an optional space) is replaced with the character matched. It uses a back reference to the character matched and memorized using the group operator (). Back-referenced characters refer to a group match using the \1 symbol.

The decompression command works as follows:

▸ s/;/;\n/g replaces ; with ;\n

▸ s/{/{\n\n/g replaces { with {\n\n

▸ s/}/\n\n}/g replaces } with \n\n}

See also

▸ The *Using sed to perform text replacement* recipe in this chapter explains the sed command

▸ The *Translate with tr* recipe in *Chapter 2, Have a Good Command*, explains the tr command

Merging multiple files as columns

There are different cases when we need to concatenate files by their columns. We may need each file's content to appear in separate columns. Usually, the `cat` command concatenates in a line (or row-wise) fashion.

How to do it...

`paste` is the command that can be used for column-wise concatenation. The `paste` command can be used with the following syntax:

```
$ paste file1 file2 file3 …
```

Let's try an example as follows:

```
$ cat file1.txt
1
2
3
4
5
$ cat file2.txt
slynux
gnu
bash
hack
$ paste file1.txt file2.txt
1slynux
2gnu
3bash
4hack
5
```

The default delimiter is tab. We can also explicitly specify the delimiter by using `-d`. For example:

```
$ paste file1.txt file2.txt -d ","
1,slynux
2,gnu
3,bash
4,hack
5,
```

See also

▸ The *Column-wise cutting of the file with cut* recipe in this chapter explains how to extract data from text files

Printing the nth word or column in a file or line

We may have a file having a number of columns, and only a few will actually be useful. For example, in a list of students in an order of their scores, we want to get, for instance, the fourth highest scorer. In this recipe, we will see how to do this.

How to do it...

The most widely-used method is to use `awk` for doing this task. It can be also done using `cut`.

1. To print the fifth column, use the following command:

   ```
   $ awk '{ print $5 }' filename
   ```

2. We can also print multiple columns and insert our custom string in between columns.

   For example, to print the permission and filename of each file in the current directory, use the following set of commands:

   ```
   $ ls -l | awk '{ print $1 " : " $8 }'
   -rw-r--r-- :  delimited_data.txt
   -rw-r--r-- :  obfuscated.txt
   -rw-r--r-- :  paste1.txt
   -rw-r--r-- :  paste2.txt
   ```

See also

▸ The *Using awk for advanced text processing* recipe in this chapter explains the `awk` command

▸ The *Column-wise cutting of the file with cut* recipe in this chapter explains how to extract data from text files

Printing text between line numbers or patterns

We may require to print a certain section of text lines, based on conditions such as a range of line numbers, and a range matched by a start and end pattern. Let's see how to do it.

Getting ready

We can use utilities such as `awk`, `grep`, and `sed` to perform the printing of a section based on conditions. Still, I found `awk` to be the simplest one to understand. Let's do it using `awk`.

How to do it...

1. To print the lines of a text in a range of line numbers, M to N, use the following syntax:

   ```
   $ awk 'NR==M, NR==N' filename
   ```

   Or, it can take the `stdin` input as follows:

   ```
   $ cat filename | awk 'NR==M, NR==N'
   ```

2. Replace M and N with numbers as follows:

   ```
   $ seq 100 | awk 'NR==4,NR==6'
   4
   5
   6
   ```

3. To print the lines of a text in a section with `start_pattern` and `end_pattern`, use the following syntax:

   ```
   $ awk '/start_pattern/, /end _pattern/' filename
   ```

   For example:

   ```
   $ cat section.txt
   line with pattern1
   line with pattern2
   line with pattern3
   line end with pattern4
   line with pattern5

   $ awk '/pa.*3/, /end/' section.txt
   line with pattern3
   line end with pattern4
   ```

   The patterns used in `awk` are regular expressions.

See also

▶ The *Using awk for advanced text processing* recipe in this chapter explains the `awk` command

Printing lines in the reverse order

This is a very simple recipe. It may not seem very useful, but it can be used to emulate the stack datastructure in Bash. This is something interesting. Let's print the lines of text in a file in reverse order.

Getting ready

A little hack with `awk` can do the task. However, there is a direct command, `tac`, to do the same as well. `tac` is the reverse of `cat`.

How to do it...

We will first see how to do this with `tac`.

1. The `tac` syntax is as follows:

   ```
   tac file1 file2 …
   ```

   It can also read from `stdin`, as follows:

   ```
   $ seq 5 | tac
   5
   4
   3
   2
   1
   ```

   In `tac`, \n is the line separator. But, we can also specify our own separator by using the `-s` "separator" option.

2. We can do it in `awk` as follows:

   ```
   $ seq 9 | \
   awk '{ lifo[NR]=$0 }
   END{ for(lno=NR;lno>-1;lno--){ print lifo[lno]; }
   }'
   ```

   \ in the shell script is used to conveniently break a single line command sequence into multiple lines.

How it works...

The `awk` script is very simple. We store each of the lines into an associative array with the line number as an array index (NR returns the line number). In the end, `awk` executes the END block. In order to get the last line number, `lno=NR` is used in the { } block. Hence, it iterates from the last line number to 0, and prints the lines stored in the array in reverse order.

Parsing e-mail addresses and URLs from text

Parsing a required text from a given file is a common task that we encounter in text processing. Items such as, e-mails and URLs can be found out with the help of correct regex sequences. Mostly, we need to parse e-mail addresses from a contact list of an e-mail client, which is composed of many unwanted characters and words, or from an HTML web page.

How to do it...

The regular expression pattern to match an e-mail address is as follows:

```
[A-Za-z0-9._]+@[A-Za-z0-9.]+\.[a-zA-Z]{2,4}
```

For example:

```
$ cat url_email.txt
this is a line of text contains,<email> #slynux@slynux.com. </email>
and email address, blog "http://www.google.com", test@yahoo.com
dfdfdfdddfdf;cool.hacks@gmail.com<br />

<a href="http://code.google.com"><h1>Heading</h1>
```

As we are using extended regular expressions (+, for instance), we should use `egrep`.

```
$ egrep -o '[A-Za-z0-9._]+@[A-Za-z0-9.]+\.[a-zA-Z]{2,4}'  url_email.txt
slynux@slynux.com
test@yahoo.com
cool.hacks@gmail.com
```

The `egrep` regex pattern for an HTTP URL is as follows:

```
http://[a-zA-Z0-9\-\.]+\.[a-zA-Z]{2,4}
```

For example:

```
$ egrep -o "http://[a-zA-Z0-9.]+\.[a-zA-Z]{2,3}" url_email.txt
http://www.google.com
http://code.google.com
```

How it works...

The regular expressions are really easy to design part-by-part. In the e-mail regex, we all know that an e-mail address takes the form `name@domain.some_2-4_letter`. Here, the same is written in the regex language as follows:

```
[A-Za-z0-9.]+@[A-Za-z0-9.]+\.[a-zA-Z]{2,4}
```

`[A-Za-z0-9.]+` means that some combination of characters in the `[]` block should appear one or more times (that is the meaning of +), before a literal @ character appears. Then, `[A-Za-z0-9.]` also should appear one or more times (+). The pattern `\.` means that a literal period should appear, and finally, the last part should be 2 to 4 alphabetic characters.

The case of an HTTP URL is similar to an e-mail, but we don't need the `name@` match part of the e-mail regex.

```
http://[a-zA-Z0-9.]+\.[a-zA-Z]{2,3}
```

See also

- ▶ The *Using sed to perform string replacement* recipe in this chapter explains the `sed` command
- ▶ The *Using regular expressions* recipe in this chapter explains how to use regular expressions

Removing a sentence in a file containing a word

Removing a sentence containing a word is a simple task when a correct regular expression is identified. This is just an exercise on solving similar problems.

Getting ready

`sed` is the best utility for making substitutions. Hence, let's use `sed` to replace the matched sentence with a blank.

How to do it...

Let's create a file with some text to carry out the substitutions. For example:

```
$ cat sentence.txt
Linux refers to the family of Unix-like computer operating systems
that use the Linux kernel. Linux can be installed on a wide variety of
computer hardware, ranging from mobile phones, tablet computers and video
game consoles, to mainframes and supercomputers. Linux is predominantly
known for its use in servers.
```

We will remove the sentence containing the words `mobile phones`. Use the following `sed` expression for this task:

```
$ sed 's/ [^.]*mobile phones[^.]*\.//g' sentence.txt
Linux refers to the family of Unix-like computer operating systems
that use the Linux kernel. Linux is predominantly known for its use in
servers.
```

 This recipe assumes that no sentence spans more than one line, for example, a sentence should always begin and end on the same line in the text.

How it works...

Let's evaluate the `sed` regex `'s/ [^.]*mobile phones[^.]*\.//g'`. It has the format `'s/substitution_pattern/replacement_string/g`. It replaces every occurrence of `substitution_pattern` with the replacement string.

Here, the substitution pattern is the regex for a sentence. Every sentence is delimited by ".", and the first character is a space. Therefore, we need to match the text that is in the format `"space" some text MATCH_STRING some text "dot"`. A sentence may contain any characters except a "dot", which is the delimiter. Hence, we have used `[^.]`. `[^.]*`matches a combination of any characters except the dot. In between, the text match string "`mobile phones`" is placed. Every match sentence is replaced by `//` (nothing).

See also

- The *Using sed to perform text replacement* recipe in this chapter explains the `sed` command
- The *Using regular expressions* recipe in this chapter explains how to use regular expressions

Replacing a pattern with text in all the files in a directory

There will be numerous occasions when we will need to replace a particular text with a new text in every file in a directory. An example would be changing a common URI everywhere in a website's source directory. Using the shell for this is one of the quickest methods out there.

How to do it...

From what we have learnt up to now, we can first use `find` to locate the files we want to perform the text replacement on. Then, we can use `sed` to do the actual replacement.

Let's say we want to replace the text `Copyright` with the word `Copyleft` in all `.cpp` files:

```
$ find . -name *.cpp -print0 |  xargs -I{} -0 sed -i 's/Copyright/
Copyleft/g' {}
```

How it works...

We use `find` on the current directory to find all the files of `.cpp`, and use `print0` to print a null-separated list of files (recall that this helps, if the filenames have spaces in them). We then pipe this list to `xargs`, which will pass these files to `sed`, which in turn will make the modifications.

There's more...

If you recall, `find` has an option `-exec`, which can be used to run a command on each of the files that `find` will match. We can use this option to achieve the same effect or replace the text with a new one, as follows:

```
$ find . -name *.cpp -exec sed -i 's/Copyright/Copyleft/g' \{\} \;
```

Or:

```
$ find . -name *.cpp -exec sed -i 's/Copyright/Copyleft/g' \{\} \+
```

While they perform the same function, the first form will call `sed` once for every file that is found, while in the second form, `find` will combine multiple filenames and pass them together to `sed`.

Text slicing and parameter operations

This recipe walks through some of the simple text-replacement techniques and parameter-expansion shorthands available in Bash. A few simple techniques can often help us avoid having to write multiple lines of code.

How to do it...

Let's get into the tasks.

Replacing some text from a variable can be done as follows:

```
$ var="This is a line of text"
$ echo ${var/line/REPLACED}
This is a REPLACED of text"
```

line is replaced with REPLACED.

We can produce a substring by specifying the start position and string length, by using the following syntax:

```
${variable_name:start_position:length}
```

To print from the fifth character onwards, use the following command:

```
$ string=abcdefghijklmnopqrstuvwxyz
$ echo ${string:4}
efghijklmnopqrstuvwxyz
```

To print eight characters starting from the fifth character, use the following command:

```
$ echo ${string:4:8}
efghijkl
```

The index is specified by counting the start letter as 0. We can also specify counting from the last letter as -1. It is used inside a parenthesis. (-1) is the index for the last letter:

```
echo ${string:(-1)}
z
$ echo ${string:(-2):2}
yz
```

See also

- ▶ The *Iterating through lines, words, and characters in a file* recipe in this chapter explains slicing of a character from a word

5
Tangled Web?
Not At All!

In this chapter, we will cover:

- ▶ Downloading from a web page
- ▶ Downloading a web page as plain text
- ▶ A primer on cURL
- ▶ Accessing unread Gmail e-mails from the command line
- ▶ Parsing data from a website
- ▶ Image crawler and downloader
- ▶ Web photo album generator
- ▶ Twitter command-line client
- ▶ Creating a "define " utility by using the Web backend
- ▶ Finding broken links in a website
- ▶ Tracking changes to a website
- ▶ Posting to a web page and reading response

Introduction

The Web is becoming the face of technology and the central access point for data processing. Though shell scripting cannot do everything that languages like PHP can do on the Web, there are still many tasks to which shell scripts are ideally suited. In this chapter, we will explore some recipes that can be used to parse website content, download and obtain data, send data to forms, and automate website-usage tasks and similar activities. We can automate many activities that we perform interactively through a browser with a few lines of scripting. Access to the functionalities provided by the HTTP protocol with command-line utilities enables us to write scripts that are suitable for solving most of the web-automation utilities. Have fun while going through the recipes of this chapter.

Downloading from a web page

Downloading a file or a web page from a given URL is simple. A few command-line download utilities are available to perform this task.

Getting ready

wget is a file download command-line utility. It is very flexible and can be configured with many options.

How to do it...

A web page or a remote file can be downloaded by using wget, as follows:

```
$ wget URL
```

For example:

```
$ wget http://slynux.org
--2010-08-01 07:51:20--  http://slynux.org/
Resolving slynux.org... 174.37.207.60
Connecting to slynux.org|174.37.207.60|:80... connected.
HTTP request sent, awaiting response... 200 OK
Length: 15280 (15K) [text/html]
Saving to: "index.html"

100%[=====================================>] 15,280      75.3K/s   in
0.2s

2010-08-01 07:51:21 (75.3 KB/s) - "index.html" saved [15280/15280]
```

It is also possible to specify multiple download URLs, as follows:

```
$ wget URL1 URL2 URL3 ..
```

How it works...

Usually, files are downloaded with the same filename as in the URL, and the download log information or progress is written to `stdout`.

You can specify the output filename with the `-O` option. If the file with the specified filename already exists, it will be truncated first and the downloaded file will be written to the specified file.

You can also specify a different `logfile` path rather than printing logs to `stdout`, by using the `-o` option:

```
$ wget ftp://example_domain.com/somefile.img -O dloaded_file.img -o log
```

By using the preceding command, nothing will be printed on screen. The log or progress will be written to the log, and the output file will be `dloaded_file.img`.

There is a chance that downloads might break due to unstable Internet connections. In that case, we can use the number of tries as an argument so that once interrupted, the utility will retry the download that many times before giving up.

To specify the number of tries, use the `-t` flag as follows:

```
$ wget -t 5 URL
```

Or to ask `wget` to keep trying infinitely, use `-t` as follows:

```
$ wget -t 0 URL
```

There's more...

The `wget` utility has several additional options that can be used under different problem domains. Let us go through a few of them.

Restricting the download speed

When we have a limited Internet bandwidth and many applications are sharing the Internet connection, and if a large file is given for download, it will suck all the bandwidth and may cause other processes to starve for the bandwidth. The `wget` command comes with a built-in option to specify the maximum bandwidth limit the download job can possess. Hence, all the applications can simultaneously access the Internet fairly.

We can restrict the speed limits in `wget` by using the `--limit-rate` argument as follows:

```
$ wget --limit-rate 20k http://example.com/file.iso
```

In this command, `k` (kilobyte) specifies the speed limit. You can also use `m` for megabyte.

We can also specify the maximum quota for the download. It will stop when the quota is exceeded. It is useful when downloading multiple files, limited by the total download size. This is useful to prevent the download from accidently using too much disk space.

Use `--quota` or `-Q` as follows:

```
$ wget -Q 100m http://example.com/file1 http://example.com/file2
```

Resume downloading and continue

If a download using `wget` gets interrupted before it is complete, we can resume the download from where we left off by using the `-c` option as follows:

```
$ wget -c URL
```

Copying a complete website (mirroring)

`wget` has an option to download the complete website by recursively collecting all the URL links in the web pages and downloading all of them like a crawler. Hence, we can completely download all the pages of a website.

In order to download the pages, use the `--mirror` option as follows:

```
$ wget --mirror --convert-links exampledomain.com
```

Or use the following command:

```
$ wget -r -N -l -k DEPTH URL
```

`-l` specifies the depth of web pages as levels. This means it will traverse only that many number of levels. It is used along with `-r` (recursive). The `-N` argument is used to enable time stamping for the file. URL is the base URL for a website for which the download needs to be initiated. The -k or `--convert-links` option instructs `wget` to convert the links to other pages in a downloaded page, to the local copy of those pages.

 Exercise discretion when mirroring other websites. Unless you have permission, only perform this for your personal use and don't do it too frequently.

Accessing pages with HTTP or FTP authentication

Some web pages require authentication for HTTP or FTP URLs. It can be obtained by using the `--user` and `--password` arguments:

```
$ wget --user username --password pass URL
```

It is also possible to ask for a password without specifying the password inline. For this, use `--ask-password` instead of the `--password` argument.

Downloading a web page as plain text

Web pages are HTML pages that contain a collection of HTML tags, along with other elements, such as JavaScript and CSS. Of these, the HTML tags define the content of a web page, which we can parse to look for a specific content, and this is something Bash scripting can help us with. When we download a web page, we receive an HTML file, and in order to view the formatted page, it should be viewed in a web browser.

In most of the circumstances, parsing a text document will be easier than parsing HTML data because we aren't required to strip off the HTML tags. **Lynx** is an interesting command-line web browser, which can get the web page as plaintext. Let us see how to do it.

How to do it...

Let's download the webpage view, in ASCII character representation, in a text file by using the `-dump` flag with the `lynx` command:

```
$ lynx URL -dump > webpage_as_text.txt
```

This command will also list all the hyperlinks (`<a href="link">`) separately under a heading `References`, as the footer of the text output. This will help us avoid parsing of links separately by using regular expressions.

For example:

```
$lynx -dump http://google.com > plain_text_page.txt
```

You can see the plaintext version of `text` by using the `cat` command, as follows:

```
$ cat plain_text_page.txt
```

A primer on cURL

cURL is a powerful utility that supports protocols, such as HTTP, HTTPS, and FTP. It supports many features including POST, cookies, authentication, downloading partial files from a specified offset, referer, user agent string, extra headers, limit speed, maximum file size, progress bar, and so on. cURL is very useful when we play around with automating a web page usage sequence, and to retrieve data. This recipe is a list of the most important features of cURL.

Getting ready

cURL mostly doesn't come with any Linux distros; you may have to install it by using the package manager. By default, distributions ship with wget.

cURL usually dumps the downloaded files to stdout, and progress information to stderr. To avoid the progress information from being shown, we use the --silent option.

How to do it...

The curl command can be used to perform different activities, such as downloading, sending different HTTP requests, and specifying HTTP headers. Let's see how we can perform different tasks with cURL:

- To dump the downloaded file onto the terminal (the downloaded data is written to stdout, use the following command:

  ```
  $ curl URL
  ```

- To prevent the curl command from displaying the progress information, mention --silent.

  ```
  $ curl URL --silent
  ```

- To write the downloaded data into a file with the filename parsed from the URL rather than writing into the standard output, use the -O option:

  ```
  $ curl URL --silent -O
  ```

- To show the # progress bar while downloading, use --progress instead of --silent:

  ```
  $ curl http://slynux.org -o index.html --progress
  ################################## 100.0%
  ```

How it works...

cURL writes a web page or file to the filename as in the URL, instead of writing to `stdout`. If the filenames are not present in the URL, it will produce an error. Hence, make sure that the URL is a URL to a remote file. `curl http://slynux.org -O --silent` will display an error, since the filename cannot be parsed from the URL. In such cases, we can manually specify the filename as follows, by using the `-o` option:

```
$ curl URL --silent -o new_filename
```

There's more...

In the preceding sections, we learned how to download files and dump HTML pages to the terminal. There are several advanced options that come along with cURL. Let us explore more of cURL.

Continuing and resuming downloads

cURL has advanced resume download features to continue at a given offset. It helps to download portions of files by specifying an offset:

```
$ curl URL/file -C offset
```

The offset is an integer value in bytes.

cURL doesn't require us to know the exact byte offset, if we want to resume downloading a file. If you want cURL to figure out the correct resume point, use the `-C -` option, as follows:

```
$ curl -C - URL
```

cURL will automatically figure out where to restart the download of the specified file.

Setting the referer string with cURL

Referer is a string in the HTTP header, used to identify the page from which the user reaches the current web page. When a user clicks on a link on web page A to go to web page B, the referer header string for page B will contain the URL of page A.

Some dynamic pages check the referer string before returning the HTML data. For example, a web page shows a Google logo attached page when a user navigates to a website by searching on Google, and shows a different page when the user navigates to the web page by manually typing the URL.

The author of a website can write a condition to return a Google page if the referer is `www.google.com`, or else return a different page.

You can use `--referer` with the `curl` command to specify the referer string as follows:

```
$ curl --referer Referer_URL target_URL
```

For example:

```
$ curl --referer http://google.com http://slynux.org
```

Cookies with cURL

By using `curl` we can specify, as well as store, the cookies that are encountered during HTTP operations.

To specify cookies, use the `--cookie "COOKIES"` option.

Cookies should be provided as `name=value`. Multiple cookies should be delimited by a semicolon (`;`). For example:

```
$ curl http://example.com --cookie "user=slynux;pass=hack"
```

To specify a file to which the cookies encountered are to be stored, use the `--cookie-jar` option. For example:

```
$ curl URL --cookie-jar cookie_file
```

Setting a user agent string with cURL

Some web pages that check the user agent won't work if there is no user agent specified. You must have noticed that certain old websites work only on **Internet Explorer (IE)**. If a different browser is used, it will show a message that it will work only on IE. This is because the website checks for a user agent. You can set the user agent with `curl`.

Using cURL it can be set using –user-agent or -A as follows:

```
$ curl URL --user-agent "Mozilla/5.0"
```

Additional headers can be passed with cURL. Use `-H "Header"` to pass multiple additional headers. For example:

```
$ curl -H "Host: www.slynux.org" -H "Accept-language: en" URL
```

 There are many different user agent strings across multiple browsers and crawlers on the web. You can find a list of some of them at `http://www. useragentstring.com/pages/useragentstring.php`.

Specifying a bandwidth limit on cURL

When the available bandwidth is limited and multiple users are sharing the Internet, in order to share bandwidth smoothly, we can limit the download rate to a specified limit in `curl` by using the `--limit-rate` option, as follows:

```
$ curl URL --limit-rate 20k
```

In this command, `k` (kilobyte) specifies the download rate limit. You can also use `m` for megabyte.

Specifying the maximum download size

The maximum download file size for cURL can be specified by using the `-max-filesize` option as follows:

```
$ curl URL --max-filesize bytes
```

It will return a non-zero exit code if the file size exceeds. It will return zero if it succeeds.

Authenticating with cURL

HTTP authentication or FTP authentication can be done by using cURL with the `-u` argument.

The username and password can be specified by using `-u username:password`. It is possible to not provide a password in such a way that it will prompt for the password while executing. For example:

```
$ curl -u user:pass http://test_auth.com
```

If you prefer to be prompted for the password, you can do that by using only `-u username`.

```
$ curl -u user http://test_auth.com
```

Printing response headers excluding the data

It is useful to print only response headers to apply many checks or statistics. For example, to check whether a page is reachable or not, we don't need to download the entire page contents; just reading the HTTP response header can be used to identify whether a page is available or not.

An example use case for checking the HTTP header, is to check the file size before downloading. We can check the `Content-length` parameter in the HTTP header to find out the length of a file before downloading. Also, several useful parameters can be retrieved from the header. The `Last-Modified` parameter enables us to know the last modification time for the remote file.

Use the `-I` or `-head` option with `curl` to dump only the HTTP headers, without downloading the remote file. For example:

```
$ curl -I http://slynux.org
HTTP/1.1 200 OK
Date: Sun, 01 Aug 2010 05:08:09 GMT
Server: Apache/1.3.42 (Unix) mod_gzip/1.3.26.1a mod_log_bytes/1.2
mod_bwlimited/1.4 mod_auth_passthrough/1.8 FrontPage/5.0.2.2635 mod_
ssl/2.8.31 OpenSSL/0.9.7a
Last-Modified: Thu, 19 Jul 2007 09:00:58 GMT
ETag: "17787f3-3bb0-469f284a"
Accept-Ranges: bytes
Content-Length: 15280
Connection: close
Content-Type: text/html
```

See also

> ▸ The *Posting to a web page and reading response* recipe in this chapter

Accessing Gmail e-mails from the command line

Gmail is a widely-used free e-mail service from Google—`http://mail.google.com/`. It allows you to read your mail via authenticated RSS feeds. We can parse the RSS feeds with the sender's name, and an e-mail with a subject. It will help us to have a look at the unread e-mails in the inbox, without opening the web browser.

How to do it...

Let's go through the shell script to parse the RSS feeds for Gmail to display the unread mails:

```
#!/bin/bash
#Desc: Fetch gmail tool

username='PUT_USERNAME_HERE'
password='PUT_PASSWORD_HERE'

SHOW_COUNT=5 # No of recent unread mails to be shown

echo
```

```
curl  -u $username:$password --silent "https://mail.google.com/mail/
feed/atom" | \
tr -d '\n' | sed 's:</entry>:\n:g'  |\
  sed -n 's/.*<title>\(.*\)<\/title.*<author><name>\([^<]*\)<\/
name><email>
\([^<]*\).*/From: \2 [\3] \nSubject: \1\n/p' | \
head -n $(( $SHOW_COUNT * 3 ))
```

The output will be as follows:

```
$ ./fetch_gmail.sh
From: SLYNUX [ slynux@slynux.com ]
Subject: Book release - 2


From: SLYNUX [ slynux@slynux.com ]
Subject: Book release - 1
.
... 5 entries
```

If you are using a Google Mail account with two factor authentication, you will have to generate a new key for this script and use it. Your regular password won't work.

How it works...

The script uses cURL to download the RSS feed by using user authentication. User authentication is provided by the -u user:pass argument. You can use -u user without providing the password. Then, while executing cURL, it will interactively ask for the password. Here, you can split the piped commands into different blocks to illustrate how they work.

tr -d '\n' removes the newline character, so that we restructure each e-mail entry with \n as the delimiter.

sed 's:</entry>:\n:g' replaces every </entry> element with a newline, so that each e-mail entry is delimited by a new line and, hence, mails can be parsed one-by-one. Have a look at the source of https://mail.google.com/mail/feed/atom for XML tags used in the RSS feeds. <entry> TAGS </entry> corresponds to a single mail entry.

The next block of script is as follows:

```
sed 's/.*<title>\(.*\)<\/title.*<author><name>\([^<]*\)<\/
name><email>
\([^<]*\).*/Author: \2 [\3] \nSubject: \1\n/'
```

This script matches the substring title by using `<title>\(.*\)<\/title`, the sender name by using `<author><name>\([^<]*\)<\/name>`, and e-mail by using `<email>\([^<]*\)`. Then back referencing is used as follows:

```
Author: \2 [\3] \nSubject: \1\n
```

This is to replace an entry for a mail with the matched items in an easy-to-read format. `\1` corresponds to the first substring match, `\2` for the second substring match, and so on.

The `SHOW_COUNT=5` variable is used to take the number of unread mail entries to be printed on the terminal.

`head` is used to display only the `SHOW_COUNT*3` lines from the first line. `SHOW_COUNT` is multiplied by three in order to show three lines of the output.

See also

> ▶ The *A primer on cURL* recipe in this chapter explains the `curl` command
> ▶ The *Basic sed primer* recipe in this chapter explains the `sed` command

Parsing data from a website

It is often useful to parse data from web pages by eliminating unnecessary details. `sed` and `awk` are the main tools that we will use for this task. You might have come across a list of actress rankings in a `grep` recipe in the *Chapter 4, Texting and driving*; it was generated by parsing the website page `http://www.johntorres.net/BoxOfficefemaleList.html`.

Let us see how we can parse the same data by using text-processing tools.

How to do it...

Let's go through the commands used to parse details of actresses from the website:

```
$ lynx -dump -nolist http://www.johntorres.net/BoxOfficefemaleList.html
| \
grep -o "Rank-.*" | \
sed -e 's/ *Rank-\([0-9]*\) *\(.*\)/\1\t\2/' | \
sort -nk 1 > actresslist.txt
```

The output will be as follows:

```
# Only 3 entries shown. All others omitted due to space limits
1    Keira Knightley
2    Natalie Portman
3    Monica Bellucci
```

How it works...

Lynx is a command-line web browser—it can dump a text version of a website as we would see in a web browser, rather than showing us the raw code. Hence, we can avoid the job of removing the HTML tags. We use the `-nolist` option for `lynx`, as we don't need the numbers that it adds automatically with each link. Parsing and formatting the lines that contain `Rank` is done by using `sed`, as follows:

```
sed -e 's/ *Rank-\([0-9]*\) *\(.*\)/\1\t\2/'
```

These lines are then sorted according to the ranks.

See also

- The *Basic sed primer* recipe in this chapter explains the `sed` command
- The *Downloading a web page as plain text* recipe in this chapter explains the `lynx` command

Image crawler and downloader

Image crawlers are very useful when we need to download all the images that appear in a web page. Instead of going through the HTML sources and picking all the images, we can use a script to parse the image files and download them automatically. Let's see how to do it.

How to do it...

Let's write a Bash script to crawl and download the images from a web page, as follows:

```bash
#!/bin/bash
#Desc: Images downloader
#Filename: img_downloader.sh

if [ $# -ne 3 ];
then
  echo "Usage: $0 URL -d DIRECTORY"
  exit -1
```

```
fi

for i in {1..4}
do
  case $1 in
  -d) shift; directory=$1; shift ;;
   *) url=${url:-$1}; shift;;
  esac
done

mkdir -p $directory;
baseurl=$(echo $url | egrep -o "https?://[a-z.]+")

echo Downloading $url
curl -s $url | egrep -o "<img src=[^>]*>" |
sed 's/<img src=\"\([^"]*\).*/\1/g' > /tmp/$$.list

sed -i "s|^/|$baseurl/|" /tmp/$$.list

cd $directory;

while read filename;
do
  echo Downloading $filename
  curl -s -O "$filename" --silent

done < /tmp/$$.list
```

An example usage is as follows:

```
$ ./img_downloader.sh http://www.flickr.com/search/?q=linux -d images
```

How it works...

The preceding image downloader script parses an HTML page, strips out all tags except
<img>, then parses src="URL" from the <img> tag, and downloads them to the specified
directory. This script accepts a web page URL and the destination directory path as command-
line arguments. The [$# -ne 3] statement checks whether the total number of
arguments to the script is three, otherwise it exits and returns a usage example.

If there are three arguments, we parse the URL and destination directory. This is done as follows:

```
while [ -n "$1" ]
do
  case $1 in
  -d) shift; directory=$1; shift ;;
   *) url=${url:-$1}; shift;;
esac
done
```

A `while` loop is used. It runs as long as there are more arguments to be processed. The `case` statement will evaluate the first argument (`$1`), and `matches` -d or any other string arguments are checked. The advantage of parsing arguments in this way is that we can place the -d argument anywhere in the command line:

```
$ ./img_downloader.sh -d DIR URL
```

Or:

```
$ ./img_downloader.sh URL -d DIR
```

`shift` is used to shift arguments to the left in such a way that when shift is called, $1 will take the next argument's value; that is, $2, and so on. Hence, we can evaluate all arguments through $1 itself.

When -d is matched, it is obvious that the next argument is the value for the destination directory. `*)` corresponds to a default match. It will match anything other than -d. Hence, while iteration $1="" or $1=URL in the default match, we need to take $1=URL, avoiding "" to overwrite. Hence, we use the expression `url=${url:-$1}`. It will return a URL value if already not "", otherwise it will assign $1.

`egrep -o "<img src=[^>]*>"` will print only the matching strings, which are the `<img>` tags including their attributes. `[^>]*` is used to match all the characters except the closing >, that is, `<img src="image.jpg" .... >`.

`sed 's/<img src=\"\([^"]*\).*/\1/g'` parses `src="url"`, so that all the image URLs can be parsed from the `<img>` tags already parsed.

There are two types of image source paths—relative and absolute. **Absolute paths** contain full URLs that start with `http://` or `https://`. Relative URLs starts with / or `image_name` itself. An example of an absolute URL is `http://example.com/image.jpg`. An example of a relative URL is `/image.jpg`.

For relative URLs, the starting / should be replaced with the base URL to transform it to `http://example.com/image.jpg`. For this transformation, we initially find out `baseurl` by parsing, and then in every URL that starts with /, we replace it with `baseurl`:

```
"s|^/|$baseurl/|" /tmp/$$.list
```

Then, a `while` loop is used to iterate each line of the list and download the images by using `curl`. The `--silent` argument is used with `curl` to avoid extra progress messages from being printed on the screen.

See also

- The *A primer on curl* recipe in this chapter explains the `curl` command
- The *Basic sed primer* recipe in this chapter explains the `sed` command
- The *Searching and mining *test* inside a file with grep* recipe in this chapter explains the `grep` command

Web photo album generator

Web developers commonly design photo album pages for websites that consist of a number of image thumbnails on the page. When thumbnails are clicked, a large version of the picture will be displayed. However, to do this, many images are required. Afterwards, copying the `<img>` tags, resizing the image to create a thumbnail, placing them in the `thumbs` directory, and so on, is a real hurdle. As with any repetitive task, this can be automated easily by writing a simple `bash` script. By writing a script, we can create thumbnails, place them in exact directories, and generate the code fragment for `<img>` tags automatically in few seconds. This recipe will do exactly this.

Getting ready

We can perform this task with a `for` loop that iterates every image in the current directory. The usual Bash utilities such as `cat` and `convert` (from the Image Magick package) are used. These will generate an HTML album, using all the images, to `index.html`.

How to do it...

Let's write a Bash script to generate an HTML album page:

```bash
#!/bin/bash
#Filename: generate_album.sh
#Description: Create a photo album using images in current directory

echo "Creating album.."
```

```
mkdir -p thumbs
cat <<EOF1 > index.html
<html>
<head>
<style>

body
{
  width:470px;
  margin:auto;
  border: 1px dashed grey;
  padding:10px;
}

img
{
  margin:5px;
  border: 1px solid black;

}
</style>
</head>
<body>
<center><h1> #Album title </h1></center>
<p>
EOF1

for img in *.jpg;
do
  convert "$img" -resize "100x" "thumbs/$img"
  echo "<a href=\"$img\" ><img src=\"thumbs/$img\" title=\"$img\" /></
a>" >> index.html
done

cat <<EOF2 >> index.html

</p>
</body>
</html>
EOF2

echo Album generated to index.html
```

Run the script as follows:

```
$ ./generate_album.sh
Creating album..
Album generated to index.html
```

How it works...

The initial part of the script is used to write the header part of the HTML page.

The following script redirects all the contents up to EOF1 to index.html:

```
cat <<EOF1 > index.html
contents...
EOF1
```

The header includes the HTML and CSS styling.

`for img in *.jpg *.JPG;` will iterate through the names of each file and will perform the necessary actions.

`convert "$img" -resize "100x" "thumbs/$img"` will create images of 100 px width as thumbnails.

The following statement will generate the required `<img>` tag and append it to `index.html`:

```
echo "<a href=\"$img\" ><img src=\"thumbs/$img\" title=\"$img\" /></
a>" >> index.html
```

Finally, the footer HTML tags are appended with `cat` as well.

See also

▸ The *Playing with file descriptors and redirection* recipe in this chapter explains EOF and `stdin` redirection

Twitter command-line client

Twitter is the hottest micro-blogging platform, as well as the latest buzz of the online social media now. We can use Twitter API to read tweets on our timeline from the command line! Let us see how to do it.

Getting ready

Recently, Twitter has stopped allowing people to log in by using plain HTTP Authentication, and we must use OAuth to authenticate ourselves. A full explanation of OAuth is out of the scope of this book, so we will use a library which makes it easy to use OAuth from `bash` scripts. Perform the following steps:

1. Download the `bash-oauth` library from `https://github.com/livibetter/bash-oauth/archive/master.zip`, and unzip it to any directory

2. Go to that directory and then inside the subdirectory `bash-oauth-master`, run `make install-all as root`.

3. Go to `https://dev.twitter.com/apps/new` and register a new app. This will make it possible to use OAuth:

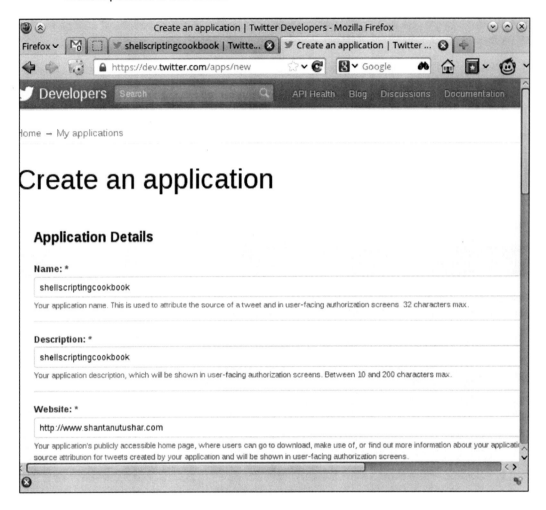

4. After registering the new app, go to your app's settings and change **Access type** to **Read and Write**:

5. Now, go to the **Details** section of the app and note two things—**Consumer Key** and **Consumer Secret**, so that you can substitute these in the script we are going to write:

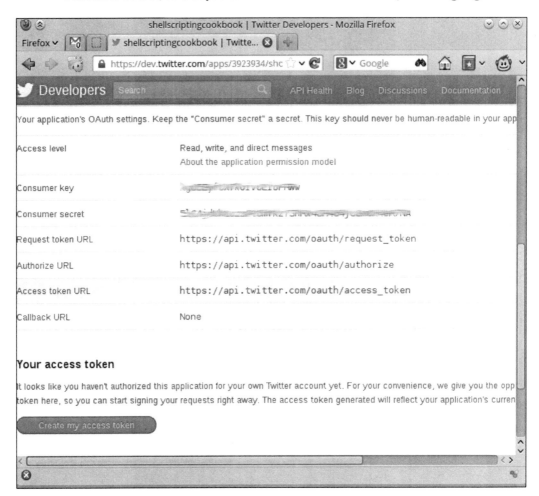

Great, now let us write the script that uses this.

How to do it...

Let's write a Bash script by using the library:

```
#!/bin/bash
#Filename: twitter.sh
#Description: Basic twitter client

oauth_consumer_key=YOUR_CONSUMER_KEY
```

```
oauth_consumer_secret=YOUR_CONSUMER_SECRET
config_file=~/.$oauth_consumer_key-$oauth_consumer_secret-rc

if [[ "$1" != "read" ]] && [[ "$1" != "tweet" ]];
then
  echo -e "Usage: $0 tweet status_message\n    OR\n      $0 read\n"
  exit -1;
fi

source TwitterOAuth.sh
TO_init

if [ ! -e $config_file ]; then
 TO_access_token_helper
 if (( $? == 0 )); then
   echo oauth_token=${TO_ret[0]} > $config_file
   echo oauth_token_secret=${TO_ret[1]} >> $config_file
 fi
fi

source $config_file

if [[ "$1" = "read" ]];
then
  TO_statuses_home_timeline '' 'shantanutushar' '10'
  echo $TO_ret | sed 's/<\([a-z]\)/\n<\1/g' | \
grep -e '^<text>' -e '^<name>' | sed 's/<name>/\ - by /g' | \
sed 's$</*[a-z]*>$$g'

elif [[ "$1" = "tweet" ]];
then
  shift
  TO_statuses_update '' "$@"
  echo 'Tweeted :)'
fi
```

Run the script as follows:

```
$./twitter.sh read
Please go to the following link to get the PIN: https://api.twitter.com/
oauth/authorize?oauth_token=GaZcfsdnhMO4HiBQuUTdeLJAzeaUamnOljWGnU
PIN: 4727143
Now you can create, edit and present Slides offline.
  - by A Googler
```

```
$./twitter.sh tweet "I am reading Packt Shell Scripting Cookbook"
Tweeted :)
$./twitter.sh read | head -2
I am reading Packt Shell Scripting Cookbook
 - by Shantanu Tushar Jha
```

How it works...

First of all, we use the `source` command to include the `TwitterOAuth.sh` library, so we can use its functions to easily access Twitter. We are required to call the `TO_init` function, so the library can initialize itself.

Now, every app needs to get an OAuth token and token secret the first time a user uses it. We check if we have already got these; if not, we use the library function `TO_access_token_helper`, which will let us get these. Once we have these, we save these to a `config` file, so we can simply source it the next time the script is run.

To read the tweets, we use the library function `TO_statuses_home_timeline`, which fetches the tweets from Twitter, and sets the XML into a variable `TO_ret`. We then use `sed` to put a newline for each tag, filter out only the `<text>` and `<name>` tags, and then finally remove the tags and replace with user-friendly text.

To post a new tweet, we use the library function `TO_statuses_update`, to which we pass an empty first parameter, which tells it to use the default format, and then we pass the message as a part of the second parameter.

See also

▸ The *Basic sed primer* recipe in this chapter explains the `sed` command

▸ The *Searching and mining text inside a file with grep* recipe in this chapter explains the `grep` command

Creating a "define" utility by using the Web backend

There are a lot of dictionaries on the Web that offer APIs that can be used to get a machine-readable definition of words. Let us use one of the APIs and see how to write a define script.

Getting ready

We are going to use `curl`, `sed`, and `grep` to write the define utility. There are a lot of dictionary websites, where you can register and use their APIs for personal use for free. In this example, we are using Merriam-Webster's dictionary API. Please perform the following steps:

1. Go to `http://www.dictionaryapi.com/register/index.htm`, and register an account for yourself. Select **Collegiate Dictionary** and **Learner's Dictionary**:

2. Log in using the newly created account and go to **My Keys** to access the keys. Note down the key for the learner's dictionary:

How to do it...

Let's go through the code for the define utility script:

```
#!/bin/bash
#Filename: define.sh
#Desc: A script to fetch definitions from dictionaryapi.com

apikey=YOUR_API_KEY_HERE

if  [ $# -ne 2 ];
then
  echo -e "Usage: $0 WORD NUMBER"
  exit -1;
fi

curl --silent http://www.dictionaryapi.com/api/v1/references/learners/
xml/$1?key=$apikey | \
grep -o \<dt\>.*\</dt\> | \
sed 's$</*[a-z]*>$$g' | \
head -n $2 | nl
```

Run the script as follows:

```
$ ./define.sh usb 1
     1  :a system for connecting a computer to another device (such as a
printer, keyboard, or mouse) by using a special kind of cord a USB cable/
port USB is an abbreviation of "Universal Serial Bus."How it works...
```

How it works...

We use `curl` to fetch the data from the dictionary API webpage by specifying our API `Key` (`$apikey`), and the word that we want the definition for (`$1`). The result contains definitions in the `<dt>` tags, which we select by using `grep` and then we remove the tags by using `sed`. We then pick the required number of lines from the definitions and use `nl` to put the line numbers in each line.

See also

- The *Basic sed primer* recipe in this chapter explains the `sed` command
- The *Searching and mining text inside a file with grep* recipe in this chapter explains the `grep` command

Finding broken links in a website

Some people manually check every page on a website to search for broken links. It is feasible for websites having very few pages, but gets difficult when the number of pages become large. It becomes really easy if we can automate the process of finding broken links. We can find the broken links by using HTTP manipulation tools. Let's see how to do it.

Getting ready

To identify the links and find the broken ones from the links, we can use `lynx` and `curl`. It has an option, namely `-traversal`, which will recursively visit pages on the website and build a list of all hyperlinks in the website. We can use cURL to verify each of the links for whether they're broken or not.

How to do it...

Let's write a Bash script with the help of the `curl` command to find out the broken links on a web page:

```bash
#!/bin/bash
#Filename: find_broken.sh
#Desc: Find broken links in a website

if [ $# -ne 1 ];
then
  echo -e "$Usage: $0 URL\n"
  exit 1;
fi


echo Broken links:

mkdir /tmp/$$.lynx
cd /tmp/$$.lynx

lynx -traversal $1 > /dev/null
count=0;

sort -u reject.dat > links.txt

while read link;
do
  output=`curl -I $link -s | grep "HTTP/.*OK"`;
  if [[ -z $output ]];
  then
    echo $link;
    let count++
  fi
done < links.txt

[ $count -eq 0 ] && echo No broken links found.
```

How it works...

`lynx -traversal URL` will produce a number of files in the working directory. It includes a file `reject.dat`, which will contain all the links in the website. `sort -u` is used to build a list by avoiding duplicates. Then, we iterate through each link and check the header response by using `curl -I`. If the header contains the first line to have `HTTP/1.0 200 OK` as the response, it means that the target is not broken. All other responses corresponding to the broken links are printed on the screen.

From its name, it might seem like `reject.dat` should contain a list of URLs, which were broken or unreachable. However, this is not the case, and lynx just adds all the URLs there.

Also note that `lynx` generates a file called `traverse.errors`, which contains all the URLs that had problems in browsing. However, `lynx` will only add URLs which return `HTTP 404 (not found)`, and so we will lose other errors (for instance, `HTTP 403 Forbidden`). This is why we manually check for statuses.

See also

▸ The *Downloading web page as formatted plain text* recipe in this chapter explains the `lynx` command

▸ The *A primer on cURL* recipe in this chapter explains the `curl` command

Tracking changes to a website

Tracking changes to a website is helpful to web developers and users. Checking a website manually in intervals is really hard and impractical. Hence, we can write a change tracker running at repeated intervals. When a change occurs, it can play an audio or send some other notification. Let us see how to write a basic tracker for the website changes.

Getting ready

Tracking changes in terms of Bash scripting means fetching websites at different times and taking the difference by using the `diff` command. We can use `curl` and `diff` to do this.

How to do it...

Let's write a Bash script by combining different commands, to track changes in a web page:

```bash
#!/bin/bash
#Filename: change_track.sh
#Desc: Script to track changes to webpage

if [ $# -ne 1 ];
then
  echo -e "$Usage: $0 URL\n"
  exit 1;
fi

first_time=0
# Not first time

if [ ! -e "last.html" ];
then
  first_time=1
  # Set it is first time run
fi

curl --silent $1 -o recent.html

if [ $first_time -ne 1 ];
then
  changes=$(diff -u last.html recent.html)
  if [ -n "$changes" ];
  then
    echo -e "Changes:\n"
    echo "$changes"
  else
    echo -e "\nWebsite has no changes"
  fi
else
  echo "[First run] Archiving.."

fi


cp recent.html last.html
```

Let's look at the output of the `track_changes.sh` script when changes are made to the webpage and when the changes are not made to the page:

- First, run the following command:

  ```
  $ ./track_changes.sh http://web.sarathlakshman.info/test.html
  [First run] Archiving..
  ```

- Second, run the following command:

  ```
  $ ./track_changes.sh http://web.sarathlakshman.info/test.html
  Website has no changes
  ```

- Third, run the following command after making changes to the web page:

  ```
  $ ./test.sh http://web.sarathlakshman.info/test_change/test.html
  Changes:

  --- last.html 2010-08-01 07:29:15.000000000 +0200
  +++ recent.html    2010-08-01 07:29:43.000000000 +0200
  @@ -1,3 +1,4 @@
  <html>
  +added line :)
  <p>data</p>
  </html>
  ```

How it works...

The script checks whether the script is running for the first time by using `[ ! -e "last.html" ];`. If `last.html` doesn't exist, it means that it is the first time and, hence, the webpage must be downloaded and copied as `last.html`.

If it is not the first time, it should download the new copy (`recent.html`) and check the difference by using the `diff` utility. If there are changes, it should print the changes and finally, copy `recent.html` to `last.html`.

See also

- The *A primer on cURL* recipe in this chapter explains the `curl` command

Posting to a web page and reading the response

POST and GET are two types of requests in HTTP to send information to, or retrieve information from a website. In a GET request, we send parameters (name-value pairs) through the webpage URL itself. In the case of POST, it won't be attached with the URL. POST is used when a form needs to be submitted. For example, a username, the password to be submitted, and the login page to be retrieved.

Posting to pages is used frequently while writing scripts based on webpage retrievals. Let us see how to work with POST. Automating the HTTP GET and POST request by sending the POST data and retrieving the output is a very important task that we practice while writing shell scripts that parse data from websites.

Getting ready

For this recipe, we will use a test website (http://book.sarathlakshman.com/lsc/mlogs/), which is used to submit the current user information, such as the hostname and username. In the home page of the website, there are two fields **HOSTNAME** and **USER**, and a **SUBMIT** button. When the user enters a hostname, a user name, and clicks on the **Submit** button, the details will be stored in the website. This process can be automated by using a single line of curl (or wget) command by automating the POST request. Let's see how to do this by using curl or wget.

How to do it...

POST and read the HTML response from a real website using curl as follows:

```
$ curl URL -d "postvar=postdata2&postvar2=postdata2"
```

For example,

```
$ curl http://book.sarathlakshman.com/lsc/mlogs/submit.php -d "host=test-host&user=slynux"
<html>
You have entered :
<p>HOST : test-host</p>
<p>USER : slynux</p>
<html>
```

curl prints the response page.

-d is the argument used for posting. The string argument for -d is similar to the GET request semantics. var=value pairs are to be delimited by &.

You can POST the data using `wget` by using `--post-data "string"`. For example:

```
$ get http://book.sarathlakshman.com/lsc/mlogs/submit.php --post-data
"host=test-host&user=slynux" -O output.html
$ cat output.html
<html>
You have entered :
<p>HOST : test-host</p>
<p>USER : slynux</p>
<html>
```

Use the same format as cURL for name-value pairs.

> The string to the post arguments (for example, to `-d` or `--post-data`) should always be given in quotes. If quotes are not used, & is interpreted by the shell to indicate that this should be a background process.

How it works...

If you look at the website source (use the **View Source** option from the web browser), you will see an HTML form defined, similar to the following code:

```
<form action="http://book.sarathlakshman.com/lsc/mlogs/submit.php"
method="post" >

<input type="text" name="host" value="HOSTNAME" >
<input type="text" name="user" value="USER" >
<input type="submit" >
</form>
```

Here, `http://book.sarathlakshman.com/lsc/mlogs/submit.php` is the target URL. When the user enters the details and clicks on the **Submit** button, the host and user inputs are sent to `submit.php` as a POST request, and the response page is returned on the browser.

See also

- The *A primer on cURL* recipe in this chapter explains the `curl` command
- The *Download a file from a website* recipe in this chapter explains the `wget` command

6
The Backup Plan

In this chapter, we will cover:

- ▸ Archiving with tar
- ▸ Archiving with cpio
- ▸ Compressing data with gzip
- ▸ Archiving and compressing with zip
- ▸ Faster archiving with pbzip2
- ▸ Creating filesystems with compression
- ▸ Backup snapshots with rsync
- ▸ Version control-based backup with Git
- ▸ Creating entire disk images using fsarchiver

Introduction

Taking snapshots and backups of data are regular tasks we come across and they are even more important when it comes to a server or large data storage systems. Shell scripting is one of the easiest ways to automate such backups, because if not automated they aren't very useful. Also, it is desirable to use various compression formats so that we don't create large backups. Encryption is another task that comes under frequent usage for protection of data. It is also important to note that in order to reduce the size of data to encrypted, usually files are archived and compressed before encrypting. Many standard encryption algorithms are available and can be handled with shell utilities. This chapter walks through different recipes for creating and maintaining files or folder archives, compression formats, and encrypting techniques with shell. Let's go through the recipes.

Archiving with tar

The `tar` command can be used to archive files, originally designed for storing data on Tape archives. It allows you to store multiple files and directories as a single file while retaining all the file attributes, such as owner, permissions, and so on. The file created by the `tar` command is often referred to as a tarball. In this recipe, we will learn how to create archives using `tar`.

Getting ready

The `tar` command comes by default with all Unix-like operating systems. It has a simple syntax and is a portable file format. It supports these arguments: A, c, d, r, t, u, x, f, and v. Each of these options can be used independently for different purposes corresponding to it.

How to do it...

We can use tar to create archives, and perform operations on existing archives. Let's see how:

1. To archive files with tar, use the following syntax:

   ```
   $ tar -cf output.tar [SOURCES]
   ```

   For example:

   ```
   $ tar -cf output.tar file1 file2 file3 folder1 ..
   ```

2. To list files in an archive, use the `-t` option:

   ```
   $ tar -tf archive.tar
   file1
   file2
   ```

3. In order to print more details while archiving or listing, use the `-v` or the `-vv` flag. This feature is called verbose (v), which for most of the commands will turn on printing more details on the terminal. For example, using verbose you could print more details, such as file permissions, owner group, modification date, and so on:

   ```
   $ tar -tvf archive.tar
   -rw-rw-r-- shaan/shaan        0 2013-04-08 21:34 file1
   -rw-rw-r-- shaan/shaan        0 2013-04-08 21:34 file2
   ```

The file name must appear immediately after the -f and it should be the last option in the argument group. For example, if you want verbose output, you should use the options like this:

```
$ tar -cvf output.tar file1 file2 file3 folder1 ..
```

How it works...

In this command, -c stands for "create file" and -f stands for "specify filename".

We can specify folders and filenames as SOURCES. We can use a list of file names or wildcards such as *.txt to specify the sources. When finished, tar will archive the source files into a file called output.tar.

We cannot pass hundreds of files or folders as command-line arguments because there is a limit. So, it is safer to use the append option (see below) if many files are to be archived.

There's more...

Let's go through additional features that are available with the tar command.

Appending files to an archive

Sometimes we may need to add files to an archive that already exists, we can use the append option -r for this.

In order to append a file into an already existing archive use:

```
$ tar -rvf original.tar new_file
```

Let's create an archive with one text file in it:

```
$ tar -cf archive.tar hello.txt
```

To list the files present in the archive, use:

```
$ tar -tf archive.tar
hello.txt
```

Now add another file to the archive and list its contents again:

```
$ tar -rf archive.tar world.txt
$ tar -tf archive.tar
hello.txt
world.txt
```

The archive now contains both the files.

Extracting files and folders from an archive

The following command extracts the contents of the archive to the current directory:

```
$ tar -xf archive.tar
```

The `-x` option stands for extract.

When `-x` is used, the `tar` command extracts the contents of the archive to the current directory. We can also specify the directory where the files need to be extracted by using the `-C` flag, as follows:

```
$ tar -xf archive.tar -C /path/to/extraction_directory
```

The command extracts the contents of an archive to a specified directory. It extracts the entire contents of the archive. We can also extract only a few files by specifying them as command arguments:

```
$ tar -xvf file.tar file1 file4
```

The command above extracts only `file1` and `file4`, and ignores other files in the archive.

stdin and stdout with tar

While archiving, we can specify `stdout` as the output file so that another command appearing through a pipe can read it as `stdin` and then do some process or extract the archive.

This is very helpful in order to transfer data through a Secure Shell (SSH) connection (while on a network). For example:

```
$ tar cvf - files/ | ssh user@example.com "tar xv -C Documents/"
```

In the preceding example, the directory files/ is added to a tar archive which is output to stdout (denoted by '-')

Concatenating two archives

We can easily merge multiple tar files with the `-A` option.

Let's pretend we have two tarballs: `file1.tar` and `file2.tar`. We can merge the contents of `file2.tar` to `file1.tar` as follows:

```
$ tar -Af file1.tar file2.tar
```

Verify it by listing the contents:

```
$ tar -tvf file1.tar
```

Updating files in an archive with a timestamp check

The append option appends any given file to the archive. If the same file is inside the archive is given to append, it will append that file and the archive will contain duplicates. We can use the update option -u to specify only append files that are newer than the file inside the archive with the same name.

```
$ tar -tf archive.tar
filea
fileb
filec
```

This command lists the files in the archive.

To append `filea` only if `filea` has been modified since the last time it was added to `archive.tar`, use:

```
$ tar -uf archive.tar filea
```

Nothing happens if the version of `filea` outside the archive and the `filea` inside `archive.tar` have the same timestamp.

Use the `touch` command to modify the file timestamp and then try the `tar` command again:

```
$ tar -uvvf archive.tar filea
-rw-r--r-- slynux/slynux      0 2010-08-14 17:53 filea
```

The file is appended since its timestamp is newer than the one inside the archive. Let's verify that:

```
$ tar -tf archive.tar
-rw-r--r-- slynux/slynux      0 2010-08-14 17:52 filea
-rw-r--r-- slynux/slynux      0 2010-08-14 17:52 fileb
-rw-r--r-- slynux/slynux      0 2010-08-14 17:52 filec
-rw-r--r-- slynux/slynux      0 2010-08-14 17:53 filea
```

As you can notice, a new `filea` has been appended to the `tar` archive. While extracting this archive, tar will pick up the latest version of `filea`.

Comparing files in the archive and file system

Sometimes it is useful to know whether files in the archive and the files with the same filename in the filesystem are the same or contain any differences. The -d flag can be used to print the differences:

```
$ tar -df archive.tar
afile: Mod time differs
afile: Size differs
```

Deleting files from the archive

We can remove files from a given archive using the -delete option. For example:

```
$ tar -f archive.tar --delete file1 file2 ..
```

Or,

```
$ tar --delete --file archive.tar [FILE LIST]
```

Let's see an example:

```
$ tar -tf archive.tar
filea
fileb
filec
```

Now let's delete filea:

```
$ tar --delete --file archive.tar filea
$ tar -tf archive.tar
fileb
filec
```

Compression with the tar archive

The `tar` command only archives files, it does not compress them. For this reason, most people usually add some form of compression when working with tarballs. This can significantly decrease the size of the files. Tarballs are often compressed into one of the following formats:

- ▶ file.tar.gz
- ▶ file.tar.bz2
- ▶ file.tar.lzma

Different `tar` flags are used to specify different compression formats:

- ▶ `-j` for bunzip2
- ▶ `-z` for gzip
- ▶ `--lzma` for lzma

They are explained in the following compression-specific recipes.

It is possible to use compression formats without explicitly specifying special options as above. `tar` can compress by looking at the given extension of the output or input file names. In order for tar to support compression automatically by looking at the extensions, use `-a` or `--auto-compress` with `tar`:

```
$ tar acvf archive.tar.gz filea fileb filec
filea
fileb
filec
$ tar tf archive.tar.gz
filea
fileb
filec
```

Excluding a set of files from archiving

It is possible to exclude a set of files from archiving by specifying patterns.Use `--exclude [PATTEN]` for excluding files matched by wildcard patterns.

For example, to exclude all `.txt` files from archiving use:

```
$ tar -cf arch.tar * --exclude "*.txt"
```

 Note, that the pattern should be enclosed within quotes to prevent the shell from expanding it.

It is also possible to exclude a list of files provided in a list file with the -X flag as follows:

```
$ cat list
filea
fileb

$ tar -cf arch.tar * -X list
```

Now it excludes `filea` and `fileb` from archiving.

Excluding version control directories

We usually use tarballs for distributing source code. In general, most source code is maintained using version control systems such as subversion, Git, mercurial, cvs, and so on. Code directories under version control will contain special directories used to manage versions like .svn or .git. However, these directories aren't needed by the code itself and so should be eliminated from the tarball of the source code.

In order to exclude version control related files and directories while archiving use the --exclude-vcs option along with tar. For example:

```
$ tar --exclude-vcs -czvvf source_code.tar.gz eye_of_gnome_svn
```

Printing total bytes

It is sometimes useful if we can print total bytes copied to the archive. To print the total bytes copied after archiving use the –totals option as follows:

```
$ tar -cf arc.tar * --exclude "*.txt" --totals
Total bytes written: 20480 (20KiB, 12MiB/s)
```

See also

> ▸ *Compressing with gzip*, explains the gzip command

Archiving with cpio

cpio is another archiving format similar to tar. It is used to store files and directories in a file with attributes such as permissions, ownership, and so on. But, it is not commonly used as much as tar. However, cpio is used in RPM package archives (which are used in distros such as Fedora), initramfs files for the Linux kernel which contain the kernel image, and so on. This recipe will give minimal usage examples of cpio.

How to do it...

cpio takes input filenames through `stdin` and it writes the archive into `stdout`. We have to redirect `stdout` to a file to receive the output cpio file as follows:

1. Create test files:

   ```
   $ touch file1 file2 file3
   ```

2. We can archive the test files as follows:

   ```
   $ echo file1 file2 file3 | cpio -ov > archive.cpio
   ```

3. In order to list files in a cpio archive use the following command:

   ```
   $ cpio -it < archive.cpio
   ```

4. In order to extract files from the cpio archive use:

   ```
   $ cpio -id < archive.cpio
   ```

How it works...

For the archiving command:

- ▶ `-o` specifies the output
- ▶ `-v` is used for printing a list of files archived

> By using cpio, we can also archive using files as absolute paths. `/usr/somedir` is an absolute path as it contains the full path starting from root (/).
>
> A relative path will not start with / but it starts the path from the current directory. For example, `test/file` means that there is a directory `test` and the `file` is inside the `test` directory.
>
> While extracting, cpio extracts to the absolute path itself. But in case of `tar` it removes the / in the absolute path and converts it as a relative path.

In the command for listing all the files in the given cpio archive:

- ▶ `-i` is for specifying the input
- ▶ `-t` is for listing

While using the command for extraction, `-d` stands for extracting and cpio overwrites files without prompting.

Compressing data with gzip

gzip is a commonly used compression format in the GNU/Linux platform. It is one of the utilities (such as `gzip`, `gunzip`, and `zcat`) that handle gzip compression. However, `gzip` can be applied only on a single file or data stream. This means that it cannot archive directories and multiple files. Hence, we must first create a `tar` archive and compress it with `gzip`. Let's see how to operate with `gzip`.

How to do it...

`gzip` can be used both to compress files and decompress them back to the original:

1. In order to compress a file with `gzip` use the following command:

   ```
   $ gzip filename
   $ ls
   filename.gz
   ```

2. Extract a `gzip` compressed file as follows:

   ```
   $ gunzip filename.gz
   $ ls
   file
   ```

3. In order to list out the properties of a compressed file use:

   ```
   $ gzip -l test.txt.gz
   compressed           uncompressed  ratio uncompressed_name
        35                         6 -33.3% test.txt
   ```

4. The `gzip` command can read a file from `stdin` and also write a compressed file into `stdout`.

   Read data from `stdin` and output the compressed data to `stdout` as follows:

   ```
   $ cat file | gzip -c > file.gz
   ```

   The `-c` option is used to specify output to `stdout`.

5. We can specify the compression level for `gzip` using `--fast` or the `--best` option to provide low and high compression ratios, respectively.

There's more...

The `gzip` command is often used with other commands and also has advanced options to specify the compression ratio. Let's see how to work with these features.

Gzip with tarball

A gzipped tarball is basically a tar archive compressed using gzip. We can use two methods to create such tarballs:

- The first method is as follows:

  ```
  $ tar -czvvf archive.tar.gz [FILES]
  ```

  or

  ```
  $ tar -cavvf archive.tar.gz [FILES]
  ```

  The `-a` option specifies that the compression format should automatically be detected from the extension.

- Alternatively, here's the second method:

  First, create a tarball:

  ```
  $ tar -cvvf archive.tar [FILES]
  ```

  Compress the tarball as follows:

  ```
  $ gzip archive.tar
  ```

If many files (a few hundreds) are to be archived in a tarball and need to be compressed, we use the second method with few changes. The issue with giving many files as command arguments to `tar` is that it can accept only a limited number of files from the command line. In order to solve this issue, we can create a `tar` file by adding files one by one using a loop with an append option (`-r`) as follows:

```
FILE_LIST="file1  file2  file3  file4  file5"

for f in $FILE_LIST;
do
tar -rvf archive.tar $f
done

gzip archive.tar
```

In order to extract a gzipped tarball, use the following command:

```
$ tar -xavvf archive.tar.gz -C extract_directory
```

In the above command, the -a option is used to detect the compression format automatically.

zcat - reading gzipped files without extracting

zcat is a command that can be used to dump an extracted file from a .gz file to stdout without manually extracting it. The .gz file remains as before but it will dump the extracted file into stdout as follows:

```
$ ls

test.gz


$ zcat test.gz

A test file

# file test contains a line "A test file"


$ ls

test.gz
```

Compression ratio

We can specify the compression ratio, which is available in range 1 to 9, where:

- 1 is the lowest, but fastest
- 9 is the best, but slowest

You can specify any ratio in that range as follows:

```
$ gzip -5 test.img
```

This should give a good balance between compression speed and ratio.

Using bzip2

bzip2 is another commonly used tool which is very similar to gzip in function and syntax. The only difference is that bzip2 offers more effective compression than gzip, while taking more time than gzip.

To compress a file using bzip2:

```
$ bzip2 filename
```

Extract a bzipped file as follows:

```
$ bunzip2 filename.bz2
```

The way to compress to and extract from tar.bz2 files is similar to tar.gz discussed earlier:

```
$ tar -xjvf archive.tar.bz2
```

where -j denotes that the archive is bzip2 format.

Using lzma

lzma is a compression tool which has even better compression ratios than gzip and bzip2. To compress a file using lzma:

```
$ lzma filename
```

Extract a lzma'd file as follows:

```
$ unlzma filename.lzma
```

A tarball can be compressed by using the --lzma option passed to the tar command while archiving and extracting.

```
$ tar -cvvf --lzma archive.tar.lzma [FILES]
```

or

```
$ tar -cavvf archive.tar.lzma [FILES]
```

In order to extract a tarball compressed with lzma compression to a specified directory, use:

```
$ tar -xvvf --lzma archive.tar.lzma -C extract_directory
```

In this command, -x is used for extraction. --lzma specifies the use of lzma to decompress the resulting file.

Or, we could also use:

```
$ tar -xavvf archive.tar.lzma -C extract_directory
```

See also

- ▶ *Archiving with tar*, explains the tar command

Archiving and compressing with zip

ZIP is a popular compression format used on many platforms. It isn't as commonly used as `gzip` or `bzip2` on Linux platforms, but files from the Internet are often saved in this format. In this recipe we will see how to use `zip` to perform compression and extraction.

How to do it...

Let's see how to use various options with `zip`:

1. In order to archive with ZIP, the following syntax is used:

    `$ zip archive_name.zip [SOURCE FILES/DIRS]`

    For example:

    `$ zip file.zip file`

    Here, the `file.zip` file will be produced.

2. Archive directories and files recursively as follows:

    `$ zip -r archive.zip folder1 folder2`

    In this command, `-r` is used for specifying recursive.

3. In order to extract files and folders in a ZIP file, use:

    `$ unzip file.zip`

It will extract the files without removing `filename.zip` (unlike `unlzma` or `gunzip`).

1. In order to update files in the archive with newer files in the filesystem, use the `-u` flag:

    `$ zip file.zip -u newfile`

2. Delete a file from a zipped archive, by using `-d` as follows:

    `$ zip -d arc.zip file.txt`

3. In order to list the files in an archive use:

    `$ unzip -l archive.zip`

How it works...

While being similar to most of the archiving and compression tools we have already discussed, `zip` unlike `lzma`, `gzip`, or `bzip2` won't remove the source file after archiving. Most importantly, while `zip` is similar to `tar`, it performs both archiving and compression while `tar` by itself does not perform compression.

Faster archiving with pbzip2

Most modern computers today are equipped with at least two CPU cores - for the user it means almost the same as two real CPUs doing your work. However, just having a multicore CPU doesn't mean your programs will run faster, it is important that the programs themselves have been designed to run faster on multicore processors.

Most of the compression commands that we saw up to now will use only one CPU and, hence, won't be very fast. `pbzip2` can use multiple cores, hence decreasing overall time taken to compress your files.

Getting ready

`pbzip2` usually doesn't come preinstalled with most distros, you will have to use your package manager to install it.

How to do it...

Let's see how to use `pbzip2` to compress files and extract them:

1. Compress a single file like this:

    `pbzip2 myfile.tar`

    pbzip2 will automatically detect the number of cores on your system and compress myfile.tar, to myfile.tar.bz2

2. To compress and archive multiple files or directories, we use `pbzip2` in combination with tar as follows:

    `tar cf myfile.tar.bz2 --use-compress-prog=pbzip2 dir_to_compress/`

    Or:

    `tar -c directory_to_compress/ | pbzip2 -c > myfile.tar.bz2`

3. Extracting a pbzip2'd file

    If it's a tar.bz2 file, we can perform the decompression and extraction in one step:

    `pbzip2 -dc myfile.tar.bz2 | tar x`

    If the archive is a single file which was pbzip2'd, use this:

    `pbzip2 -d myfile.tar.bz2`

How it works...

`pbzip2` internally uses the same compression algorithms as `bzip2`, but it compresses separate chunks of data simultaneously using pthreads - a threading library. However, this is all transparent to the user and all that happens is a much faster compression.

Just like `gzip` or `bzip2`, `pbzip2` does not create archives itself, it can only work on a single file. Hence, to compress multiple files and directories, we use it in conjunction with tar.

There's more...

There are other useful options we can use with `pbzip2`:

Manually specifying the number of CPUs

Use the `-p` option to `pbzip2` to specify the number of CPU cores manually. This is useful if the automatic detection fails or you want some CPU cores to be free for some other job.

```
pbzip2 -p4 myfile.tar
```

This will tell `pbzip2` to use 4 CPUs.

Specifying the compression ratio

Just like other compression tools we saw up to now, we can use the options from 1 to 9 to specify the fastest and best compression ratios respectively.

Creating filesystems with compression

`squashfs` is a heavy-compression based read-only filesystem that is capable of compressing 2 to 3 GB of data onto a 700 MB file. If you have ever used a Linux LiveCD (or LiveUSB), they are built using `squashfs` . These CDs make use of a read-only compressed filesystem which keeps the root filesystem on a compressed file. It can be loopback mounted and loads a complete Linux environment. Thus, when some files are required by processes, they are decompressed and loaded onto the RAM and used.

`squashfs` can be useful when it is required to keep files heavily compressed and to access a few of them without extracting all the files. This is because completely extracting a large compressed archive takes a long time. However, if an archive is loopback mounted, it will be very fast since only the required portion of the compressed archive is decompressed when requested. Let's see how we can use `squashfs`.

Getting ready

squashfs internally uses compression algorithms such as gzip and lzma and is supported in all modern Linux distros. However, in order to create squashfs files we need to install **squashfs-tools** using the package manager.

How to do it...

Let's see how to create and mount squashfs files:

1. In order to create a squashfs file by adding source directories and files, use:

    ```
    $ mksquashfs SOURCES compressedfs.squashfs
    ```

    Sources can be wildcards, or file, or folder paths.

    For example:

    ```
    $ sudo mksquashfs /etc test.squashfs
    Parallel mksquashfs: Using 2 processors
    Creating 4.0 filesystem on test.squashfs, block size 131072.
    [=====================================] 1867/1867 100%
    ```

     More details will be printed on the terminal. The output is stripped to save space

2. To mount the squashfs file to a mount point, use loopback mounting as follows:

    ```
    # mkdir /mnt/squash
    # mount -o loop compressedfs.squashfs /mnt/squash
    ```

You can access the contents at /mnt/squashfs.

There's more...

The squashfs file system can be customized by specifying additional parameters. Let's go through the additional options.

Excluding files while creating a squashfs file

While creating a squashfs file, we can exclude a list of files or a file pattern specified using wildcards.

To exclude a list of files specified as command-line arguments use the `-e` option. For example:

```
$ sudo mksquashfs /etc test.squashfs -e /etc/passwd /etc/shadow
```

The `-e` option is used to exclude `passwd` and `shadow` files.

It is also possible to specify a list of exclude files given in a file with `-ef` as follows:

```
$ cat excludelist
/etc/passwd
/etc/shadow


$ sudo mksquashfs /etc test.squashfs -ef excludelist
```

If we want to support wildcards in excludes lists, use `-wildcard` as an argument.

Backup snapshots with rsync

Backing up data is something that most sysadmins need to do regularly. In addition to backing up local files, we may need to backup data from a web server or from remote locations. `rsync` is a command that can be used to synchronize files and directories from one location to another while minimizing data transfer using file difference calculations and compression. The advantage of `rsync` over the `cp` command is that `rsync` uses strong difference algorithms. Additionally, it supports data transfer across remote machines. While making copies, it compares the files in the original and destination locations and will only copy the files that are newer. It also supports compression, encryption, and a lot more. Let us see how to work with `rsync`.

How to do it...

Let's see how to copy files and create backups with `rsync`:

1. To copy a source directory to a destination use:

   ```
   $ rsync -av source_path destination_path
   For example,
   $ rsync -av /home/slynux/data slynux@192.168.0.6:/home/backups/
   data
   ```

   In this command:

   - `-a` stands for archiving
   - `-v` (verbose) prints the details or progress on `stdout`

   The above command will recursively copy all the files from the source path to the destination path. We can specify paths as remote or local paths.

2. In order to backup data to a remote server or host, use:

```
$ rsync -av source_dir username@host:PATH
```

To keep a mirror at the destination, run the same `rsync` command scheduled at regular intervals. It will copy only changed files to the destination.

3. Restore the data from the remote host to `localhost` as follows:

```
$ rsync -av username@host:PATH destination
```

The `rsync` command uses SSH to connect to the remote machine, hence you should provide the remote machine's address in the format `user@host`, where user is the username and host is the IP address or host name attached to the remote machine. `PATH` is the path on the remote machine from where the data needs to be copied.

Make sure that OpenSSH server is installed and running on the remote machine. Additionally, to prevent the prompt for a password for the remote machine, see the recipe "*Password-less auto-login with SSH*" from Chapter 7.

4. Compressing data while transferring through the network can significantly optimize the speed of the transfer. We can use the `rsync` option `-z` to specify to compress data while transferring through a network. For example:

```
$ rsync -avz source destination
```

5. Synchronize one directory to another directory as follows:

```
$ rsync -av /home/test/ /home/backups
```

This command copies the source (`/home/test`) to an existing folder called backups.

6. Copy a full directory inside another directory as follows:

```
$ rsync -av /home/test /home/backups
```

This command copies the source (`/home/test`) to a directory named backups by creating that directory.

For the PATH format, if we use / at the end of the source, `rsync` will copy contents of that end directory specified in the `source_path` to the destination.

If / is not present at the end of the source, `rsync` will copy that end directory itself to the destination.

For example, the following command copies the content of the test directory:

The following command copies the test directory to the destination:

> If / is at the end of destination_path, rsync will copy the source to the destination directory.
>
> If / is not used at the end of the destination path, rsync will create a folder, named similar to the source directory, at the end of the destination path and copy the source into that directory.

For example:

```
$ rsync -av /home/test /home/backups/
$ rsync -av /home/test /home/backups
```

How it works...

rsync works with source and destination paths which can be either local or remote. Most importantly, even both the paths can be remote paths. Usually the remote connections are made using SSH so that rsync can calculate what files to copy and what not to. Local and remote paths look like this:

- ▸ /home/slynux/data   (local path)
- ▸ slynux@192.168.0.6:/home/backups/data   (remote path)

/home/slynux/data specifies the absolute path in the machine in which the rsync command is executed. slynux@192.168.0.6:/home/backups/data specifies that the path is /home/backups/data in the machine with IP address 192.168.0.6 and is logged in as user slynux.

There's more...

The rsync command has several additional functionalities that can be specified using its command-line options. Let's go through them.

Excluding files while archiving with rsync

Some files need not be updated while archiving to a remote location. It is possible to tell rsync to exclude certain files from the current operation. Files can be excluded by two options:

```
--exclude PATTERN
```

We can specify a wildcard pattern of files to be excluded. For example:

```
$ rsync -avz /home/code/some_code /mnt/disk/backup/code --exclude "*.txt"
```

This command excludes .txt files from backing up.

Or, we can specify a list of files to be excluded by providing a list file.

Use --exclude-from FILEPATH.

Deleting non-existent files while updating rsync backup

By default, rsync does not remove files from the destination if they no longer exist at the source. In order to remove the files from the destination that do not exist at the source, use the rsync --delete option:

```
$ rsync -avz SOURCE DESTINATION --delete
```

Scheduling backups at intervals

You can create a cron job to schedule backups at regular intervals.

A sample is as follows:

```
$ crontab -ev
```

Add the following line:

```
0 */10 * * * rsync -avz /home/code user@IP_ADDRESS:/home/backups
```

The above crontab entry schedules the rsync to be executed every 10 hours.

*/10 is the hour position of the crontab syntax. /10 specifies to execute the backup every 10 hours. If */10 is written in the minutes position, it will execute every 10 minutes.

Have a look at the *Scheduling with cron* recipe in *Chapter 9, Administration Calls* to understand how to configure crontab.

Version control-based backup with Git

People use different strategies for backing up data. Out of these, differential backups are more efficient than making copies of the entire source directory to a target of the backup directory with the version number using date or time of a day as it causes wastage of space. We only need to copy the changes that occurred to files from the second time that the backups occur - this is also called incremental backup. We can manually create incremental backups using tools like rsync but restoring this sort of backup can be difficult. The best way to maintain and restore changes is to use version control systems. They are very much used in software development and maintenance of code, since coding frequently undergoes changes. Git is the most famous and the most efficient version control system available. Let us use Git for the backup of regular files in a non-programming context.

Getting ready

We have a directory that contains several files and subdirectories. We need to keep track of changes occurring to the directory contents and back them up. If data becomes corrupted or goes missing, we must be able to restore a previous copy of that data. We will either need to take the backup at different locations in the local machine, or to a remote machine. To install git, just use your distro's package manager and let's get started:

How to do it...

Let's see how to use git to version control data, in this case backups:

1. In the directory which is to be backed up use:

   ```
   $ cd /home/data/source
   ```

   Let it be the directory source to be tracked.

2. Set up and initiate the remote backup directory. In the remote machine, create the backup destination directory:

   ```
   $ mkdir -p /home/backups/backup.git
   $ cd /home/backups/backup.git
   $ git init --bare
   ```

The following steps are to be performed in the source host machine:

1. Add user details to Git in the source host machine:

   ```
   $ git config --global user.name  "Sarath Lakshman"

   $ git config --global user.email slynux@slynux.com
   ```

2. Initiate the source directory to backup from the host machine. In the source directory in the host machine whose files are to be backed up, execute the following commands:

   ```
   $ git init
   Initialized empty Git repository in /home/backups/backup.git/


   $ git commit --allow-empty -am "Init"
   [master (root-commit) b595488] Init
   ```

3. In the source directory, execute the following command to add the remote git directory and synchronize backup:

    ```
    $ git remote add origin user@remotehost:/home/backups/backup.git
    ```

    ```
    $ git push origin master
    Counting objects: 2, done.
    Writing objects: 100% (2/2), 153 bytes, done.
    Total 2 (delta 0), reused 0 (delta 0)
    To user@remotehost:/home/backups/backup.git
     * [new branch]      master -> master
    ```

4. Add or remove files for Git tracking.

    The following command adds all files and folders in the current directory to the backup list:

    ```
    $ git add *
    ```

    We can conditionally add certain files only to the backup list as follows:

    ```
    $ git add *.txt
    ```

    ```
    $ git add *.py
    ```

    We can remove the files and folders not required to be tracked by using:

    ```
    $ git rm file
    ```

    It can be a folder or even a wildcard as follows:

    ```
    $ git rm *.txt
    ```

5. Check-pointing or marking backup points.

    We can mark checkpoints for the backup with a message using the following command:

    ```
    $ git commit -m "Commit Message"
    ```

    We need to update the backup at the remote location at regular intervals. Hence, set up a cron job (for example, backing up every five hours):

    Create a file crontab entry with lines:

    ```
    0 */5 * * *   /home/data/backup.sh
    ```

    Create a script /home/data/backup.sh as follows:

    ```
    #!/bin/ bash
    cd /home/data/source
    git add .
    git commit -am "Backup taken at @ $(date)"
    git push
    ```

Now we have set up the backup system.

6. To view all backup versions:

```
$ git log
```

7. To revert back to any previous state or version, look into the commit ID, which is a 32-character hex string. Use the commit ID with `git checkout`.

For commit ID 3131f9661ec1739f72c213ec5769bc0abefa85a9 it will be:

```
$ git checkout 3131f9661ec1739f72c213ec5769bc0abefa85a9
```

To make this revert permanent:

```
$ git commit -am "Restore @ $(date) commit ID:
3131f9661ec1739f72c213ec5769bc0abefa85a9"
```

In order to view the details about versions again, use:

```
$ git log
```

8. If the working directory is broken due to some issues, we need to fix the directory with the backup at the remote location. We can recreate the contents from the backup at the remote location as follows:

```
$ git clone user@remotehost:/home/backups/backup.git
```

It will create a directory backup with all contents.

While `git` is pretty good for keeping versioned copies of text files which includes documents, source code and so on, it's not a good idea to use `git` for a large amount of binary-only data. For example, it's not sensible to use `git` to backup/version control your photo collection. The reason for this is `git` keeps whole files instead of differences when it comes to binary files, and this will make it occupy a huge amount of space.

Creating entire disk images using fsarchiver

`fsarchiver` is a tool which can save the contents of a complete `filesystem` to a compressed archive file. Due to these abilities, it is one of the most complete and easy to use tools for backup.

`fsarchiver` is the successor of `partimage` - the well-known **filesystem** backup solution. `fsarchiver` has the advantage of supporting newer **filesystems** like **ext4** when compared to `partimage`, however the latter has a minimal GUI that makes it somewhat easier to use.

Getting ready

`fsarchiver` is not installed in most of the distros by default. You will have to manually install it using your package manager. If you want more information, go to `http://www.fsarchiver.org/Installation`

How to do it...

1. Creating a backup of a filesystem/partition

    Use the `savefs` option of `fsarchiver` like this:

    `fsarchiver savefs backup.fsa /dev/sda1`

    where backup.fsa is the final backup file and /dev/sda1 is the partition to backup

2. Backup more than one partition at the same time

    Use the `savefs` option as earlier and pass the partitions as the last parameters to `fsarchiver`:

    `fsarchiver savefs backup.fsa /dev/sda1 /dev/sda2`

3. Restore a partition from a backup archive

    Use the `restfs` option of `fsarchiver` like this:

    `fsarchiver restfs backup.fsa id=0,dest=/dev/sda1`

    `id=0` denotes that we want to pick the first partition from the archive to the partition specified as `dest=/dev/sda1`

4. Restore multiple partitions from a backup archive

As earlier, use the `restfs` option as follows:

`fsarchiver restfs backup.fsa id=0,dest=/dev/sda1 id=1,dest=/dev/sdb1`

Here, we use two sets of the `id,dest` parameter to tell `fsarchiver` to restore the first two partitions from the backup to two physical partitions.

How it works...

Very similar to the way tar works, `fsarchiver` goes through the filesystem to create a list of files and then saves them to a compressed archive file. The advantage here is that unlike tar which only saves information about the files, `fsarchiver` performs a backup of the filesystem as well. This means that it is easier to restore the backup on a fresh system as it is not necessary to recreate the filesystem.

If you are seeing the `/dev/sda1` notation for partitions for the first time, this deserves some explanation. `/dev` in Linux holds special files called device files which refer to a physical device. The `sd` in `sda1` refers to **SATA d**isk, the next letter can be a, b, c and so on, followed by the partition number.

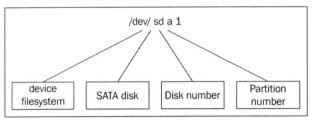

Diagram showing the various parts of a disk device's filename in Linux

7

The Old-boy Network

In this chapter, we will cover:

- ▸ Setting up the network
- ▸ Let us ping!
- ▸ Listing all the machines alive on a network
- ▸ Running commands on a remote host with SSH
- ▸ Transferring files through the network
- ▸ Connecting to a wireless network
- ▸ Password-less auto-login with SSH
- ▸ Port forwarding using SSH
- ▸ Mounting a remote drive at a local mount point
- ▸ Network traffic and port analysis
- ▸ Creating arbitrary sockets
- ▸ Sharing an Internet connection
- ▸ Basic firewall using iptables

Introduction

Networking is the act of interconnecting machines to form a network so that the machines can interchange information. The most widely used networking stack is TCP/IP, where each node is assigned a unique IP address for identification. There are many parameters in networking, such as subnet mask, route, ports, host names, and so on which require a basic understanding to follow.

Several applications that make use of a network operate by opening and connecting to something called ports, which denote services such as data transfer, remote shell login, and so on. Several interesting management tasks can be performed on a network consisting of many machines. Shell scripts can be used to configure the nodes in a network, test the availability of machines, automate execution of commands at remote hosts, and so on. This chapter focuses on different recipes that introduce interesting tools or commands related to networking, and also how they can be used for solving different problems.

Setting up the network

Before digging through recipes based on networking, it is essential to have a basic understanding of setting up a network, terminologies, and commands for assigning IP address, adding routes, and so on. This recipe will give an overview of different commands used in GNU/Linux for networking and their usages from the basics.

Getting ready

A network interface is used to connect a machine to a network. Usually, Linux denotes network interfaces using names like eth0, eth1 (referring to Ethernet interfaces). Other interfaces, such as usb0, wlan0, and so on are available for USB network interfaces, wireless LAN respectively.

In this recipe, we will use these commands: `ifconfig`, `route`, `nslookup`, and `host`.

`ifconfig` is the command that is used to configure and display details about network interfaces, subnet mask, and so on. On a typical system, it should be available at `/sbin/ifconfig`.

How to do it...

1. List the current network interface configuration:

```
$ ifconfig
lo         Link encap:Local Loopback
inet addr:127.0.0.1  Mask:255.0.0.0
inet6addr: ::1/128 Scope:Host
          UP LOOPBACK RUNNING  MTU:16436  Metric:1
          RX packets:6078 errors:0 dropped:0 overruns:0 frame:0
          TX packets:6078 errors:0 dropped:0 overruns:0 carrier:0
collisions:0 txqueuelen:0
          RX bytes:634520 (634.5 KB)  TX bytes:634520 (634.5 KB)
```

```
wlan0      Link encap:EthernetHWaddr 00:1c:bf:87:25:d2
inet addr:192.168.0.82  Bcast:192.168.3.255  Mask:255.255.252.0
inet6addr: fe80::21c:bfff:fe87:25d2/64 Scope:Link
           UP BROADCAST RUNNING MULTICAST  MTU:1500  Metric:1
           RX packets:420917 errors:0 dropped:0 overruns:0 frame:0
           TX packets:86820 errors:0 dropped:0 overruns:0 carrier:0
collisions:0 txqueuelen:1000
           RX bytes:98027420 (98.0 MB)  TX bytes:22602672 (22.6 MB)
```

The left-most column in the `ifconfig` output lists the names of network interfaces, and the right-hand columns show the details related to the corresponding network interface.

2. In order to manually set the IP address for a network interface, use:

   ```
   # ifconfig wlan0 192.168.0.80
   ```

   You will need to run the preceding command .as root. `192.168.0.80` is the address to be set,

   Set the subnet mask along with the IP address as follows:

   ```
   # ifconfig wlan0 192.168.0.80  netmask 255.255.252.0
   ```

3. Automatically configure network interfaces. If you are connecting to, let's say a wired network which supports automatically assigning IPs, just use this to configure the network interface:

   ```
   # dhclient eth0
   ```

There's more...

Let's go through a few more essential commands and their usage.

Printing the list of network interfaces

Here is a one-line command sequence to print the list of network interfaces available on a system:

```
$ ifconfig | cut -c-10 | tr -d ' ' | tr -s '\n'
lo
wlan0
```

The first 10 characters of each line in `ifconfig` output is reserved for writing names of network interfaces. Hence, we use `cut` to extract the first 10 characters of each line. `tr -d ' '` deletes every space character in each line. Now, the \n newline character is squeezed using `tr -s '\n'` to produce a list of interface names.

Displaying IP addresses

The `ifconfig` command displays details of every active network interface available on the system. However, we can restrict it to a specific interface using:

```
$ ifconfig iface_name
```

For example:

```
$ ifconfig wlan0
wlan0       Link encap:EthernetHWaddr 00:1c:bf:87:25:d2
inet addr:192.168.0.82  Bcast:192.168.3.255
    Mask:255.255.252.0
```

From the outputs of the previously mentioned command, our interests lie in the IP address, broadcast address, hardware address, and subnet mask. They are as follows:

- ▸ `HWaddr 00:1c:bf:87:25:d2` is the hardware address (MAC address)
- ▸ `inet addr:192.168.0.82` is the IP address
- ▸ `Bcast:192.168.3.255` is the broadcast address
- ▸ `Mask:255.255.252.0` is the subnet mask

In several scripting contexts, we may need to extract any of these addresses from the script for further manipulations. Extracting the IP address is a frequently needed task. In order to extract the IP address from the `ifconfig` output use:

```
$ ifconfig wlan0 | egrep -o "inet addr:[^ ]*" | grep -o "[0-9.]*"
192.168.0.82
```

Here ,the first command `egrep -o "inet addr:[^ ]*"` will print `inet addr:192.168.0.82`. The pattern starts with `inet addr:` and ends with some non-space character sequence (specified by `[^ ]*`). Now in the next pipe, it prints the character combination of digits and `'.'`.

Spoofing the hardware address (MAC address)

In certain circumstances where authentication or filtering of computers on a network are based on the hardware address, we can use hardware address spoofing. The hardware address appears in `ifconfig` output as `HWaddr 00:1c:bf:87:25:d2`.

We can spoof the hardware address at the software level as follows:

```
# ifconfig eth0 hw ether 00:1c:bf:87:25:d5
```

In the preceding command, `00:1c:bf:87:25:d5` is the new MAC address to be assigned. This can be useful when we need to access the Internet through MAC-authenticated service providers that provide access to the Internet for a single machine. However, note that this only lasts until a machine restarts.

Name server and DNS (Domain Name Service)

The elementary addressing scheme for the Internet is IP addressing (dotted decimal form, for example, `202.11.32.75`). However, the resources on the Internet (for example, websites) are accessed through a combination of ASCII characters called **URLs** or **domain names**. For example, `www.google.com` is a domain name and it corresponds to one (or more) IP address. Typing the IP address in the browser can also access the URL `www.google.com`.

This technique of abstracting IP addresses with symbolic names is called **Domain Name Service** (**DNS**). When we enter www.google.com, our computer uses the DNS servers configured with the network to resolve the domain name into the corresponding IP address. While on a local network, we set up the local DNS for naming local machines on the network symbolically using their hostnames.

Name servers assigned to the current system can be viewed by reading `/etc/resolv.conf`, for example:

```
$ cat /etc/resolv.conf
nameserver 8.8.8.8
```

We can add name servers manually as follows:

```
# echo nameserver IP_ADDRESS >> /etc/resolv.conf
```

How can we obtain the IP address for a corresponding domain name? The easiest method to obtain an IP address is by trying to ping the given domain name and looking at the echo reply. For example:

```
$ ping google.com
PING google.com (64.233.181.106) 56(84) bytes of data.
Here 64.233.181.106 is the corresponding IP address.
```

A domain name can have multiple IP addresses assigned. In that case, `ping` will show one address among the list of IP addresses. To obtain all the addresses assigned to the domain name, we should use a DNS lookup utility.

DNS lookup

There are different DNS lookup utilities available from the command line, which will request a DNS server for an IP address resolution. `host` and `nslookup` are two of such DNS lookup utilities.

When `host` is executed it will list out all of the IP addresses attached to the domain name. `nslookup` is another command that is similar to `host`, which can be used to query details related to DNS and resolving of names. For example:

```
$ host google.com
google.com has address 64.233.181.105
google.com has address 64.233.181.99
google.com has address 64.233.181.147
google.com has address 64.233.181.106
google.com has address 64.233.181.103
google.com has address 64.233.181.104
```

We can also list out all the DNS resource records as follows:

```
$ nslookup google.com
Server:       8.8.8.8
Address:      8.8.8.8#53

Non-authoritative answer:
Name:   google.com
Address: 64.233.181.105
Name:   google.com
Address: 64.233.181.99
Name:   google.com
Address: 64.233.181.147
Name:   google.com
Address: 64.233.181.106
Name:   google.com
Address: 64.233.181.103
Name:   google.com
Address: 64.233.181.104

Server:       8.8.8.8
```

The last line in the preceding command-line snippet corresponds to the default name server used for resolution.

Without using the DNS server, it is possible to add a symbolic name to the IP address resolution just by adding entries into the file /etc/hosts. In order to add an entry, use the following syntax:

```
# echo IP_ADDRESS symbolic_name >> /etc/hosts
```

For example:

```
# echo 192.168.0.9 backupserver >> /etc/hosts
```

After adding this entry, whenever resolution to backupserver occurs, it will resolve to 192.168.0.9.

Showing routing table information

Having more than one network connected with each other is a very common scenario. An example of this is in a college, where different departments may be on separate networks. In this case, when a device on one network wants to communicate with a device on the other network, it needs to go through a device which is common to the two networks. This special device is called a **gateway** and its function is to route packets to and from different networks.

The operating system maintains a table called the **routing table**, which contains the information on how packets are to be forwarded through machines on the network. The routing table can be displayed as follows:

```
$ route
Kernel IP routing table
Destination       Gateway     Genmask         Flags  Metric  Ref   UseIface
192.168.0.0          *        255.255.252.0   U      2       0     0wlan0
link-local           *        255.255.0.0     U      1000    0     0wlan0
default           p4.local    0.0.0.0         UG     0       0     0wlan0
```

Or, you can also use:

```
$ route -n
Kernel IP routing table
Destination   Gateway      Genmask         Flags Metric Ref   Use   Iface
192.168.0.0   0.0.0.0      255.255.252.0   U     2      0     0     wlan0
169.254.0.0   0.0.0.0      255.255.0.0     U     1000   0     0     wlan0
0.0.0.0       192.168.0.4  0.0.0.0         UG    0      0     0     wlan0
```

Using -n specifies to display the numerical addresses. When -n is used it will display every entry with a numerical IP address, else it will show symbolic hostnames instead of IP addresses in DNS entries for IP addresses that are available.

A default gateway is set as follows:

```
# route add default gw IP_ADDRESS INTERFACE_NAME
```

For example:

```
# route add default gw 192.168.0.1 wlan0
```

See also

- The *Playing with variables and environment variables* recipe of *Chapter 1, Shell Something Out*, explains the PATH variable
- The *Searching and mining text inside a file with grep* recipe of *Chapter 4, Texting and Driving*, explains the grep command

Let us ping!

ping is the most basic network command every user should first know and is available on all major Operating Systems. It is also a diagnostic tool used for verifying the connectivity between two hosts on a network. It can be used to find out which machines are alive on a network. Let us see how to use ping.

How to do it...

In order to check the connectivity of two hosts on a network, the ping command uses **Internet Control Message Protocol (ICMP)** echo packets. When these echo packets are sent towards a host, the host responds back with a reply if it is reachable or alive.

Check whether a host is reachable as follows:

```
$ ping ADDRESS
```

The ADDRESS can be a hostname, domain name, or an IP address itself.

ping will continuously send packets and the reply information is printed on the terminal. Stop the pinging process by pressing *Ctrl + C*.

For example:

- When a host is reachable, the output will be similar to the following:
  ```
  $ ping 192.168.0.1
  PING 192.168.0.1 (192.168.0.1) 56(84) bytes of data.
  64 bytes from 192.168.0.1: icmp_seq=1 ttl=64 time=1.44 ms
  ^C
  ```

```
--- 192.168.0.1 ping statistics ---

1 packets transmitted, 1 received, 0% packet loss, time 0ms

rtt min/avg/max/mdev = 1.440/1.440/1.440/0.000 ms


$ ping google.com

PING google.com (209.85.153.104) 56(84) bytes of data.

64 bytes from bom01s01-in-f104.1e100.net (209.85.153.104): icmp_
seq=1 ttl=53 time=123 ms

^C

--- google.com ping statistics ---

1 packets transmitted, 1 received, 0% packet loss, time 0ms

rtt min/avg/max/mdev = 123.388/123.388/123.388/0.000 ms
```

▶   When a host is unreachable, the output will be similar to:

```
$ ping 192.168.0.99

PING 192.168.0.99 (192.168.0.99) 56(84) bytes of data.

From 192.168.0.82 icmp_seq=1 Destination Host Unreachable

From 192.168.0.82 icmp_seq=2 Destination Host Unreachable
```

Once the host is not reachable, the ping returns with the `Destination Host Unreachable` error message.

 Network administrators generally configure devices such as routers not to respond to `ping`. This is done to lower security risks, as `ping` can be used by attackers (using brute-force) to find out IP addresses of machines.

There's more

In addition to checking the connectivity between two points in a network, the `ping` command can be used with additional options to get useful information. Let us go through the additional options of `ping`.

Round trip time

The `ping` command can be used to find out the **Round Trip Time** (**RTT**) between two hosts on a network. RTT is the time required for the packet to reach the destination host and come back to the source host. RTT in milliseconds can be obtained from `ping`. An example is as follows:

```
--- google.com ping statistics ---
5 packets transmitted, 5 received, 0% packet loss, time 4000ms
rtt min/avg/max/mdev = 118.012/206.630/347.186/77.713 ms
```

Here, the minimum RTT is `118.012ms`, the average RTT is `206.630ms`, and the maximum RTT is `347.186ms`. The `mdev` (`77.713ms`) parameter in the ping output stands for mean deviation.

Limiting the number of packets to be sent

The `ping` command sends echo packets and waits for the reply of echo indefinitely until it is stopped by pressing *Ctrl + C*. However, we can limit the count of echo packets to be sent by using the `-c` flag. The usage is as follows:

```
-c COUNT
```

For example:

```
$ ping 192.168.0.1 -c 2
PING 192.168.0.1 (192.168.0.1) 56(84) bytes of data.
64 bytes from 192.168.0.1: icmp_seq=1 ttl=64 time=4.02 ms
64 bytes from 192.168.0.1: icmp_seq=2 ttl=64 time=1.03 ms

--- 192.168.0.1 ping statistics ---
2 packets transmitted, 2 received, 0% packet loss, time 1001ms
rtt min/avg/max/mdev = 1.039/2.533/4.028/1.495 ms
```

In the previous example, the `ping` command sends two echo packets and stops. This is useful when we need to ping multiple machines from a list of IP addresses through a script and check its statuses.

Return status of the ping command

The `ping` command returns exit status `0` when it succeeds and returns non-zero when it fails. `Successful` means destination host is reachable, whereas `Failure` is when the destination host is unreachable.

The return status can be easily obtained as follows:

```
$ ping domain -c2
if [ $? -eq 0 ];
then
   echo Successful ;
else
   echo Failure
fi
```

Traceroute

When an application requests a service through the Internet, the server may be at a distant location and connected through many number of gateways or device nodes. The packets travel through several gateways and reach the destination. There is an interesting command traceroute that displays the address of all intermediate gateways through which a packet travelled to reach a particular destination. traceroute information helps us to understand how many hops each packet should take in order to reach the destination. The number of intermediate gateways or routers gives a metric to measure the distance between two nodes connected in a large network. An example of traceroute is as follows:

```
$ traceroute google.com
traceroute to google.com (74.125.77.104), 30 hops max, 60 byte packets
1   gw-c6509.lxb.as5577.net (195.26.4.1)   0.313 ms   0.371 ms   0.457 ms
2   40g.lxb-fra.as5577.net (83.243.12.2)   4.684 ms   4.754 ms   4.823 ms
3   de-cix10.net.google.com (80.81.192.108)   5.312 ms   5.348 ms   5.327 ms
4   209.85.255.170 (209.85.255.170)   5.816 ms   5.791 ms 209.85.255.172
(209.85.255.172)   5.678 ms
5   209.85.250.140 (209.85.250.140)   10.126 ms   9.867 ms   10.754 ms
6   64.233.175.246 (64.233.175.246)   12.940 ms 72.14.233.114
(72.14.233.114)   13.736 ms   13.803 ms
7   72.14.239.199 (72.14.239.199)   14.618 ms 209.85.255.166
(209.85.255.166)   12.755 ms 209.85.255.143 (209.85.255.143)   13.803 ms
8   209.85.255.98 (209.85.255.98)   22.625 ms 209.85.255.110
(209.85.255.110)   14.122 ms
*
9   ew-in-f104.1e100.net (74.125.77.104)   13.061 ms   13.256 ms   13.484 ms
```

Modern Linux distributions also ship with a command `mtr`, which is similar to `traceroute` but shows real-time data which keeps refreshing. It is very useful to check your network carrier quality and so on.

Listing all the machines alive on a network

When we deal with a large local area network, we may need to check the availability of other machines in the network. A machine may not be alive in two conditions: either it is not powered on, or due to a problem in the network. By using shell scripting, we can easily find out and report which machines are alive on the network. Let's see how to do it.

Getting ready

In this recipe, we use two methods. The first method uses `ping` and the second method uses `fping`. `fping` is easier to use for scripts and has more features as compared to the `ping` command. Usually it won't be shipped with your Linux distribution by default, so manually install it using your package manager.

How to do it...

Let's go through the script to find out all the live machines on the network and alternate methods to find out the same.

1. The first method is as follows:

   We can write our own script using the `ping` command to query a list of IP addresses and check whether they are alive or not as follows:

   ```
   #!/bin/bash
   #Filename: ping.sh
   # Change base address 192.168.0 according to your network.

   for ip in 192.168.0.{1..255} ;
   do
     ping $ip -c 2 &> /dev/null ;

     if [ $? -eq 0 ];
     then
       echo $ip is alive
     fi
   ```

```
done
```

The output is as follows:

```
$ ./ping.sh
192.168.0.1 is alive
192.168.0.90 is alive
```

2. Using `fping`, the second method is as follows:

We can use an existing command-line utility to query the status of machines on a network as follows:

```
$ fping -a 192.160.1/24 -g 2> /dev/null
192.168.0.1
192.168.0.90
```

Or, use:

```
$ fping -a 192.168.0.1 192.168.0.255 -g
```

How it works...

In the first method, we used the `ping` command to find out the alive machines on the network. We used a `for` loop for iterating through a list of IP addresses generated using the expression `192.168.0.{1..255}`. The `{start..end}` notation will expand and will generate a list of IP addresses, such as `192.168.0.1, 192.168.0.2, 192.168.0.3` up to `192.168.0.255`.

`ping $ip -c 2 &> /dev/null` will run a `ping` command to the corresponding IP address in each execution of the loop. The `-c` option is used to restrict the number of echo packets to be sent to a specified number. `&> /dev/null` is used to redirect both `stderr` and `stdout` to `/dev/null` so that it won't be printed on the terminal. Using `$?` we evaluate the exit status. If it is successful, the exit status is `0` else non-zero. Hence, the IP addresses which replied to our ping are printed.

In this script, each `ping` command for the IP address is executed one after the other. Even though all the IP addresses are independent of each other, the `ping` command is executed as a sequential program, it takes a delay of sending two echo packets and receiving them or the time-out for a reply for executing the next `ping` command.

There's more...

We discussed a method for finding out the alive machines on a network. Let's see some enhancements and another method to do the same thing.

Parallel pings

When it comes to 255 addresses, the delay gets accumulated and becomes large. We can run all the `ping` commands in parallel to make this faster. To make the `ping` commands run in parallel, we enclose the loop body in ( ) &. ( ) encloses a block of commands to run as a subshell and & sends it to the background. For example:

```
#!/bin/bash
#Filename: fast_ping.sh
# Change base address 192.168.0 according to your network.

for ip in 192.168.0.{1..255} ;
do
    (
        ping $ip -c2 &> /dev/null ;

        if [ $? -eq 0 ];
        then
          echo $ip is alive
        fi
    ) &
  done
wait
```

In the `for` loop, we execute many background processes and come out of the loop, terminating the script. In order to prevent the script to terminate until all its entire child processes end, we have a command called `wait`. Place `wait` at the end of the script, so that it waits for the time until all the child ( ) subshell processes complete.

Using fping

The second method uses a different command called `fping`. It can ping a list of IP addresses simultaneously and respond very quickly. The options available with `fping` are as follows:

- ▸ The `-a` option with `fping` specifies to print all alive machine's IP addresses
- ▸ The `-u` option with `fping` specifies to print all unreachable machines
- ▸ The `-g` option specifies to generate a range of IP addresses from slash-subnet mask notation specified as IP/mask or start and end IP addresses as:

  $ fping -a 192.160.1/24 -g

  Or

  $ fping -a 192.160.1 192.168.0.255 -g

- ▸ `2>/dev/null` is used to dump error messages printed due to an unreachable host to null device

It is also possible to manually specify a list of IP addresses as command-line arguments or as a list through `stdin`. For example:

```
$ fping -a 192.168.0.1 192.168.0.5 192.168.0.6
# Passes IP address as arguments
$ fping -a < ip.list
# Passes a list of IP addresses from a file
```

See also

▸ The *Playing with file descriptors and redirection* recipe of *Chapter 1, Shell Something Out*, explains the data redirection

▸ The *Comparisons and tests* recipe of *Chapter 1, Shell Something Out*, explains numeric comparisons

Running commands on a remote host with SSH

SSH is an interesting system administration tool that gives you access to a shell on a remote computer which you can use to run commands. **SSH** stands for **Secure Shell** as it transfers the network data transfer over an encrypted tunnel. This recipe will introduce different ways in which commands can be executed at a remote host.

Getting ready

SSH doesn't come preinstalled with all GNU/Linux distributions, and you may have to install the `openssh-server` and `openssh-client` packages using a package manager. SSH service runs at default port number 22.

How to do it...

1. To connect to a remote host with the SSH server running, use:

   ```
   $ ssh username@remote_host
   ```

   In this command:

   ❑ `username` is the user that exists at the remote host

   ❑ `remote_host` can be the domain name or IP address

For example:

```
$ ssh mec@192.168.0.1
```

```
The authenticity of host '192.168.0.1 (192.168.0.1)' can't be
established.
```

```
RSA key fingerprint is 2b:b4:90:79:49:0a:f1:b3:8a:db:9f:73:2d:75:d
6:f9.
```

```
Are you sure you want to continue connecting (yes/no)? yes
```

```
Warning: Permanently added '192.168.0.1' (RSA) to the list of
known hosts.
```

```
Password:
```

```
Last login: Fri Sep  3 05:15:21 2010 from 192.168.0.82
```

```
mec@proxy-1:~$
```

It will interactively ask for a user password, and upon successful authentication it will return the shell for the user.

> SSH performs a fingerprint verification to make sure that we are actually connecting to the remote computer we want to. This is to avoid what is called a **man-in-the-middle attack**, where an attacker tries to impersonate another computer. SSH will, by default, store the fingerprint the first time we connect to a server and verify that it does not change for future connections.

By default, the SSH server runs at port 22. But certain servers run SSH service at different ports. In that case, use -p port_num with the ssh command to specify the port.

2. In order to connect to an SSH server running at port 422, use:

```
$ ssh user@locahost -p 422
```

You can execute commands in the shell that corresponds to the remote host. However, when using ssh in shell scripts, we do not want an interactive shell as we require to execute several commands and display or store their output.

> Issuing a password every time is not practical for an automated script, hence password-less login using SSH keys should be configured. The *Password-less auto-login with SSH* recipe explains the SSH commands to set this up.

3. To run a command at the remote host and display its output on the local shell, use the following syntax:

```
$ ssh user@host 'COMMANDS'
```

For example:

```
$ ssh mec@192.168.0.1 'whoami'
mec
```

Multiple commands can be given by using a semicolon delimiter in between the commands as:

```
$ ssh user@host "command1 ; command2 ; command3"
```

For example:

```
$ ssh mec@192.168.0.1   "echo user: $(whoami);echo OS: $(uname)"
Password:
user: mec
OS: Linux
```

In this example, the commands executed at the remote host are:

```
echo user: $(whoami);
echo OS: $(uname)
```

It can be generalized as:

```
COMMANDS="command1; command2; command3"
$ ssh user@hostname   "$COMMANDS"
```

We can also pass a more complex subshell in the command sequence by using the ( ) subshell operator.

4. Let's write an SSH-based shell script that collects the uptime of a list of remote hosts. Uptime is the time for which the system is powered on and the uptime command is used to display this information.

It is assumed that all systems in IP_LIST have a common user test.

```
#!/bin/bash
#Filename: uptime.sh
#Description: Uptime monitor

IP_LIST="192.168.0.1 192.168.0.5 192.168.0.9"
USER="test"

for IP in $IP_LIST;
```

```
do
  utime=$(ssh ${USER}@${IP} uptime   | awk '{ print $3 }' )
  echo $IP uptime:   $utime
done
```

Expected output:

```
$ ./uptime.sh
192.168.0.1 uptime: 1:50,
192.168.0.5 uptime: 2:15,
192.168.0.9 uptime: 10:15,
```

There's more...

The `ssh` command can be executed with several additional options. Let's go through them.

SSH with compression

The SSH protocol also supports data transfer with compression, which comes in handy when bandwidth is an issue. Use the `-C` option with the `ssh` command to enable compression as follows:

```
$ ssh -C user@hostname COMMANDS
```

Redirecting data into stdin of remote host shell commands

Sometimes, we need to redirect some data into `stdin` of remote shell commands. Let's see how to do it. An example is as follows:

```
$ echo 'text' | ssh user@remote_host 'echo'

text
```

Or

```
# Redirect data from file as:
$ ssh user@remote_host 'echo'   < file
```

`echo` on the remote host prints the data received through `stdin` which in turn is passed to `stdin` from localhost.

Running graphical commands on a remote machine

If you attempt to use this recipe with a command that needs to show some kind of GUI to the user, you will see an error similar to "cannot open display". This is because the `ssh` shell is not able to connect to the X server running on the remote machine. For this you need to set the `$DISPLAY` variable like this:

```
ssh user@host "export DISPLAY=:0 ; command1; command2"""
```

This will launch the graphical output on the remote machine. If you want to show the graphical output on your local machine, use SSH's X11 forwarding option as follows:

```
ssh -X user@host "command1; command2"
```

This will run the commands on the remote machine, but it will bring the graphical output to your machine.

See also

► The *Password less auto-login with SSH* recipe, explains how to configure auto-login to execute commands without prompting for a password.

Transferring files through the network

The major driver for networking of computers is resource sharing, and file sharing is the most prominent shared resource. There are different methods by which we can transfer files between different nodes on a network. This recipe discusses how to transfer files using commonly used protocols FTP, SFTP, RSYNC, and SCP.

Getting ready

The commands for performing file transfer over the network are mostly available by default with Linux installation. Files can be transferred via FTP using the `lftp` command. Files can be transferred via a SSH connection using `sftp`. Further, we can use RSYNC over SSH with `rsync` command and transfer files through SSH using `scp`.

How to do it...

File Transfer Protocol (**FTP**) is a very old file transfer protocol for transferring files between machines on a network. We can use the command `lftp` for accessing FTP-enabled servers for file transfer. FTP can only be used if the FTP server is installed on the remote machine. FTP is used in many public websites to share files and the service usually runs on port 21.

To connect to an FTP server and transfer files in between, use:

```
$ lftp username@ftphost
```

It will prompt for a password and then display a logged in prompt as follows:

```
lftp username@ftphost:~>
```

You can type commands in this prompt. For example:

- ▸ To change to a directory, use `cd directory`
- ▸ To change the directory of a local machine, use `lcd`
- ▸ To create a directory use `mkdir`
- ▸ To list files in the current directory on the remote machine, use `ls`
- ▸ To download a file, use `get filename` as follows:

  `lftp username@ftphost:~> get filename`

- ▸ To upload a file from the current directory, use `put filename` as follows:

  `lftp username@ftphost:~> put filename`

- ▸ An `lftp` session can be terminated by using the `quit` command

Autocompletion is supported by in the `lftp` prompt.

There's more...

Let's go through additional techniques and commands used for file transfer through a network.

Automated FTP transfer

`ftp` is another command used for FTP-based file transfer. `lftp` is more flexible for usage. `lftp` and the `ftp` commands open an interactive session with the user (it prompts for user input by displaying messages). What if we want to automate file transfer instead of an interactive mode? We can automate FTP file transfers by writing a shell script as follows:

```
#!/bin/bash
#Filename: ftp.sh
#Automated FTP transfer
HOST='domain.com'
USER='foo'
PASSWD='password'
ftp -i -n $HOST <<EOF
user ${USER} ${PASSWD}
binary
cd /home/slynux
puttestfile.jpg
getserverfile.jpg
quit
EOF
```

The preceding script has the following structure:

```
<<EOF
DATA
EOF
```

This is used to send data through `stdin` to the `ftp` command. The *Playing with file descriptors and redirection* recipe of *Chapter 1, Shell Something Out,* explains various methods for redirection into stdin.

The `-i` option of `ftp` turns off the interactive session with user. `user ${USER} ${PASSWD}` sets the username and password. `binary` sets the file mode to binary. The `-n` option tells `ftp` to not attempt automatically logging in and use the username and password we supply it.

SFTP (Secure FTP)

SFTP is a FTP-like file transfer system that runs on top of an SSH connection and emulates as an FTP interface. It doesn't require an FTP server at the remote end to perform file transfer, but it requires an OpenSSH server to be installed and running. It is an interactive command, which offers an `sftp` prompt.

The following commands are used to perform the file transfer. All other commands remain the same for every automated FTP session with a specific HOST, USER, and PASSWORD:

cd /home/slynux

put testfile.jpg

get serverfile.jpg

In order to run `sftp`, use:

$ sftp user@domainname

Similar to `lftp`, an `sftp` session can be terminated by typing the `quit` command.

Sometimes, the SSH server will not be running at the default port 22. If it is running at a different port, we can specify the port along with `sftp` as `-oPort=PORTNO`. For example:

$ sftp -oPort=422 user@slynux.org

`-oPort` should be the first argument of the `sftp` command.

The rsync command

`rsync` is an important command-line utility that is widely used for copying files over networks and for taking backup snapshots. This is better explained in the *Backup snapshots with rsync* recipe of *Chapter 6, The Backup Plan,* that explains the usage of `rsync`.

SCP (secure copy program)

SCP is a file copy technique which is more secure than the traditional remote copy tool called `rcp`. The files are transferred through an encrypted channel. SSH is used over an encryption channel and we can easily transfer files to a remote machine as follows:

```
$ scp filename user@remotehost:/home/path
```

This will prompt for a password and can be made password-less by using the auto-login SSH technique. The *Password-less auto-login with SSH* recipe explains SSH auto-login. Therefore, file transfer using `scp` doesn't require specific scripting. Once SSH login is automated, the `scp` command can be executed without an interactive prompt for the password.

Here, `remotehost` can be an IP address or domain name. The format of the scp command is:

```
$ scp SOURCE DESTINATION
```

SOURCE or DESTINATION can be in the format `username@host:/path`, for example:

```
$ scp user@remotehost:/home/path/filename filename
```

The preceding command copies a file from the remote host to the current directory with the given filename.

If SSH is running at a different port than 22, use `-oPort` with the same syntax, `sftp`.

Recursive copying with SCP

By using `scp`, we can recursively copy a directory between two machines on a network as follows with the `-r` parameter:

```
$ scp -r /home/slynux user@remotehost:/home/backups
# Copies the directory /home/slynux recursively recurisvely to a remote
location
```

`scp` can also copy files by preserving permissions and modes by using the `-p` parameter.

See also

- The *Playing with file descriptors and redirection* recipe of *Chapter 1, Shell Something Out*, explains the standard input using EOF

Connecting to a wireless network

An Ethernet connection is simple to configure, since it is connected through wired cables with no special requirements like authentication. However, wireless LAN may require authentication like a secret key as well as ESSID of the wireless network to connect. **ESSID**, or **Extended Service Set Identification**, is the name of the network. Let's see how to connect to a wireless network by writing a shell script.

Getting ready

To connect to a wired network, we need to assign an IP address and subnet mask by using the `ifconfig` utility. But for a wireless network connection, it will require additional utilities such as `iwconfig` and `iwlist` to configure more parameters.

How to do it...

Let's write a script for connecting to a wireless LAN with **WEP** (**Wired Equivalent Privacy**):

```
#!/bin/bash
#Filename: wlan_connect.sh
#Description: Connect to Wireless LAN

#Modify the parameters below according to your settings
######### PARAMETERS ###########
IFACE=wlan0
IP_ADDR=192.168.1.5
SUBNET_MASK=255.255.255.0
GW=192.168.1.1
HW_ADDR='00:1c:bf:87:25:d2'
#Comment above line if you don't want to spoof mac address

ESSID="homenet"
WEP_KEY=8b140b20e7
FREQ=2.462G
################################

KEY_PART=""

if [[ -n $WEP_KEY ]];
then
  KEY_PART="key $WEP_KEY"
fi
```

```
# Turn the interface down before setting new config
/sbin/ifconfig $IFACE down

if [ $UID -ne 0 ];
then
  echo "Run as root"
  exit 1;
fi

if [[ -n $HW_ADDR ]];
then
  /sbin/ifconfig $IFACE hw ether $HW_ADDR
  echo Spoofed MAC ADDRESS to $HW_ADDR
fi

/sbin/iwconfig $IFACE essid $ESSID $KEY_PART freq $FREQ

/sbin/ifconfig $IFACE $IP_ADDR netmask $SUBNET_MASK

route add default gw $GW $IFACE

echo Successfully configured $IFACE
```

How it works...

The commands `ifconfig`, `iwconfig`, and `route` are to be run as root. Hence, a check for the root user is performed before performing any actions in the scripts.

Wireless LAN requires some parameters such as **essid, key**, and **frequency** to connect to the network. essid is the name of the wireless network to which we need to connect. Some networks use a WEP key for authentication, which is usually a 5 or 10 letter hex passphrase. Another parameter is the frequency assigned to the network which the `iwconfig` command uses to attach the wireless card with the proper wireless network.

We can scan and list the available wireless network using the utility `iwlist`. To scan, use the following command:

```
# iwlist scan

wlan0     Scan completed :
          Cell 01 - Address: 00:12:17:7B:1C:65
                    Channel:11
                    Frequency:2.462 GHz (Channel 11)
                    Quality=33/70   Signal level=-77 dBm
                    Encryption key:on
                    ESSID:"model-2"
```

The `Frequency` parameter can be extracted from the scan result, from the line
`Frequency:2.462 GHz (Channel 11)`.

 WEP is used in this example for simplicity, but its worthy to note that currently it is considered insecure. If you are administering the wireless network, make sure that you use a variant of **Wi-Fi Protected Access2 (WPA2)** to be secure.

See also

▶ The *Comparisons and tests* recipe of *Chapter 1, Shell Something Out*, explains string comparisons

Password-less auto-login with SSH

SSH is widely used with automation scripting, as it makes it possible to remotely execute commands at remote hosts and read their outputs. Usually, SSH is authenticated by using a username and password, which are prompted during the execution of SSH commands. However, providing passwords in automated scripts is impractical, so we need to automate logins. SSH has an in-built feature by which SSH can auto-login using SSH keys. This recipe describes how to create SSH keys and facilitate auto-login.

Getting ready

SSH uses an encryption technique called **asymmetric keys** consisting of two keys: a public key and a private key for automatic authentication. We can create an authentication key pair using the `ssh-keygen` command. For automating the authentication, the public key must be placed at the server (by appending the public key to the `~/.ssh/authorized_keys` file) and its private key file of the pair should be present at the `~/.ssh` directory of the user at the client machine, which is the computer you are logging in from. Several configurations (for example, path and name of the `authorized_keys` file) regarding the SSH can be configured by altering the configuration file `/etc/ssh/sshd_config`.

How to do it...

There are two steps towards setup of automatic authentication with SSH. They are:

▶ Creating the SSH key on the machine, which requires a login to a remote machine

▶ Transferring the public key generated to the remote host and appending it to `~/.ssh/authorized_keys`

In order to create an SSH key, enter the ssh-keygen command with the encryption algorithm type specified as RSA as follows:

```
$ ssh-keygen -t rsa
Generating public/private rsa key pair.
Enter file in which to save the key (/home/slynux/.ssh/id_rsa):
Created directory '/home/slynux/.ssh'.
Enter passphrase (empty for no passphrase):
Enter same passphrase again:
Your identification has been saved in /home/slynux/.ssh/id_rsa.
Your public key has been saved in /home/slynux/.ssh/id_rsa.pub.
The key fingerprint is:
f7:17:c6:4d:c9:ee:17:00:af:0f:b3:27:a6:9c:0a:05 slynux@slynux-laptop
The key's randomart image is:
+--[ RSA 2048]----+
|           .     |
|          o . .|
|     E      o o.|
|      ...oo |
|      .S .+  +o.|
|      .  . .=....|
|     .+.o...|
|      . . + o.  .|
|        ..+      |
+-----------------+
```

You need to enter a passphrase for generating the public-private key pair. It is also possible to generate the key pair without entering a passphrase, but it is insecure. We can write monitoring scripts that use automated login from the script to several machines. In such cases, you should leave the passphrase empty while running the ssh-keygen command to prevent the script from asking for a passphrase while running.

Now ~/.ssh/id_rsa.pub and ~/.ssh/id_rsa have been generated. id_rsa.pub is the generated public key and id_rsa is the private key. The public key has to be appended to the ~/.ssh/authorized_keys file on remote servers where we need to auto-login from the current host.

In order to append a key file, use:

```
$ ssh USER@REMOTE_HOST "cat >> ~/.ssh/authorized_keys" < ~/.ssh/id_rsa.pub
Password:
```

Provide the login password in the previous command.

The auto-login has been set up and from now onwards, SSH will not prompt for passwords during execution. Test this with the following command:

```
$ ssh USER@REMOTE_HOST uname
Linux
```

You will not be prompted for a password.

> Most Linux distros ship with a tool called ssh-copy-id which will automatically add your private key to the authorized_keys file on the remote server. Use it like this:
>
> ```
> ssh-copy-id USER@REMOTE_HOST
> ```

Port forwarding using SSH

Port forwarding is a technique by which you can enable other computers to connect to a particular service on a remote server using your machine. To understand this with an example, let's say your machine is assigned the IP 192.168.1.2 on a network and it has an Internet connection as well. Now, if you forward your machine's port 8000 to port 80 of `www.kernel.org`, it will be possible for some other computer to access the Linux Kernel website by going to `http://192.168.1.2:8000` using a browser. Let's see how to do this.

How to do it...

You can either forward a port on your local machine to another machine and it's also possible to forward a port on a remote machine to another machine. In the following methods, you will eventually get a shell prompt once the forwarding is complete. Keep this shell open to use the port forward and exit it whenever you want to stop the port forward.

1. Use this command to forward a port 8000 on your local machine to port 80 of `www.kernel.org`:

   ```
   ssh -L 8000:www.kernel.org:80 user@localhost
   ```

   Here, replace `user` with the username on your local machine.

2. Use this command to forward a port 8000 on a remote machine to port 80 of `www.kernel.org`:

   ```
   ssh -L 8000:www.kernel.org:80 user@REMOTE_MACHINE
   ```

   Here, replace `REMOTE_MACHINE` with the hostname or IP address of the remote machine and `user` with the username that you have SSH access to.

There's more...

Port forwarding can be made more useful using non-interactive mode or reverse port forwarding. Let's see these.

Non-interactive port forward

If you want to just set the port forwarding instead of having a shell to be kept open for the port forwarding to be effective, use the following form of `ssh`:

```
ssh -fL 8000:www.kernel.org:80 user@localhost -N
```

The -f instructs `ssh` to fork to background just before executing the command, and -l for the login name for the remote host machine. -N tells `ssh` that there is no command to run; we only want to forward ports.

Reverse port forwarding

Reverse port forwarding is one of the most powerful features of SSH. This is most useful in situations where you have a machine which isn't publicly accessible from the Internet, but you want others to be able to access a service on this machine. In this case, if you have SSH access to a remote machine which is publicly accessible on the Internet, you can set up a reverse port forward on that remote machine to the local machine which is running the service.

Reverse port forwarding is very similar to port forwarding:

```
ssh -R 8000:localhost:80 user@REMOTE_MACHINE
```

This will forward port 8000 on the remote machine to port 80 on the local machine. As always, don't forget to replace REMOTE_MACHINE with the hostname of the IP address of the remote machine.

Using this method, if you browse to `http://localhost` on the remote machine, you will actually connect to a web server running on port 8000 of the local machine.

Mounting a remote drive at a local mount point

Having a local mount point to access the remote host filesystem is really helpful while carrying out both read and write data transfer operations. SSH is the common transfer protocol available in a network and hence, we can make use of it with `sshfs` which enables you to mount a remote filesystem to a local mount point. Let's see how to do it.

Getting ready

sshfs doesn't come by default with GNU/Linux distributions. Install sshfs by using a package manager. sshfs is an extension to the FUSE filesystem package that allows supported OSs to mount a wide variety of data as if it were a local filesystem.

For more information on FUSE, visit its website at http://fuse.sourceforge.net/.

How to do it...

In order to mount a filesystem location at a remote host to a local mount point, use:

```
# sshfs -o allow_other user@remotehost:/home/path /mnt/mountpoint
Password:
```

Issue the password when prompted, and data at /home/path on the remote host can be accessed via a local mount point /mnt/mountpoint.

In order to unmount after completing the work, use:

```
# umount /mnt/mountpoint
```

See also

► The *Running commands on remote host with SSH* recipe, explains the ssh command

Network traffic and port analysis

Network ports are essential parameters of network-based applications. Applications open ports on the host and communicate to a remote host through opened ports at the remote host. Having awareness of opened and closed ports is essential for security context. Malwares and root kits may be running on the system with custom ports and custom services that allow attackers to capture unauthorized access to data and resources. By getting the list of opened ports and services running on the ports, we can analyze and defend the system from being controlled by root kits and helps to remove them efficiently. The list of opened ports is not only helpful for malware detection, but is also useful for collecting information about opened ports on the system which enables us to debug network-based applications. It helps to analyze whether certain port connections and port listening functionalities are working fine. This recipe discusses various utilities for port analysis.

Getting ready

Various commands are available for listing ports and services running on each port (for example, `lsof` and `netstat`). These commands are, by default, available on all GNU/Linux distributions.

How to do it...

In order to list all opened ports on the system along with the details on each service attached to it, use:

```
$ lsof -i
COMMAND     PID    USER    FD    TYPE DEVICE SIZE/OFF NODE NAME
firefox-b 2261 slynux    78u   IPv4   63729      0t0   TCP localhost:47797-
>localhost:42486 (ESTABLISHED)
firefox-b 2261 slynux    80u   IPv4   68270      0t0   TCP slynux-laptop.
local:41204->192.168.0.2:3128 (CLOSE_WAIT)
firefox-b 2261 slynux    82u   IPv4   68195      0t0   TCP slynux-laptop.
local:41197->192.168.0.2:3128 (ESTABLISHED)
ssh         3570 slynux     3u   IPv6   30025      0t0   TCP localhost:39263-
>localhost:ssh (ESTABLISHED)
ssh         3836 slynux     3u   IPv4   43431      0t0   TCP slynux-laptop.
local:40414->boneym.mtveurope.org:422 (ESTABLISHED)
GoogleTal 4022 slynux    12u   IPv4   55370      0t0   TCP localhost:42486
(LISTEN)
GoogleTal 4022 slynux    13u   IPv4   55379      0t0   TCP localhost:42486-
>localhost:32955 (ESTABLISHED)
```

Each entry in the output of `lsof` corresponds to each service that opens a port for communication. The last column of output consists of lines similar to:

```
laptop.local:41197->192.168.0.2:3128
```

In this output, `laptop.local:41197` corresponds to the localhost and `192.168.0.2:3128` corresponds to the remote host. `41197` is the port opened from the current machine, and `3128` is the port to which the service connects at the remote host.

In order to list out the opened ports from the current machine, use:

```
$ lsof -i | grep ":[0-9]\+->" -o | grep "[0-9]\+" -o  | sort | uniq
```

How it works...

The `: [0-9] \+- >` regex for `grep` is used to extract the host port portion (`:34395->`) from the `lsof` output. The next `grep` is used to extract the port number (which is numeric). Multiple connections may occur through the same port and hence, multiple entries of the same port may occur. In order to display each port once, they are sorted and the unique ones are printed.

There's more...

Let's go through additional utilities that can be used for viewing the opened port and network traffic related information.

Opened port and services using netstat

`netstat` is another command for the network service analysis. Explaining all the features of `netstat` is not in the scope of this recipe. We will now look at how to list services and port numbers.

Use `netstat -tnp` to list opened port and services as follows:

```
$ netstat -tnp
(Not all processes could be identified, non-owned process info
will not be shown, you would have to be root to see it all.)
Active Internet connections (w/o servers)
Proto Recv-Q Send-Q Local Address          Foreign Address         State
PID/Program name
tcp        0      0 192.168.0.82:38163     192.168.0.2:3128
ESTABLISHED 2261/firefox-bin
tcp        0      0 192.168.0.82:38164     192.168.0.2:3128        TIME_
WAIT    -
tcp        0      0 192.168.0.82:40414     193.107.206.24:422
ESTABLISHED 3836/ssh
tcp        0      0 127.0.0.1:42486        127.0.0.1:32955
ESTABLISHED 4022/GoogleTalkPlug
tcp        0      0 192.168.0.82:38152     192.168.0.2:3128
ESTABLISHED 2261/firefox-bin
tcp6       0      0 ::1:22                 ::1:39263
ESTABLISHED -
tcp6       0      0 ::1:39263              ::1:22
ESTABLISHED 3570/ssh
```

Creating arbitrary sockets

For defined operations such as file transfer, remote shells, and so on, we have prebuilt tools such as `ftp` and `ssh` respectively. However, in some cases you will find the need to do a customized network operation. An example for this might be writing a script which will do something when a remote client connects to your machine. In this recipe, we will create simple network sockets and use them for communication.

Getting ready

To perform these things, we will need to create network sockets which enable us to do data transfer over a TCP/IP network. The easiest way to do this is by using the command `netcat` (or `nc`). We need two sockets: one listens for connections and the other connects to this one.

How to do it...

1. Set up the listening socket using the following:

   ```
   nc -l 1234
   ```

   This will create a listening socket on port 1234 on the local machine.

2. Connect to the socket using the following:

   ```
   nc HOST 1234
   ```

   If you are running this on the same machine that the listening socket is, replace HOST with localhost, otherwise replace it with the IP address or hostname of the machine.

3. To actually send messages, type something and press *Enter* on the terminal where you performed step 2. The message will appear on the terminal where you performed step 1.

There's more...

Network sockets can be used for more than just text communication; let's see how.

Quickly copying files over the network

We can exploit `netcat` and shell redirection to easily copy files over the network:

1. On the receiver machine, run the following command:

   ```
   nc -l 1234 > destination_filename
   ```

2. On the sender machine, run the following command:

   ```
   nc HOST 1234 < source_filename
   ```

Sharing an Internet connection

In the modern computing world, we are using different kinds of devices in our day-to-day life. We use desktop computers, netbooks, laptop computers, tablets, smartphones and so on. Additionally, we feel the need to keep all of these connected to the Internet for which people usually keep a wireless router which distributes an Internet connection across these devices. But what if you don't have a router (or your router just blew up) and you need to share the Internet? No problem! Linux, iptables and some scripting are at your rescue.

Getting ready

This recipe uses `iptables` for setting up **Network Address Translation** (**NAT**) which lets a networking device share a connection with other devices. You will need the name of your wireless interface for which just use the `iwconfig` command.

How to do it...

1. Connect to the Internet. In this recipe, we are assuming that the primary wired network connection, eth0 is connected to Internet. Change it according to your setup.

2. Using your distro's network management tool, create a new ad hoc wireless connection with the following settings:

    ❑   IP address: 10.99.66.55

    ❑   Subnet mask: 255.255.0.0 (16)

3. Use the following shell script to share the internet connection:

    ```bash
    #!/bin/bash
    #filename: netsharing.sh
    echo 1 > /proc/sys/net/ipv4/ip_forward
    iptables -A FORWARD -i $1 -o $2 -s 10.99.0.0/16 -m conntrack
    --ctstate NEW -j ACCEPT
    iptables -A FORWARD -m conntrack --ctstate ESTABLISHED,RELATED -j
    ACCEPT
    iptables -A POSTROUTING -t nat -j MASQUERADE
    ```

4. Run the script as follows:

    ```bash
    ./netsharing.sh eth0 wlan0
    ```

    Where `eth0` is the interface which is connected to the Internet and `wlan0` is the wireless interface which is supposed to share the Internet to other devices.

5. Connect your devices to the wireless network you just created with the following settings:

   ❑ IP address: 10.99.66.56 (and so on)

   ❑ Subnet mask: 255.255.0.0

 To make this more convenient, you might want to install a DHCP and DNS server on your machine, so it's not necessary to configure IPs on devices manually. A handy tool for this is dnsmasq which you can use for performing both DHCP and DNS operations.

Basic firewall using iptables

A firewall is a network service which is used to filter network traffic for unwanted traffic, block it, and allow the desired traffic to pass. The most powerful tool on Linux is iptables, which has kernel integration in recent versions of the kernels.

How to do it...

iptables is present, by default, on all modern Linux distributions. We will see how to configure iptables for common scenarios.

1. Block traffic to a specific IP address:

   ```
   #iptables -A OUTPUT -d 8.8.8.8 -j DROP
   ```

   If you run PING 8.8.8.8 in another terminal before running the iptables command, you will see this:

   ```
   PING 8.8.8.8 (8.8.8.8) 56(84) bytes of data.
   64 bytes from 8.8.8.8: icmp_req=1 ttl=56 time=221 ms
   64 bytes from 8.8.8.8: icmp_req=2 ttl=56 time=221 ms
   ping: sendmsg: Operation not permitted
   ping: sendmsg: Operation not permitted
   ```

   Here, the ping fails the third time because we used the iptables command to drop all traffic to 8.8.8.8.

2. Block traffic to a specific port:

   ```
   #iptables -A OUTPUT -p tcp -dport 21 -j DROP
   $ ftp ftp.kde.org
   ftp: connect: Connection timed out
   ```

How it works...

`iptables` is the standard command used for firewall on Linux. The first argument in `iptables` is -A which instructs `iptables` to append a new rule to the **chain** specified as the next parameter. A chain is simply a collection of rules, and in this recipe we have used the OUTPUT chain which runs on all the outgoing traffic.

In the first step, the -d parameter specifies the destination to match with the packet being sent. After that, we use the parameter -j to instruct `iptables` to DROP the packet.

Similarly, in the second one, we use the -p parameter to specify that this rule should match only TCP on the port specified with -dport. Using this we can block all the outbound FTP traffic.

There's more...

While playing with `iptables` commands, you might want to clear the changes made to the `iptables` chains. To do this, just use:

```
#iptables --flush
```

8

Put on the Monitor's Cap

In this chapter, we will cover:

- ► Monitoring disk usage
- ► Calculating the execution time for a command
- ► Collecting information about logged in users, boot logs, and boot failures
- ► Listing the top 10 CPU consuming processes in an hour
- ► Monitoring command outputs with watch
- ► Logging access to files and directories
- ► Logfile management with logrotate
- ► Logging with syslog
- ► Monitoring user logins to find intruders
- ► Remote disk usage health monitor
- ► Finding out active user hours on a system
- ► Measuring and optimizing power usage
- ► Monitoring disk activity
- ► Checking disks and filesystems for errors

Introduction

An operating system consists of a collection of system software that is designed for different purposes. It is a good idea to monitor each of these programs in order to know whether they are working properly or not. We will also use a technique called logging by which we can get important information in a file while the program is running. The content of this file can be used to understand the timeline of operations that are taking place in a running program or daemon. For instance, if an application or a service crashes, this information helps to debug the issue and enables us to fix any issues.

This chapter deals with different commands that can be used to monitor different activities. It also goes through logging techniques and their usages.

Monitoring disk usage

Disk space is a limited resource. We frequently perform disk usage calculation on storage media (such as hard disks) to find out the free space available on them. When free space becomes scarce, we find out large files to be deleted or moved in order to create free space. In addition to this, disk usage manipulations are also used in shell scripting contexts. This recipe will illustrate various commands used for disk manipulations with a variety of options.

Getting ready

df and du are the two significant commands that are used for calculating disk usage in Linux. The command df stands for disk free and du stands for disk usage. Let's see how we can use them to perform various tasks that involve disk usage calculation.

How to do it...

To find the disk space used by a file (or files), use:

```
$ du  FILENAME1 FILENAME2 ..
```

For example:

```
$ du file.txt
4
```

 The result is, by default, shown as size in bytes.

To obtain the disk usage for all files inside a directory along with the individual disk usage for each file showed in each line, use:

```
$ du -a DIRECTORY
```

-a outputs results for all files in the specified directory or directories recursively.

 Running du DIRECTORY will output a similar result, but it will show only the size consumed by subdirectories. However, this does not show the disk usage for each of the files. For printing the disk usage by files, -a is mandatory.

For example:

```
$  du -a test
4   test/output.txt
4   test/process_log.sh
4   test/pcpu.sh
16  test
```

An example of using du DIRECTORY is as follows:

```
$ du test
16   test
```

There's more...

Let's go through additional usage practices for the du command.

Displaying disk usage in KB, MB, or Blocks

By default, the disk usage command displays the total bytes used by a file. A more human-readable format is expressed in units such as KB, MB, or GB. In order to print the disk usage in a display-friendly format, use -h as follows:

```
du -h FILENAME
```

For example:

```
$ du -h test/pcpu.sh
4.0K   test/pcpu.sh
# Multiple file arguments are accepted
```

Or

```
# du -h DIRECTORY
$ du -h hack/
16K   hack/
```

Displaying the grand total sum of disk usage

If we need to calculate the total size taken by all the files or directories, displaying individual file sizes won't help. du has an option -c such that it will output the total disk usage of all files and directories given as an argument. It appends a line SIZE total with the result. The syntax is as follows:

```
$ du -c FILENAME1 FILENAME2..
```

For example:

```
du -c process_log.shpcpu.sh
4   process_log.sh
4   pcpu.sh
8   total
```

Or

```
$ du   -c DIRECTORY
```

For example:

```
$ du -c test/
16   test/
16   total
```

Or

```
$ du -c *.txt
# Wildcards
```

-c can be used along with other options like -a and -h, in which case they will produce their usual output with an extra line containing the total size.

There is another option -s (summarize), which will print only the grand total as the output. It will print the total sum, and the flag -h can be used along with it to print in human-readable format. This combination has frequent use in practice:

```
$ du -s FILES(s)
$ du -sh DIRECTORY
```

For example:

```
$ du -sh slynux
680K   slynux
```

Printing files in specified units

We can force du to print the disk usage in specified units. For example:

> ▸ Print the size in bytes (by default) by using:
>
> ```
> $ du -b FILE(s)
> ```

> ▸ Print the size in kilobytes by using:
>
> ```
> $ du -k FILE(s)
> ```

- ▶ Print the size in megabytes by using:

  ```
  $ du -m FILE(s)
  ```

- ▶ Print the size in the given BLOCK size specified by using:

  ```
  $ du -B BLOCK_SIZE FILE(s)
  ```

  Here, BLOCK_SIZE is specified in bytes.

An example consisting of all the commands is as follows:

```
$ du pcpu.sh
4   pcpu.sh
$ du -b pcpu.sh
439     pcpu.sh
$ du -k pcpu.sh
4   pcpu.sh
$ du -m pcpu.sh
1   pcpu.sh
$ du -B 4  pcpu.sh
1024  pcpu.sh
```

Excluding files from the disk usage calculation

There are circumstances when we need to exclude certain files from the disk usage calculation. Such excluded files can be specified in two ways:

- ▶ **Wildcards**: We can specify a wildcard as follows:

  ```
  $ du --exclude "WILDCARD" DIRECTORY
  ```

  For example:

  ```
  $ du --exclude "*.txt" FILES(s)
  # Excludes all .txt files from calculation
  ```

- ▶ **Exclude list**: We can specify a list of files to be excluded from a file as follows:

  ```
  $ du --exclude-from EXCLUDE.txt DIRECTORY
  # EXCLUDE.txt is the file containing list
  ```

There are also some other handy options available with du to restrict the disk usage calculation. With the `--max-depth` parameter, we can specify the maximum depth of the hierarchy du should traverse while calculating disk usage. Specifying a depth of 1 calculates the size of files in the current directory, a depth of 2, specifies to calculate files in the current directory and the next subdirectory, and so on. For example:

```
$ du --max-depth 2 DIRECTORY
```

> du can be restricted to traverse only one filesystem by using the `-x` argument. Suppose du `DIRECTORY` is run, it will traverse through every possible subdirectory of `DIRECTORY` recursively. A subdirectory in the directory hierarchy may be a mount point (for example, `/mnt/sda1` is a subdirectory of `/mnt` and it is a mount point for the device `/dev/sda1`). du will traverse that mount point and calculate the sum of disk usage for that device filesystem also. `-x` is used to prevent du from doing this. For example, du `-x` `/` will exclude all mount points in `/mnt/` for the disk usage calculation.

While using du make sure that the directories or files it traverses have the proper read permissions.

Finding the 10 largest size files from a given directory

Finding large files is a task we come across regularly so that we can delete or move them. We can easily find out such files using du and `sort` commands like this:

```
$ du -ak SOURCE_DIR | sort -nrk 1 | head
```

Here, `-a` makes du traverse the `SOURCE_DIR` and calculates the size of all files and directories. The first column of the output contains the size in kilobytes since `-k` is specified, and the second column contains the file or folder name.

`sort` is used to perform a numerical sort with column 1 and reverse it. head is used to parse the first 10 lines from the output. For example:

```
$ du -ak /home/slynux | sort -nrk 1 | head -n 4
50220 /home/slynux
43296 /home/slynux/.mozilla
43284 /home/slynux/.mozilla/firefox
43276 /home/slynux/.mozilla/firefox/8c22khxc.default
```

One of the drawbacks of the preceding one-liner is that it includes directories in the result. However, when we need to find only the largest files and not directories, we can improve the one-liner to output only the large files as follows:

```
$ find . -type f -exec du -k {} \; | sort -nrk 1 | head
```

We used `find` to filter only files to `du` rather than allow `du` to traverse recursively by itself.

Disk free information

The `du` command provides information about the usage, whereas `df` provides information about free disk space. Use `-h` with `df` to print the disk space in human-readable format. For example:

```
$ df -h
Filesystem              Size   Used  Avail  Use%  Mounted on
/dev/sda1               9.2G   2.2G   6.6G   25%  /
none                    497M   240K   497M    1%  /dev
none                    502M   168K   501M    1%  /dev/shm
none                    502M    88K   501M    1%  /var/run
none                    502M      0   502M    0%  /var/lock
none                    502M      0   502M    0%  /lib/init/rw
none                    9.2G   2.2G   6.6G   25%  /var/lib/ureadahead/debugfs
```

Calculating the execution time for a command

While testing an application's efficiency or comparing different algorithms to solve a given problem, the execution time taken is very critical. A good algorithm should execute in a minimum amount of time. Let's see how to calculate the execution time.

How to do it...

1. To measure the execution time, just prefix `time` to the command you want to run.

   For example:

   ```
   $ time COMMAND
   ```

   The command will execute and its output will be shown. Along with the output, the `time` command appends the time taken in `stderr`. An example is as follows:

   ```
   $ time ls
   test.txt
   next.txt
   real    0m0.008s
   user    0m0.001s
   sys     0m0.003s
   ```

   It will show real, user, and system times for execution.

An executable binary of the `time` command is available at `/usr/bin/time`, as well as a shell built-in named `time` exists. When we run time, it calls the shell built-in by default. The shell built-in `time` has limited options. Hence, we should use an absolute path for the executable (`/usr/bin/time`) for performing additional functionalities.

2. We can write these time statistics to a file using the -o filename option as follows:

```
$ /usr/bin/time -o output.txt COMMAND
```

The filename should always appear after the -o flag.

In order to append the time statistics to a file without overwriting, use the -a flag along with the -o option as follows:

```
$ /usr/bin/time -a -o output.txt COMMAND
```

3. We can also format the time outputs using format strings with -f option. A format string consists of parameters corresponding to specific options prefixed with %. Format strings for real time, user time, and sys time are as follows:

- Real time: %e
- User: %U
- sys: %S

By combining parameter strings, we can create a formatted output as follows:

```
$ /usr/bin/time -f "FORMAT STRING" COMMAND
```

For example:

```
$ /usr/bin/time -f "Time: %U" -a -o timing.log uname
Linux
```

Here %U is the parameter for user time.

When a formatted output is produced, the formatted output of the command is written to the standard output and the output of the COMMAND, which is timed, is written to standard error. We can redirect the formatted output using a redirection operator (>) and redirect the time information output using the (2>) error redirection operator.

For example:

```
$ /usr/bin/time -f "Time: %U" uname> command_output.txt 2>time.log
$ cat time.log
Time: 0.00
$ cat command_output.txt
Linux
```

4. To show the page size, use the `%Z` parameters as follows:

```
$ /usr/bin/time -f "Page size: %Z bytes" ls> /dev/null
Page size: 4096 bytes
```

Here the output of the timed command is not required and hence, the standard output is directed to the `/dev/null` device in order to prevent it from writing to the terminal.

More format string parameters are available. Try `man time` for more details.

How it works...

The three different times can be defined as follows:

- **Real** is wall clock time—the time from start to finish of the call. This is all elapsed time including time slices used by other processes and the time that the process spends when blocked (for example, if it is waiting for I/O to complete).

- **User** is the amount of CPU time spent in user-mode code (outside the kernel) within the process. This is only the actual CPU time used in executing the process. Other processes, and the time that the process spends when blocked do not count towards this figure.

- **Sys** is the amount of CPU time spent in the kernel within the process. This means executing the CPU time spent in system calls within the kernel, as opposed to the library code, which is still running in the user space. Like user time, this is only the CPU time used by the process. Refer to the following table for a brief description of kernel mode (also known as supervisor mode) and the system call mechanism.

Many details regarding a process can be collected using the `time` command. The important details include, exit status, number of signals received, number of context switches made, and so on. Each parameter can be displayed by using a suitable format string.

The following table shows some of the interesting parameters that can be used:

Parameter	Description
`%C`	Name and command-line arguments of the command being timed.
`%D`	Average size of the process's unshared data area, in kilobytes.
`%E`	Elapsed real (wall clock) time used by the process in [hours:]minutes:seconds.
`%x`	Exit status of the command.
`%k`	Number of signals delivered to the process.
`%W`	Number of times the process was swapped out of the main memory.
`%Z`	System's page size in bytes. This is a per-system constant, but varies between systems.

Parameter	Description
%P	Percentage of the CPU that this job got. This is just user + system times divided by the total running time. It also prints a percentage sign.
%K	Average total (data + stack + text) memory usage of the process, in Kilobytes.
%w	Number of times that the program was context-switched voluntarily, for instance while waiting for an I/O operation to complete.
%c	Number of times the process was context-switched involuntarily (because the time slice expired).

Collecting information about logged in users, boot logs, and boot failures

Collecting information about the operating environment, logged in users, the time for which the computer has been powered on, and boot failures are very helpful. This recipe will go through a few commands used to gather information about a live machine.

Getting ready

This recipe will introduce commands who, w, users, uptime, last, and lastb.

How to do it...

1. To obtain information about users currently logged into the machine use:

```
$ who
slynux    pts/0    2010-09-29 05:24 (slynuxs-macbook-pro.local)
slynux    tty7     2010-09-29 07:08 (:0)
```

This output lists the login name, the TTY used by the users, login time, and remote hostname (or X display information) about logged in users.

>
> **TTY** (the term comes from **TeleTYpewriter**) is the device file associated with a text terminal which is created in /dev when a terminal is newly spawned by the user (for example, /dev/pts/3). The device path for the current terminal can be found out by typing and executing the command tty.

2. To obtain more detailed information about the logged in users, use:

```
$ w
 07:09:05 up  1:45,  2 users,  load average: 0.12, 0.06, 0.02
USER      TTY      FROM     LOGIN@   IDLE  JCPU PCPU WHAT
slynux    pts/0    slynuxs 05:24   0.00s  0.65s 0.11s sshd: slynux
slynux    tty7     :0      07:08   1:45m  3.28s 0.26s gnome-session
```

This first line lists the current time, system uptime, number of users currently logged on, and the system load averages for the past 1, 5, and 15 minutes. Following this, the details about each login are displayed with each line containing the login name, the TTY name, the remote host, login time, idle time, total CPU time used by the user since login, CPU time of the currently running process, and the command line of their current process.

Load average in the `uptime` command's output is a parameter that indicates system load. This is explained in more detail in *Chapter 9, Administration Calls*.

3. In order to list only the usernames of the users currently logged into the machine, use:

```
$ users
```

slynux slynux slynux hacker

If a user has opened multiple terminals, it will show that many entries for the same user. In the preceding output, the user `slynux` has opened three pseudo terminals. The easiest way to print unique users is to use `sort` and `uniq` to filter as follows:

```
$ users | tr ' ' '\n' | sort | uniq
slynux
hacker
```

We have used `tr` to replace ' ' with '\n'. Then a combination of `sort` and `uniq` will produce unique entries for each user.

4. In order to see how long the system has been powered on, use:

```
$ uptime
 21:44:33 up  3:17,  8 users,  load average: 0.09, 0.14, 0.09
```

The time that follows the word `up` indicates the time for which the system has been powered on. We can write a simple one-liner to extract the uptime only:

```
$ uptime | grep -Po '\d{2}\:\d{2}\:\d{2}'
```

This uses `grep` with a perl-style regex to extract only three two-digit numbers separated by colons.

5. In order to get information about previous boot and user logged sessions, use:

```
$ last
slynux    tty7            :0              Tue Sep 28 18:27    still
logged in
reboot    system boot  2.6.32-21-generic Tue Sep 28 18:10 - 21:46
(03:35)
slynux    pts/0           :0.0            Tue Sep 28 05:31 - crash
(12:39)
```

The `last` command will provide information about logged in sessions. It is actually a log of system logins that consists of information, such as `tty` from which it has logged in, login time, status, and so on.

The `last` command uses the log file `/var/log/wtmp` for the input log data. It is also possible to explicitly specify the log file for the `last` command using the `-f` option. For example:

```
$ last -f /var/log/wtmp
```

6. In order to obtain information about login sessions for a single user, use:

```
$ last USER
```

7. Get information about reboot sessions as follows:

```
$ last reboot
reboot    system boot  2.6.32-21-generi Tue Sep 28 18:10 - 21:48
(03:37)
reboot    system boot  2.6.32-21-generi Tue Sep 28 05:14 - 21:48
(16:33)
```

8. In order to get information about failed user login sessions, use:

```
# lastb
test      tty8            :0              Wed Dec 15 03:56 - 03:56
(00:00)
slynux    tty8            :0              Wed Dec 15 03:55 - 03:55
(00:00)
```

You should run `lastb` as the root user.

Listing the top 10 CPU consuming processes in an hour

CPU is a major resource and it is good to keep a track of the processes that consume most of the CPU in a period of time. By monitoring the CPU usage for a certain period, we can identify the processes that keep the CPU busy all the time and troubleshoot them to efficiently use the CPU. In this recipe, we will discuss process monitoring and logging.

Getting ready

`ps` command is used for collecting details about the processes running on the system. It can be used to gather details, such as CPU usage, commands under execution, memory usage, status of processes, and so on. Processes that consume the CPU for one hour can be logged, and the top 10 can be determined by proper usage of `ps` and text processing. For more details on the ps command, refer to *Chapter 9, Administration Calls*.

How to do it...

Let's go through the following shell script for monitoring and calculating CPU usages in one hour:

```
#!/bin/bash
#Name: pcpu_usage.sh
#Description: Script to calculate cpu usage by processes for 1 hour

SECS=3600
UNIT_TIME=60

#Change the SECS to total seconds for which monitoring is to be
performed.
#UNIT_TIME is the interval in seconds between each sampling

STEPS=$(( $SECS / $UNIT_TIME ))

echo Watching CPU usage... ;

for((i=0;i<STEPS;i++))
do
  ps -eocomm,pcpu | tail -n +2 >> /tmp/cpu_usage.$$
```

```
   sleep $UNIT_TIME
done


echo
echo CPU eaters :


cat /tmp/cpu_usage.$$ | \
awk '
{ process[$1]+=$2; }
END{
  for(i in process)
  {
    printf("%-20s %s\n",i, process[i]) ;
  }

  }' | sort -nrk 2 | head


rm /tmp/cpu_usage.$$
#Remove the temporary log file
```

A sample output is as follows:

```
$ ./pcpu_usage.sh
Watching CPU usage...
CPU eaters :
Xorg          20
firefox-bin   15
bash          3
evince        2
pulseaudio    1.0
pcpu.sh         0.3
wpa_supplicant 0
wnck-applet   0
watchdog/0    0
usb-storage   0
```

How it works...

In the preceding script, the major input source is `ps -eocomm,pcpu`. `comm` stands for command name and `pcpu` stands for the CPU usage in percent. It will output all the process names and the CPU usage in percent. For each process there exists a line in the output. Since we need to monitor the CPU usage for one hour, we repeatedly take usage statistics using `ps -eocomm,pcpu | tail -n +2` and append to a file `/tmp/cpu_usage.$$` running inside a `for` loop with 60 seconds wait in each iteration. This wait is provided by `sleep 60`. It will execute `ps` once in each minute. `tail -n +2` is used to strip off the header and COMMAND %CPU in the `ps` output.

`$$` in `cpu_usage.$$` signifies that it is the process ID of the current script. Suppose PID is `1345`; during execution it will be replaced as `/tmp/cpu_usage.1345`. We place this file in `/tmp` since it is a temporary file.

The statistics file will be ready after one hour and will contain 60 sets of entries, each set containing entries corresponding to the process status for each minute. Then `awk` is used to sum the total CPU usage for each process. An associative array process is used for the summation of CPU usages. It uses the process name as array index. Finally, it sorts the result with a numeric reverse sort according to the total CPU usage and pass through `head` to obtain the top 10 usage entries.

See also

- ▸ The *Using awk for advanced text processing* recipe of *Chapter 4, Texting and Driving*, explains the `awk` command
- ▸ The *Using head and tail for printing the last or first 10 lines* recipe of *Chapter 3, File In, File Out*, explains the `tail` command

Monitoring command outputs with watch

We might need to continuously watch the output of a command for a period of time in equal intervals. For example, while copying a large file, we might need to watch the growth of the file size. In order to do that, we can use the `watch` command to execute the `du` command and output repeatedly. This recipe explains how to do that.

How to do it...

The `watch` command can be used to monitor the output of a command on the terminal at regular intervals. The syntax of the `watch` command is as follows:

```
$ watch COMMAND
```

For example:

```
$ watch ls
```

Or

```
$ watch 'COMMANDS'
```

For example:

```
$ watch 'ls -l | grep "^d"'
# list only directories
```

This command will update the output at a default interval of two seconds.

We can also specify the time interval at which the output needs to be updated, by using
`-n SECONDS`. For example:

```
$ watch -n 5 'ls -l'
#Monitor the output of ls -l at regular intervals of 5 seconds
```

There's more

Let's explore an additional feature of the `watch` command.

Highlighting the differences in the watch output

In `watch`, there is an option for updating the differences that occur during the execution of
the command at an update interval to be highlighted using colors. Difference highlighting can
be enabled by using the `-d` option as follows:

```
$ watch -d 'COMMANDS'
```

Logging access to files and directories

Logging of file and directory access is very helpful to keep a track of changes that are
happening to files and folders. This recipe will describe how to log such accesses.

Getting ready

The `inotifywait` command can be used to gather information about file accesses. It
doesn't come by default with every Linux distro. You have to install the `inotify-tools`
package by using a package manager. It also requires the Linux kernel to be compiled with
`inotify` support. Most of the new GNU/Linux distributions come with `inotify` enabled in
the kernel.

How to do it...

Let's walk through the shell script to monitor the directory access:

```
#/bin/bash
#Filename: watchdir.sh
#Description: Watch directory access
path=$1
#Provide path of directory or file as argument to script

inotifywait -m -r -e create,move,delete $path  -q
```

A sample output is as follows:

```
$ ./watchdir.sh .
./ CREATE new
./ MOVED_FROM new
./ MOVED_TO news
./ DELETE news
```

How it works...

The previous script will log events, create, move, and delete files and folders from the given path. The -m option is given for monitoring the changes continuously, rather than going to exit after an event happens, and -r enables a recursive watch of the directories (symbolic links are ignored). Finally, -e specifies the list of events to be watched and -q is to reduce the verbose messages and print only the required ones. This output can be redirected to a log file.

We can add or remove the event list. Important events available are as follows:

Event	Description
access	When a read happens to a file.
modify	When file contents are modified.
attrib	When metadata is changed.
move	When a file undergoes a move operation.
create	When a new file is created.
open	When a file undergoes an open operation.
close	When a file undergoes a close operation.
delete	When a file is removed.

Logfile management with logrotate

Logfiles are essential components of a Linux system to keep track of events happening on different services on the system. This helps to debug issues as well as provide statistics on the live machine. Management of logfiles is required because as time passes, the size of a logfile gets bigger and bigger. Therefore, we use techniques called **rotation** such that we limit the size of the logfile and if the logfile reaches a size beyond the limit, it will strip the logfile with that size and store the older entries in the logfile archived in log directories. Hence, older logs can be stored and kept for future references. Let's see how to rotate logs and store them.

Getting ready

`logrotate` is a command every Linux system admin should know. It helps to restrict the size of the logfile to the given SIZE. In a logfile, the logger appends information to the log file. Hence, the recent information appears at the bottom of the log file. `logrotate` will scan specific logfiles according to the configuration file. It will keep the last 100 kilobytes (for example, specified SIZE = 100 k) from the logfile and move rest of the data (older log data) to a new file `logfile_name.1` with older entries. When more entries occur in the logfile (`logfile_name.1`) and it exceeds the SIZE, it updates the logfile with recent entries and creates `logfile_name.2` with older logs. This process can easily be configured with `logrotate`. `logrotate` can also compress the older logs as `logfile_name.1.gz`, `logfile_name2.gz`, and so on. The option of whether older log files are to be compressed or not is available with the `logrotate` configuration.

How to do it...

`logrotate` has the configuration directory at `/etc/logrotate.d`. If you look at this directory by listing its contents, many other logfile configurations can be found.

We can write our custom configuration for our logfile (say `/var/log/program.log`) as follows:

```
$ cat /etc/logrotate.d/program
/var/log/program.log {
missingok
notifempty
size 30k
  compress
weekly
  rotate 5
create 0600 root root
}
```

Now the configuration is complete. `/var/log/program.log` in the configuration specifies the logfile path. It will archive old logs in the same directory path.

How it works...

Let's see what each of the parameters in the configuration mean:

Parameter	Description
`missingok`	Ignore if the logfile is missing and return without rotating the log.
`notifempty`	Only rotate the log if the source logfile is not empty.
`size 30k`	Limit the size of the logfile for which the rotation is to be made. It can be 1 M for 1 MB.
`compress`	Enable compression with gzip for older logs.
`weekly`	Specify the interval at which the rotation is to be performed. It can be weekly, yearly, or daily.
`rotate 5`	It is the number of older copies of logfile archives to be kept. Since 5 is specified, there will be `program.log.1.gz`, `program.log.2.gz`, and so on up to `program.log.5.gz`.
`create 0600 root root`	Specify the mode, user, and the group of the logfile archive to be created.

The options specified in the table are optional; we can specify the required options only in the `logrotate` configuration file. There are numerous options available with `logrotate`, please refer to the man pages (`http://linux.die.net/man/8/logrotate`) for more information on `logrotate`.

Logging with syslog

Usually, logfiles related to different daemons and applications are located in the `/var/log` directory, as it is the common directory for storing log files. If you read through a few lines of the logfiles, you can see that lines in the log are in a common format. In Linux, creating and writing log information to logfiles at `/var/log` are handled by a protocol called **syslog**, handled by the `syslogd` daemon. Every standard application makes use of syslog for logging information. In this recipe, we will discuss how to make use of `syslogd` for logging information from a shell script.

Getting ready

Logfiles are very good for helping you deduce what is going wrong with a system. Hence, while writing critical applications, it is always a good practice to log the progress of an application with messages into a logfile. We will learn the command `logger` to log into log files with `syslogd`. Before getting to know how to write into logfiles, let's go through a list of important logfiles used in Linux:

Logfile	Description
`/var/log/boot.log`	Boot log information.
`/var/log/httpd`	Apache web server log.
`/var/log/messages`	Post boot kernel information.
`/var/log/auth.log`	User authentication log.
`/var/log/dmesg`	System boot up messages.
`/var/log/mail.log`	Mail server log.
`/var/log/Xorg.0.log`	X Server log.

How to do it...

Let's see how to use `logger` to create and manage log messages:

1. In order to log to the syslog file `/var/log/messages`, use:

   ```
   $ logger LOG_MESSAGE
   ```

   For example:

   ```
   $ logger This is a test log line
   ```

   ```
   $ tail -n 1 /var/log/messages
   Sep 29 07:47:44 slynux-laptop slynux: This is a test log line
   ```

   The logfile `/var/log/messages` is a general purpose logfile. When the `logger` command is used, it logs to `/var/log/messages` by default.

2. In order to log to the syslog with a specified tag, use:

   ```
   $ logger -t TAG This is a message
   ```

   ```
   $ tail -n 1 /var/log/messages
   Sep 29 07:48:42 slynux-laptop TAG: This is a message
   ```

syslog handles a number of logfiles in /var/log. However, while logger sends a message, it uses the tag string to determine in which logfile it needs to be logged. syslogd decides to which file the log should be made by using the TAG associated with the log. You can see the tag strings and associated logfiles from the configuration files located in the /etc/rsyslog.d/ directory.

3. In order to log in to the system log with the last line from another logfile, use:

```
$ logger -f /var/log/source.log
```

See also

▸ The *Using head and tail for printing the last or first 10 lines* recipe of *Chapter 3, File In, File Out*, explains the head and tail commands

Monitoring user logins to find intruders

Logfiles can be used to gather details about the state of the system. Here is an interesting scripting problem statement:

We have a system connected to the Internet with SSH enabled. Many attackers are trying to log in to the system, and we need to design an intrusion detection system by writing a shell script. Intruders are defined as users who are trying to log in with multiple attempts for more than two minutes and whose attempts are all failing. Such users are to be detected, and a report should be generated with the following details:

▸ User account to which a login is attempted

▸ Number of attempts

▸ IP address of the attacker

▸ Host mapping for the IP address

▸ Time for which login attempts were performed

Getting ready

We can write a shell script that scans through the logfiles and gather the required information from them. For dealing with SSH login failures, it is useful to know that the user authentication session log is written to the logfile /var/log/auth.log. The script should scan the logfile to detect the failure login attempts and perform different checks on the log to infer the data. We can use the host command to find out the host mapping from the IP address.

How to do it...

Let's write the intruder detection script that can generate a report to intruders by using a authentication logfile as follows:

```bash
#!/bin/bash
#Filename: intruder_detect.sh
#Description: Intruder reporting tool with auth.log input
AUTHLOG=/var/log/auth.log

if [[ -n $1 ]];
then
  AUTHLOG=$1
  echo Using Log file : $AUTHLOG
fi

LOG=/tmp/valid.$$.log
grep -v "invalid" $AUTHLOG > $LOG
users=$(grep "Failed password" $LOG | awk '{ print $(NF-5) }' | sort |
uniq)


printf "%-5s|%-10s|%-10s|%-13s|%-33s|%s\n" "Sr#" "User" "Attempts" "IP
address" "Host_Mapping" "Time range"


ucount=0;

ip_list="$(egrep -o "[0-9]+\.[0-9]+\.[0-9]+\.[0-9]+" $LOG | sort |
uniq)"

for ip in $ip_list;
do
  grep $ip $LOG > /tmp/temp.$$.log


  for user in $users;
  do
    grep $user /tmp/temp.$$.log> /tmp/$$.log
    cut -c-16 /tmp/$$.log > $$.time
    tstart=$(head -1 $$.time);
    start=$(date -d "$tstart" "+%s");
```

```
    tend=$(tail -1 $$.time);
    end=$(date -d "$tend" "+%s")

    limit=$(( $end - $start ))

    if [ $limit -gt 120 ];
    then
       let ucount++;



       IP=$(egrep -o "[0-9]+\.[0-9]+\.[0-9]+\.[0-9]+" /tmp/$$.log |
head -1 );

       TIME_RANGE="$tstart-->$tend"

       ATTEMPTS=$(cat /tmp/$$.log|wc -l);

       HOST=$(host $IP | awk '{ print $NF }' )


    printf "%-5s|%-10s|%-10s|%-10s|%-33s|%-s\n" "$ucount" "$user"
"$ATTEMPTS" "$IP" "$HOST" "$TIME_RANGE";
       fi
   done
done

   rm /tmp/valid.$$.log /tmp/$$.log $$.time /tmp/temp.$$.log 2> /dev/null
```

A sample output is as follows:

```
slynux@slynux-laptop:~$ ./intruder_detect.sh sampleauth.log
Using Log file : sampleauth.log

Sr#  |User    |Attempts|IP address     |Host_Mapping |Time range
1    |alice   |3       |203.110.250.34|attk1.foo.com|Oct 29 05:28:59 -->Oct 29 05:31:59
2    |bob1    |3       |203.110.251.31|attk2.foo.com|Oct 29 05:21:52 -->Oct 29 05:29:52
3    |bob2    |3       |203.110.250.34|attk1.foo.com|Oct 29 05:22:59 -->Oct 29 05:25:52
4    |gvraju  |20      |203.110.251.31|attk2.foo.com|Oct 28 04:37:10 -->Oct 29 05:19:09
5    |root    |21      |203.110.253.32|attk3.foo.com|Oct 29 05:18:01 -->Oct 29 05:37:01
```

How it works...

In the `intruder_detect.sh` script, we use the `auth.log` file as input. We can either provide a logfile as input to the script by using a command-line argument to the script or, by default, it reads the `/var/log/auth.log` file. We need to log details about login attempts for valid usernames only. When a login attempt for an invalid user occurs, a log similar to `Failed password for invalid user bob from 203.83.248.32 port 7016 ssh2` is logged to `auth.log`. Hence, we need to exclude all lines in the logfile having the word `invalid`. The `grep` command with the invert option (`-v`) is used to remove all logs corresponding to invalid users. The next step is to find out the list of users for which login attempts occurred and failed. The SSH will log lines similar to `sshd[21197]: Failed password for bob1 from 203.83.248.32 port 50035 ssh2` for a failed password. Hence, we should find all the lines with words `Failed password`.

Next, all the unique IP addresses are to be found out for extracting all the log lines corresponding to each IP address. The list of IP addresses is extracted by using a regular expression for the IP address and the `egrep` command. A `for` loop is used to iterate through the IP address, and the corresponding log lines are found using `grep` and are written to a temporary file. The sixth word from the last word in the log line is the username (for example, bob1). The `awk` command is used to extract the sixth word from the last word. `NF` returns the column number of the last word. Therefore, `NF-5` gives the column number of the sixth word from the last word. We use `sort` and `uniq` commands to produce a list of users without duplication.

Now, we should collect the failed login log lines containing the name of each user. A `for` loop is used for reading the lines corresponding to each user and the lines are written to a temporary file. The first 16 characters in each of the log lines is the timestamp. The `cut` command is used to extract the timestamp. Once we have all the timestamps for failed login attempts for a user, we should check the difference in time between the first attempt and the last attempt. The first log line corresponds to the first attempt and the last log line corresponds to the last attempt. We have used `head -1` to extract the first line and `tail -1` to extract the last line. Now, we have a timestamp for first (`tstart`) and last attempt (`tends`) in string format. Using the `date` command, we can convert the date in string representation to total seconds in Unix Epoch time (the *Getting, setting dates, and delays* recipe of *Chapter 1, Shell Something Out*, explains Epoch time).

The variable's start and end has the time in seconds corresponding to the start and end timestamps in the date string. Now, take the difference between them and check whether it exceeds two minutes (120 seconds). Thus, the particular user is termed as an intruder and the corresponding entry with details are to be produced as a log. IP addresses can be extracted from the log by using a regular expression for the IP address and the `egrep` command. The number of attempts is the number of log lines for the user. The number of lines can be found out by using the `wc` command. The hostname mapping can be extracted from the output of the host command by running with the IP address as the argument. The time range can be printed using the timestamp we extracted. Finally, the temporary files used in the script are removed.

The previous script is aimed only at illustrating a model for scanning the log and producing a report from it. It has tried to make the script smaller and simpler to leave out the complexity. Hence, it has few bugs. You can improve the script by using a better logic.

Remote disk usage health monitor

A network consists of several machines with different users and requires centralized monitoring of disk usage of remote machines. The system administrator of the network needs to log the disk usage of all the machines in the network every day. Each log line should contain details like the date, IP address of the machine, device, capacity of device, used space, free space, percentage usage, and health status. If the disk usage of any of the partitions in any remote machine exceeds 80 percent, the health status should be set as ALERT, else it should be set as SAFE. This recipe will illustrate how to write a monitoring script that can collect details from remote machines in a network.

Getting ready

We need to collect the disk usage statistics from each machine on the network, individually, and write a logfile in the central machine. A script that collects the details and writes the log can be scheduled to run every day at a particular time. SSH can be used to log in to remote systems to collect disk usage data.

How to do it...

First, we have to set up a common user account on all the remote machines in the network. It is for the disklog program to log in to the system. We should configure auto-login with SSH for that particular user (the *Password less auto-login with SSH* recipe of *Chapter 7, The Old-boy Network*, explains configuration of auto-login). We assume that there is a user test in all remote machines configured with auto-login. Let's go through the shell script:

```
#!/bin/bash
#Filename: disklog.sh
#Description: Monitor disk usage health for remote systems


logfile="diskusage.log"

if [[ -n $1 ]]
then
  logfile=$1
fi

if [ ! -e $logfile ]
```

```
then

    printf "%-8s %-14s %-9s %-8s %-6s %-6s %-6s %s\n" "Date" "IP
address" "Device" "Capacity" "Used" "Free" "Percent" "Status" >
$logfile
fi

IP_LIST="127.0.0.1 0.0.0.0"
#provide the list of remote machine IP addresses

(
for ip in $IP_LIST;
do
    #slynux is the username, change as necessary
    ssh slynux@$ip 'df -H' | grep ^/dev/ > /tmp/$$.df

    while read line;
    do
        cur_date=$(date +%D)
        printf "%-8s %-14s " $cur_date $ip
        echo $line | awk '{ printf("%-9s %-8s %-6s %-6s
%-8s",$1,$2,$3,$4,$5); }'

    pusg=$(echo $line | egrep -o "[0-9]+%")
    pusg=${pusg/\%/};
    if [ $pusg -lt 80 ];
    then
        echo SAFE
    else
        echo ALERT
    fi

    done< /tmp/$$.df
done

) >> $logfile
```

We can use the `cron` utility to run the script at regular intervals. For example, to run the script every day at 10 a.m., write the following entry in the `crontab`:

```
00 10 * * * /home/path/disklog.sh /home/user/diskusg.log
```

Run the command `crontab -e` and add the preceding line. You can run the script manually as follows:

```
$ ./disklog.sh
```

A sample output log for the previous script is as follows:

```
slynux@slynux-laptop:~/book$ cat diskusage.log
Date        IP address      Device      Capacity Used    Free    Percent Status
12/15/10 127.0.0.1         /dev/sda1 9.9G     2.4G    7.0G    26%     SAFE
12/15/10 0.0.0.0           /dev/sda1 9.9G     2.4G    7.0G    26%     SAFE
```

How it works...

In the `disklog.sh` script, we can provide the logfile path as a command-line argument or else it will use the default logfile. If the logfile does not exist, it will write the logfile header text into the new file. `-e $logfile` is used to check whether the file exists or not. The list of IP addresses of remote machines are stored in the variable `IP_LIST` delimited with spaces. It should be made sure that all the remote systems listed in the `IP_LIST` have a common user `test` with auto-login with SSH configured. A `for` loop is used to iterate through each of the IP addresses. A remote command `df -H` is executed to get the disk free usage data using the `ssh` command. It is stored in a temporary file. A `while` loop is used to read the file line by line. Data is extracted using `awk` and is printed. The date is also printed. The percentage usage is extracted using the `egrep` command and `%` is replaced with nothing to get the numeric value of percent. It is checked whether the percentage value exceeds 80. If it is less than 80, the status is set as `SAFE` and if greater than, or equal to 80, the status is set as `ALERT`. The entire printed data should be redirected to the logfile. Hence, the portion of code is enclosed in a subshell `()` and the standard output is redirected to the logfile.

See also

▶ The *Scheduling with cron* recipe in *Chapter 9, Administration Calls*, explains the `crontab` command

Finding out active user hours on a system

Consider a web server with shared hosting. Many users log in and log out to the server every day and the user activity gets logged in the server's system log. This recipe is a practice task to make use of the system logs and to find out how many hours each of the users have spent on the server and rank them according to the total usage hours. A report should be generated with the details, such as rank, user, first logged in date, last logged in date, number of times logged in, and total usage hours. Let's see how we can approach this problem.

Getting ready

The `last` command is used to list the details about the login sessions of the users in a system. The log data is stored in the `/var/log/wtmp` file. By individually adding the session hours for each user, we can find out the total usage hours.

How to do it...

Let's go through the script to find out active users and generate the report:

```
#!/bin/bash
#Filename: active_users.sh
#Description: Reporting tool to find out active users

log=/var/log/wtmp

if [[ -n $1 ]];
then
  log=$1
fi

printf "%-4s %-10s %-10s %-6s %-8s\n" "Rank" "User" "Start" "Logins"
"Usage hours"

last -f $log | head -n -2   > /tmp/ulog.$$

cat /tmp/ulog.$$ |  cut -d' ' -f1 | sort | uniq> /tmp/users.$$

(
while read user;
do
  grep ^$user /tmp/ulog.$$ > /tmp/user.$$
  minutes=0

  while read t
  do
    s=$(echo $t | awk -F: '{ print ($1 * 60) + $2 }')
    let minutes=minutes+s
  done< <(cat /tmp/user.$$ | awk '{ print $NF }' | tr -d ')(')

  firstlog=$(tail -n 1 /tmp/user.$$ | awk '{ print $5,$6 }')
  nlogins=$(cat /tmp/user.$$ | wc -l)
  hours=$(echo "$minutes / 60.0" | bc)

  printf "%-10s %-10s %-6s %-8s\n"  $user "$firstlog" $nlogins $hours
done< /tmp/users.$$

) | sort -nrk 4 | awk '{ printf("%-4s %s\n", NR, $0) }'
rm /tmp/users.$$ /tmp/user.$$ /tmp/ulog.$$
```

A sample output is as follows:

```
$ ./active_users.sh
Rank User       Start      Logins Usage hours
1    easyibaa   Dec 11     531    349
2    demoproj   Dec 10     350    230
3    kjayaram   Dec 9      213    55
4    cinenews   Dec 11     85     139
5    thebenga   Dec 10     54     35
6    gateway2   Dec 11     52     34
7    soft132    Dec 12     49     25
8    sarathla   Nov 1      45     29
9    gtsminis   Dec 11     41     26
10   agentcde   Dec 13     39     32
```

How it works...

In the `active_users.sh` script, we can either provide the `wtmp` logfile as a command-line argument or it will use the default `wtmp` log file. The `last -f` command is used to print the logfile contents. The first column in the logfile is the username. By using `cut`, we extract the first column from the logfile. Then, the unique users are found out by using the `sort` and `uniq` commands. Now for each user, the log lines corresponding to their login sessions are found out using `grep` and are written to a temporary file. The last column in the last log is the duration for which the user logged in to the session. Hence, in order to find out the total usage hours for a user, the session duration is to be added. The usage duration is in (`HOUR:SEC`) format and it is converted into minutes using a simple awk script.

In order to extract the session hours for the users, we have used the `awk` command. For removing the parenthesis, `tr -d` is used. The list of the usage hour string is passed to the standard input for the `while` loop using the `< ( COMMANDS )` operator, which acts as a file input. Each hour string is converted into seconds by using the `date` command and added to the variable `seconds`. The first login time for a user is in the last line and it is extracted. The number of login attempts is the number of log lines. In order to calculate the rank of each user according to the total usage hours, the data record is to be sorted in the descending order with usage hours as the key. For specifying the number reverse sort, the `-nr` option is used along with `sort` command. `-k4` is used to specify the key column (usage hour). Finally, the output of the sort is passed to `awk`. The `awk` command prefixes a line number to each of the lines, which becomes the rank for each user.

Measuring and optimizing power usage

Power consumption is one of the factors that one must keep on monitoring, especially on mobile devices, such as notebook computers, tablets, and so on. There are few tools available for Linux systems to measure power consumption, one such command is `powertop` which we are going to use for this recipe.

Getting ready

`powertop` doesn't come preinstalled with most Linux distributions, you will have to install it using your package manager.

How to do it...

Let's see how to use `powertop` to measure and optimize power consumption:

1. Using `powertop` is pretty easy, just run:

   ```
   # powertop
   ```

   `powertop` will start taking some measurements and once it's done, it will show a screen which will have detailed information about power usage, the processes using the most power, and so on:

```
PowerTOP 2.1      Overview   Idle stats   Frequency stats   Device stats   Tunables

The battery reports a discharge rate of 17.6 W
The estimated remaining time is 0 hours, 58 minutes

Summary: 186.4 wakeups/second,  0.5 GPU ops/seconds, 0.0 VFS ops/sec and 2.0% CPU use

Power est.          Usage      Events/s  Category      Description
  1.46 W     0.0 pkts/s                  Device        Network interface: eth0 (r8169)
  931 mW     100.0%                       Device        Audio codec hwC0D0: Realtek
  931 mW     100.0%                       Device        Audio codec hwC0D3: Intel
  230 mW     0.0 pkts/s                   Device        Network interface: wlan0 (rtl8192se)
  142 mW     4.0 ms/s       0.24         kWork         rfkill_poll
 80.8 mW     2.3 ms/s       2.9          Process       /usr/bin/yakuake
 65.4 mW     1.8 ms/s       0.24         Process       powertop
 62.3 mW     1.8 ms/s       7.3          Process       /usr/bin/quasselcore --logfile=/var/log/quassel/core.log --loglevel=Info --configdir=/var/lib/qu
 41.0 mW     1.2 ms/s       0.7          Process       /usr/bin/quasselclient
 23.8 mW     674.7 us/s     0.7          Process       /usr/sbin/owncloud
 22.3 mW     630.6 us/s     1.0          Process       /usr/lib/telepathy/telepathy-gabble
 18.7 mW     528.6 us/s     22.9         Process       /usr/sbin/mysqld
 18.0 mW     509.5 us/s     0.5          Process       /usr/bin/X :0 -core -auth /var/run/lightdm/root/:0 -nolisten tcp vt7 -novtswitch -background non
 11.5 mW     324.4 us/s     35.0         Interrupt     [42] i915
 11.3 mW     217.5 us/s     2.3          Process       kwin
 10.9 mW     309.4 us/s     2.0          Process       kdeinit4: kded4 [kdeinit]
 10.9 mW     309.2 us/s     1.8          Process       /usr/bin/python /usr/bin/hp-systray
 9.89 mW     279.8 us/s     0.00         Process       dbus-daemon --system --fork
 7.87 mW     222.8 us/s     0.00         Process       [kworker/0:2]
 7.87 mW     222.7 us/s     1.7          Process       /usr/lib/upower/upowerd
 7.78 mW     220.1 us/s     1.1          Interrupt     [7] sched(softirq)
 7.72 mW     218.4 us/s     5.3          Interrupt     [23] ehci_hcd:usb2
 7.63 mW     215.9 us/s     33.8         Timer         tick_sched_timer

<ESC> Exit |

Shell  Shell No. 2  Shell No. 3
shaan : sudo - KDE Terminal Emulator
```

2. For generating HTML reports, use:

   ```
   # powertop --html
   ```

   `powertop` will take measurements over a period of time and generate an HTML
   report with the default filename `PowerTOP.html`, which you can open using any
   web browser.

3. For optimizing power usage, use:

   When `powertop` is running, use the arrow keys to switch to the **Tunables** tab; this
   will show you a list of things that `powertop` can tune so that they consume less
   power. Just choose whichever ones you want, press *Enter* to toggle from **Bad**
   to **Good**:

If you want to monitor the power consumption from a portable device's
battery, it is required to remove the charger and use the battery for
`powertop` to make measurements.

Monitoring disk activity

Going by the popular naming convention of monitoring tools ending in the word `'top'`
(the command used to monitor processes), the tool to monitor disk I/O is called `iotop`.

Getting ready

`iotop` doesn't come preinstalled with most Linux distributions, you will have to install it using your package manager.

How to do it...

There are multiple ways of using `iotop` to perform I/O monitoring, some of which we will see in this recipe:

1. For interactive monitoring, use:

   ```
   # iotop -o
   ```

   The `-o` option to `iotop` tells it to show only those processes which are doing active I/O while it is running. It is a useful option to reduce the noise in the output.

2. For non-interactive use from shell scripts, use:

   ```
   # iotop -b -n 2
   ```

   This will tell iotop to print the statistics two times and then exit, which is useful if we want this output in a shell script and do some manipulation on it.

3. Monitor a specific process using the following:

   ```
   # iotop -p PID
   ```

   Put PID of the process that you wish to monitor, and `iotop` will restrict the output to it and show statistics.

> In most modern distros, instead of finding the PID and supplying it to `iotop`, you can use the `pidof` command and write the preceding command as:
>
> ```
> # iotop -p `pidof cp`
> ```

Checking disks and filesystems for errors

Data is the most important thing in any computer system. Naturally, it is important to monitor the consistency of data stored on physical media.

Getting ready

We will use the standard tool, `fsck` to check for errors in the filesystems. This command should be preinstalled on all modern distros. If not, use your package manager to install it.

How to do it...

Let us see how to use `fsck` with its various options to check filesystems for errors, and optionally fix them.

1. To check for errors on a partition or filesystem, just pass its path to `fsck`:

   ```
   # fsck /dev/sdb3
   fsck from util-linux 2.20.1
   e2fsck 1.42.5 (29-Jul-2012)
   HDD2 has been mounted 26 times without being checked, check
   forced.
   Pass 1: Checking inodes, blocks, and sizes
   Pass 2: Checking directory structure
   Pass 3: Checking directory connectivity
   Pass 4: Checking reference counts
   Pass 5: Checking group summary information
   HDD2: 75540/16138240 files (0.7% non-contiguous),
   48756390/64529088 blocks
   ```

2. To check all the filesystems configured in `/etc/fstab`, we can use the following syntax:

   ```
   # fsck -A
   ```

   This will go through the `/etc/fstab` file sequentially, checking each of the filesystems one-by-one. The `fstab` file basically configures a mapping between disks and mount points which makes it easy to mount filesystems. This also makes it possible to mount certain filesystems during boot.

3. Instruct `fsck` to automatically attempt fixing errors, instead of interactively asking us whether or not to repair, we can use this form of `fsck`:

   ```
   # fsck -a /dev/sda2
   ```

4. To simulate the actions, `fsck` is going to perform:

   ```
   # fsck -AN
   fsck from util-linux 2.20.1
   [/sbin/fsck.ext4 (1) -- /] fsck.ext4 /dev/sda8
   [/sbin/fsck.ext4 (1) -- /home] fsck.ext4 /dev/sda7
   [/sbin/fsck.ext3 (1) -- /media/Data] fsck.ext3 /dev/sda6
   ```

   This will print information on what actions will be performed, which is checking all the filesystems.

How it works...

`fsck` is just a frontend for filesystem specific `fsck` programs written for those filesystems. When we run `fsck`, it automatically detects the type of the filesystem and runs the appropriate `fsck.fstype` command where `fstype` is the type of the filesystem. For example, if we run `fsck` on an `ext4` filesystem, it will end up calling the `fsck.ext4` command.

Because of this, you will find that `fsck` itself supports only the common options across all such filesystem-specific tools. To find more detailed options, look at the man pages of specific commands such as `fsck.ext4`.

Further, simulating the actions `fsck` performs is useful when there is a suspicion of a filesystem being corrupt and we run `fsck` to fix it, it is sometimes important to make sure that `fsck` doesn't perform an operation which we don't want. An example maybe that `fsck` might want to mark some sectors as bad, but we might want to try recovering data from it. In this case, we ask `fsck` to just do a dry run and print the actions instead of actually performing the actions.

9
Administration Calls

In this chapter, we will cover:

- ▸ Gathering information about processes
- ▸ Killing processes and send or respond to signals
- ▸ Sending messages to user terminals
- ▸ Gathering system information
- ▸ Using /proc for gathering information
- ▸ Scheduling with cron
- ▸ Writing and reading the MySQL database from Bash
- ▸ User administration script
- ▸ Bulk image resizing and format conversion
- ▸ Taking screenshots from the terminal
- ▸ Managing multiple terminals from one

Introduction

A GNU/Linux ecosystem consists of running programs, services, connected devices, filesystems, users, and a lot more. Having an overview of the entire system and managing the OS as a whole is the primary purpose of system administration. One should be armed with enough knowledge of commonly-used commands and proper usage practices to gather system information and manage resources. It also helps in writing script and automation tools that perform management tasks. This chapter will introduce several such tools.

Gathering information about processes

Processes are the running instance of a program. Several processes run on a computer, and each process is assigned a unique identification number called a **process ID** (**PID**). Multiple instances of the same program with the same name can be executed at the same time, but they all will have different PIDs. A process consists of several attributes, such as which user owns the process, the amount of memory used by the program, CPU time used by the program, and so on. This recipe shows how to gather information about processes.

Getting ready

Important commands related to process management are top, ps, and pgrep. Let's see how we can gather information about processes.

How to do it...

ps is an important tool for gathering information about the processes. It provides information on which user owns the process, the time when a process started, the command path used for executing the process, PID, the terminal it is attached with (TTY), the memory used by the process, CPU time used by the process, and so on. For example:

```
$ ps
  PID TTY          TIME CMD
 1220 pts/0    00:00:00 bash
 1242 pts/0    00:00:00 ps
```

The ps command is usually used with a set of parameters. When it is run without any parameter, ps will display processes that are running on the current terminal (TTY). The first column shows the process ID (PID), the second column is the TTY (terminal), the third column is how much time has elapsed since the process started, and finally CMD (the command).

In order to show more columns consisting of more information, use -f (stands for **full**) as follows:

```
$ ps -f
UID         PID  PPID  C STIME TTY          TIME CMD
slynux     1220  1219  0 18:18 pts/0    00:00:00 -bash
slynux     1587  1220  0 18:59 pts/0    00:00:00 ps -f
```

The preceding ps commands are not useful, as it does not provide any information about processes other than the ones attached to the current terminal. In order to get information about every process running on the system, add the -e (**every**) option. The -ax (**all**) option will also produce an identical output.

The -x argument along with -a specifies to remove the default TTY restriction imparted by ps. Usually, using ps without arguments prints processes that are attached to the terminal only.

Run one of these commands: ps -e, ps -ef, ps -ax, or ps -axf.

```
$ ps -e | head
   PID TTY              TIME CMD
1  ?           00:00:00 init
2  ?           00:00:00 kthreadd
3  ?           00:00:00 migration/0
4  ?           00:00:00 ksoftirqd/0
5  ?           00:00:00 watchdog/0
6  ?           00:00:00 events/0
7  ?           00:00:00 cpuset
8  ?           00:00:00 khelper
9  ?           00:00:00 netns
```

It will be a long list. The example filters the output using head, so we only get the first 10 entries.

The ps command supports several details to be displayed along with the process name and PID. By default, ps shows the information as different columns, and some of them may not be useful for us. We can specify the columns to be displayed using the -o flag and hence, thereby print only the required columns. Different parameters associated with a process are specified with options for that parameter. The list of parameters and usage of -o are discussed next.

In order to display the required columns of output using ps, use:

```
$ ps [OTHER OPTIONS] -o parameter1,parameter2,parameter3 ..
```

Parameters for -o are delimited by using the comma (,) operator. It should be noted that there is no space in between the comma operator and the next parameter. Usually, the -o option is combined with the -e (every) option (-oe), as it should list every process running in the system. However, when certain filters are used along with -o, such as those used for listing the processes owned by specified users, -e is not used along with -o. Usage of -e with a filter will nullify the filter and it will show all process entries.

An example is as follows. Here, comm stands for COMMAND and pcpu is percent of CPU usage:

```
$ ps -eo comm,pcpu | head
COMMAND         %CPU
init             0.0
kthreadd         0.0
migration/0      0.0
ksoftirqd/0      0.0
watchdog/0       0.0
events/0         0.0
cpuset           0.0
khelper          0.0
netns            0.0
```

How it works...

The different parameters that can be used with the -o option and their descriptions are as follows:

Parameter	Description
pcpu	Percentage of CPU
pid	Process ID
ppid	Parent Process ID
pmem	Percentage of memory
comm	Executable filename
cmd	Simple command
user	The user who started the process
nice	The priority (niceness)
time	Cumulative CPU time
etime	Elapsed time since the process started
tty	The associated TTY device
euid	The effective user
stat	Process state

There's more...

Let's go through additional usage examples of process manipulation commands.

top

`top` is a very important command for system administrators. The `top` command will, by default, output a list of top CPU consuming processes. The output is updated every few seconds, and is used as follows:

```
$ top
```

It will display several parameters along with the top CPU consuming processes:

```
top - 23:21:11 up 38 min,   4 users,  load average: 1.13, 0.96, 1.11
KiB Mem:   3925048 total,  3627108 used,    297940 free,    187536 buffers
KiB Swap:  1998844 total,        0 used,   1998844 free,   2094184 cached

  PID USER       PR  NI  VIRT   RES   SHR S  %CPU %MEM     TIME+  COMMAND
 3061 shaan      20   0  526m  131m  39m S   10.9  3.4   3:01.05 plasma-mediacen
 1362 root       20   0  184m   80m  60m S    8.6  2.1   2:40.96 Xorg
 2503 shaan      20   0  286m   46m  29m S    6.0  1.2   1:46.16 kwin
 2511 shaan      20   0  403m  139m  52m S    4.6  3.6   2:44.36 plasma-desktop
 5401 shaan      20   0  875m  227m  39m S    2.3  5.9   2:16.76 firefox
 2559 shaan      20   0  115m   31m  24m S    2.0  0.8   0:08.01 yakuake
 2572 shaan       9 -11  161m  5920 4140 S    1.3  0.2   0:35.77 pulseaudio
 3095 shaan      -4   0 13416  9.9m 1128 S    1.3  0.3   1:04.17 wineserver
 6238 shaan      20   0 96520   21m  17m S    1.0  0.6   0:01.18 ksnapshot
 1663 quasselc   20   0 88960   17m 8096 S    0.7  0.5   0:04.47 quasselcore
 6125 root       20   0     0     0    0 S    0.7  0.0   0:00.58 kworker/2:0
   10 root       20   0     0     0    0 S    0.3  0.0   0:01.41 ksoftirqd/1
   33 root       20   0     0     0    0 S    0.3  0.0   0:01.49 kworker/3:1
  240 root       20   0     0     0    0 S    0.3  0.0   0:00.27 usb-storage
  714 root       20   0     0     0    0 S    0.3  0.0   0:00.31 ips-monitor
 1324 mysql      20   0  310m   32m 5692 S    0.3  0.9   0:01.94 mysqld
 1956 shaan      20   0  5492   380  216 S    0.3  0.0   0:00.06 gpg-agent
 Shell  Shell No. 2
 shaan : top - KDE Terminal Emulator
```

Sorting the ps output with respect to a parameter

Output of the `ps` command can be sorted according to specified columns with the `--sort` parameter. The ascending or descending order can be specified by using the + (ascending) or - (descending) prefix to the parameter as follows:

```
$ ps [OPTIONS] --sort -paramter1,+parameter2,parameter3..
```

For example, to list the top 10 CPU consuming processes, use:

```
$ ps -eo comm,pcpu --sort -pcpu | head
COMMAND           %CPU
Xorg              0.1
hald-addon-stor   0.0
ata/0             0.0
scsi_eh_0         0.0
gnome-settings-   0.0
init              0.0
hald              0.0
pulseaudio        0.0
gdm-simple-gree   0.0
```

Here, processes are sorted in the descending order by percentage of CPU usage, and head is applied to extract the top 10 processes.

We can use grep to extract entries in the ps output related to a given process name or another parameter. In order to find out entries about running Bash processes, use:

```
$ ps -eo comm,pid,pcpu,pmem | grep bash
bash              1255  0.0  0.3
bash              1680  5.5  0.3
```

Finding the process ID when given command names

Suppose several instances of a command are being executed, we may need to identify the PID of the processes. This information can be found by using the ps or the pgrep command. We can use ps as follows:

```
$ ps -C COMMAND_NAME
```

Or

```
$ ps -C COMMAND_NAME -o pid=
```

The -o user-defined format specifier was described in the earlier part of the recipe. But here, you can see = appended with pid. This is to remove the header PID in the output of ps. In order to remove headers for each column, append = to the parameter. For example:

```
$ ps -C bash -o pid=
 1255
 1680
```

This command lists the process IDs of Bash processes.

Alternately, there is a handy command called `pgrep`. You should use `pgrep` to get a quick list of process IDs for a particular command. For example:

```
$ pgrep COMMAND
$ pgrep bash
1255
1680
```

 `pgrep` requires only a portion of the command name as its input argument to extract a Bash command, for example, `pgrep ash` or `pgrep bas` will also work. But `ps` requires you to type the exact command.

`pgrep` accepts many more output-filtering options. In order to specify a delimiter character for output rather than using a newline as the delimiter, use:

```
$ pgrep COMMAND -d DELIMITER_STRING
$ pgrep bash -d ":"
1255:1680
```

Specify a list of owners of the user for the matching processes as follows:

```
$ pgrep -u root,slynux COMMAND
```

In this command, `root` and `slynux` are users. Return the count of matching processes as follows:

```
$ pgrep -c COMMAND
```

Filters with ps for real user or ID, effective user or ID

With `ps`, it is possible to group processes based on the real and effective username or ID specified. Specified arguments can be used to filter the `ps` output by checking whether each entry belongs to a specific, effective user, or real user from the list of arguments and shows only the entries matching them. This can be done as follows:

- ▸ Specify an effective users' list by using `-u EUSER1, EUSER2`, and so on
- ▸ Specify a real users' list by using `-U RUSER1, RUSER2`, and so on

For example:

```
$ ps -u root -U root -o user,pcpu
```

This command will show all processes running with `root` as the effective user ID and real user ID, and will also show the user and percentage CPU usage columns.

Mostly, we find -o along with -e as -eo, but when filters are applied -o should act alone, as mentioned in this section.

TTY filter for ps

The ps output can be selected by specifying the TTY to which the process is attached. Use the -t option to specify the TTY list, as follows:

```
$ ps -t TTY1, TTY2 ..
```

For example:

```
$ ps -t pts/0,pts/1
  PID TTY          TIME CMD
 1238 pts/0    00:00:00 bash
 1835 pts/1    00:00:00 bash
 1864 pts/0    00:00:00 ps
```

Information about process threads

Usually, information about process threads are hidden in the ps output. We can show information about threads in the ps output by adding the -L option. Then, it will show two columns NLWP and NLP. NLWP is the thread count for a process and NLP is the thread ID for each entry in ps. For example:

```
$ ps -eLf
```

Or

```
$ ps -eLf --sort -nlwp | head
UID          PID  PPID   LWP  C NLWP STIME TTY          TIME CMD
root         647     1   647  0   64 14:39 ?        00:00:00 /usr/sbin/
console-kit-daemon --no-daemon
root         647     1   654  0   64 14:39 ?        00:00:00 /usr/sbin/
console-kit-daemon --no-daemon
root         647     1   656  0   64 14:39 ?        00:00:00 /usr/sbin/
console-kit-daemon --no-daemon
root         647     1   657  0   64 14:39 ?        00:00:00 /usr/sbin/
console-kit-daemon --no-daemon
root         647     1   658  0   64 14:39 ?        00:00:00 /usr/sbin/
console-kit-daemon --no-daemon
root         647     1   659  0   64 14:39 ?        00:00:00 /usr/sbin/
console-kit-daemon --no-daemon
```

```
root          647     1    660   0    64 14:39 ?        00:00:00 /usr/sbin/
console-kit-daemon --no-daemon
root          647     1    662   0    64 14:39 ?        00:00:00 /usr/sbin/
console-kit-daemon --no-daemon
root          647     1    663   0    64 14:39 ?        00:00:00 /usr/sbin/
console-kit-daemon --no-daemon
```

This command lists 10 processes with a maximum number of threads.

Specifying output width and columns to be displayed

We can specify the columns to be displayed in the `ps` output using the user-defined output format specifier `-o`. Another way to specify the output format is with standard options. Practice them according to your usage style. Try these options:

- `-f`   `ps -ef`
- `u`   `ps  -e u`
- `ps`   `ps  -e w` (w stands for wide output)

Showing environment variables for a process

Understanding which environment variables a process is dependent on is a very useful bit of information we might need. The way a process behaves might be heavily dependent on the environmental variables set. We can debug and make use of environment data for fixing several problems related to the running of processes.

In order to list environment variables along with `ps` entries, use:

`$ ps -eo cmd e`

For example:

```
$ ps -eo pid,cmd   e | tail -n 3
 1162 hald-addon-acpi: listening on acpid socket /var/run/acpid.socket
 1172 sshd: slynux [priv]
 1237 sshd: slynux@pts/0
 1238 -bash USER=slynux LOGNAME=slynux HOME=/home/slynux PATH=/usr/
local/sbin:/usr/local/bin:/usr/sbin:/usr/bin:/sbin:/bin:/usr/games
MAIL=/var/mail/slynux SHELL=/bin/bash SSH_CLIENT=10.211.55.2 49277 22
SSH_CONNECTION=10.211.55.2 49277 10.211.55.4 22 SSH_TTY=/dev/pts/0
TERM=xterm-color LANG=en_IN XDG_SESSION_COOKIE=d1e96f5cc8a7a3bc3a0a73e44c
95121a-1286499339.592429-1573657095
```

An example of where this type of environment tracing can come in handy is in tracing problems with the apt-get package manager. If you use an HTTP proxy to connect to the Internet, you may need to set environment variables `http_proxy=host:port`. Let's say you forgot to set the environment variables in a script, the `apt-get` command will not select the proxy and hence, it returns an error. Then, you can actually look at an environment variable and track the issue.

We may need some applications to be run automatically with scheduling tools, such as `cron`. But it might be dependent on some environment variables. Suppose, if we want to open a GUI-windowed application at a given time. We schedule it using `crontab` at a specified time, but this will not work:

```
00 10 * * * /usr/bin/windowapp
```

It is because a windowed application always depends on the `DISPLAY` environment variable. To figure out the environment variables needed, run `windowapp` manually, and then run `ps -C windowapp -eo cmd e`.

Find out the environment variables and prefix them before a command name appears in `crontab` as follows:

```
00 10 * * * DISPLAY=:0 /usr/bin/windowapp
```

Here, `DISPLAY=:0` was obtained from the `ps` output.

About which, whereis, file, whatis, and load average

There are a few commands which are useful for exploring other commands and such. Let's discuss them:

- `which`: The `which` command is used to find the location of a command. We type commands in the terminal without knowing the location where the executable file is stored.

- When we type a command, the terminal looks for the command in a set of locations and executes the executable file if found at the location. These sets of locations are specified using an environment variable `PATH`. For example:

```
$ echo $PATH
/usr/local/sbin:/usr/local/bin:/usr/sbin:/usr/bin:/sbin:/bin:/usr/
games
```

- We can export `PATH` and can add our own locations to be searched when command names are typed. For example, to add `/home/slynux/bin` to `PATH`, use the following command:

```
$ export PATH=$PATH:/home/slynux/bin
# /home/slynux/bin is added to PATH
```

▸ The `which` command outputs the location of the command given as the argument. For example:

```
$ which ls
/bin/ls
```

▸ `whereis`: `whereis` is similar to the which command. But it not only returns the path of the command, it will also print the location of the man page, if available, and also the path of the source code for the command if available. For example:

```
$ whereis ls
ls: /bin/ls /usr/share/man/man1/ls.1.gz
```

▸ `file`: The `file` command is an interesting and frequently-used command. It is used for determining the file type:

```
$ file FILENAME
```

▸ This will print the details of the file regarding its file type.

▸ An example is as follows:

```
$ file /bin/ls
/bin/ls: ELF 32-bit LSB executable, Intel 80386, version 1 (SYSV),
dynamically linked (uses shared libs), for GNU/Linux 2.6.15,
stripped
```

▸ `whatis`: The `whatis` command outputs a one-line description of the command given as the argument. It parses information from the man page. For example:

```
$ whatis ls
ls (1)                    - list directory contents
```

apropos

Sometimes, we need to search if some command related to a word exists. Then, we can search the man pages for strings in the command. For this we can use:

```
apropos COMMAND
```

▸ `load average`: `load average` is an important parameter for the total load on the running system. It specifies the average of the total number of runnable processes on the system. It is specified by three values. The first value indicates the average in one minute, the second indicates the average in five minutes, and the third indicates the average in 15 minutes.

▸ It can be obtained by running uptime. For example:

```
$ uptime
 12:40:53 up  6:16,  2 users,  load average: 0.00, 0.00, 0.00
```

See also

▸ The *Scheduling with cron* recipe explains how to schedule tasks

Killing processes and send or respond to signals

Termination of processes is an important task we always come across, including the need to terminate all the instances of a program. The command line provides several options for terminating programs. An important concept regarding processes in Unix-like environments is that of **signals**. Signals are an inter-process communication mechanism used to interrupt a running process to perform some action. Termination of a program is also performed by using the same technique. This recipe is an introduction to signals and their usage.

Getting ready

Signals are an inter-process mechanism available in Linux. We can interrupt a process using a specific signal, which is associated with an integer value. When a process receives a signal, it responds by executing a signal handler. It is possible to send and receive signals and respond according to the signals in shell scripts as well. KILL is a signal used to terminate a process. The events such as *Ctrl + C*, and *Ctrl + Z* also send two types of signals. The kill command is used to send signals to processes and the trap command is used to handle the received signals.

How to do it...

1. In order to list all the signals available, use:

   ```
   $ kill -l
   ```

   It will print signal numbers and corresponding signal names.

2. Terminate a process as follows:

   ```
   $ kill PROCESS_ID_LIST
   ```

   The kill command issues a TERM signal by default. The process ID list is to be specified with space as a delimiter between process IDs.

3. In order to specify a signal to be sent to a process via the kill command, use:

   ```
   $ kill -s SIGNAL PID
   ```

   The `SIGNAL` argument is either a signal name or a signal number. Though there are many signals specified for different purposes, we frequently use only a few signals. They are as follows:

   - `SIGHUP 1`: Hangup detection on death of the controlling process or terminal
   - `SIGINT 2`: Signal which is emitted when *Ctrl + C* is pressed
   - `SIGKILL 9`: Signal used to force kill the process
   - `SIGTERM 15`: Signal used to terminate a process by default
   - `SIGTSTP 20`: Signal emitted when *Ctrl + Z* is pressed

4. We frequently use force kill for processes. In order to force kill a process, use:

   ```
   $ kill -s SIGKILL PROCESS_ID
   ```

   Or:

   ```
   $ kill -9 PROCESS_ID
   ```

There's more...

Let's walk through the additional commands used for terminating and signalling processes.

The kill family of commands

The `kill` command takes the process ID as the argument. There are also a few other commands in the `kill` family that accept the command name as the argument and send a signal to the process.

The `killall` command terminates the process by name as follows:

```
$ killall process_name
```

In order to send a signal to a process by name, use:

```
$ killall -s SIGNAL process_name
```

In order to force kill a process by name, use:

```
$ killall -9 process_name
```

For example:

```
$ killall -9 gedit
```

Specify the process by name, which is specified by users who own it, by using:

```
$ killall -u USERNAME process_name
```

If you want `killall` to interactively confirm before killing processes, use the `-i` argument.

The `pkill` command is similar to the `kill` command but it, by default, accepts a process name instead of a process ID. For example:

```
$ pkill process_name
$ pkill -s SIGNAL process_name
```

`SIGNAL` is the signal number. The `SIGNAL` name is not supported with `pkill`. It provides many of the same options that the `kill` command does. Check the `pkill` man pages for more details.

Capturing and responding to signals

`trap` is a command used to assign signal handler to signals in a script. Once a function is assigned to a signal using the `trap` command, while the script runs and it receives a signal, this function is executed upon reception of a corresponding signal.

The syntax is as follows:

```
trap 'signal_handler_function_name' SIGNAL LIST
```

`SIGNAL LIST` is delimited by space. It can be a signal number or a signal name.

Let's write a shell script that responds to the `SIGINT` signal:

```
#/bin/bash
#Filename: sighandle.sh
#Description: Signal handler

function handler()
{
  echo Hey, received signal : SIGINT
}

echo My process ID is $$
# $$ is a special variable that returns process ID of current process/
script
trap 'handler' SIGINT
#handler is the name of the signal handler function for SIGINT signal

while true;
do
  sleep 1
done
```

Run this script in a terminal. When the script is running, if you press *Ctrl + C*, it will show the message by executing the signal handler associated with it. *Ctrl + C* corresponds to a `SIGINT` signal.

The `while` loop is used to keep the process running in an infinite loop without getting terminated. This is done so that it can respond to the signals that are sent to the process asynchronously by another process. The loop that is used to keep the process alive infinitely is often called the **event loop**.

We can send a signal to the script by using the `kill` command and the process ID of the script:

```
$ kill -s SIGINT PROCESS_ID
```

`PROCESS_ID` of the preceding script will be printed when it is executed, or you can find it out by using the `ps` command.

If no signal handlers are specified for signals, it will call the default signal handlers assigned by the operating system. Generally, pressing *Ctrl + C* will terminate a program, as the default handler provided by the operating system will terminate the process. But the custom handler defined here specifies a custom action upon receipt of the signal.

We can define signal handlers for any signals available (`kill -l`) by using the `trap` command. It is also possible to set a single signal handler for multiple signals.

Sending messages to user terminals

A system administrator may need to send messages to the terminal of every user or a specified user on all the machines over a network. This recipe is a guide on how to perform this task.

Getting ready

`wall` is a command that is used to write messages on the terminals of all logged in users. It can be used to convey messages to all logged in users on a server or multiple access machines. Sending messages to all users may not be useful at all times. Terminals are treated as devices in a Linux system and hence, these opened terminals will have a corresponding device node file at `/dev/pts/`. Writing data to a specific device will display messages on the corresponding terminal.

How to do it...

In order to broadcast a message to all users and all logged in terminals, use:

```
$ cat message | wall
```

Or:

```
$ wall< message
Broadcast Message from slynux@slynux-laptop
        (/dev/pts/1) at 12:54 ...

This is a message
```

The message outline will show who sent the message (which user and which host). It is noteworthy that the message gets displayed to the current terminal only if the **write message** option is enabled. In most distros, **write message** is enabled by default. If the sender of the message is root, then the message gets displayed on the screen irrespective of whether the **write message** option is enabled or disabled by the user.

In order to enable write messages, use:

```
$ mesg y
```

In order to disable write messages, use:

```
$ mesg n
```

Let's write a script for sending messages specifically to a given user's terminal:

```bash
#/bin/bash
#Filename: message_user.sh
#Description: Script to send message to specified user logged
terminals.
USERNAME=$1

devices=`ls /dev/pts/* -l | awk '{ print $3,$10 }' | grep $USERNAME |
awk '{ print $2 }'`
for dev in $devices;
do
  cat /dev/stdin > $dev
done
```

Run the script as:

```
./message_user.sh USERNAME < message.txt
# Pass message through stdin and username as argument
```

The output will be as follows:

```
$ cat message.txt
A message to slynux. Happy Hacking!
# ./message_user.sh slynux  < message.txt
# Run message_user.sh as root since the message is to be send to specific
user.
```

Now, the `slynux` command's terminal will receive the message text.

How it works...

The `/dev/pts` directory will contain character devices corresponding to each of the logged in terminals on the system. We can find out who logged into which terminal by looking at the owner of the device files from the `ls -l` output. This information is extracted by using `awk`, and then `grep` is used to extract the lines corresponding to the specified user only. The username is accepted as the first argument for the script and stored as variable USERNAME. `$devices` contains a list of terminals for a given user, which is iterated using a `for` loop. `/dev/stdin` will contain standard input data passed to the current process, which is redirected to the corresponding terminal (TTY) devices.

Gathering system information

Collecting information about the current system from the command line is very important in logging system data. The different system information data includes hostname, kernel version, Linux distro name, CPU information, memory information, disk partition information, and so on. This recipe will show you different sources in a Linux system to gather information about the system.

How to do it...

1. In order to print the hostname of the current system, use:

   ```
   $ hostname
   ```

   Or:

   ```
   $ uname -n
   ```

2. Print long details about the Linux kernel version, hardware architecture, and more by using:

   ```
   $ uname -a
   ```

3. In order to print the kernel release, use:

   ```
   $ uname -r
   ```

4. Print the machine type as follows:

```
$ uname -m
```

5. In order to print details about the CPU, use:

```
$ cat /proc/cpuinfo
```

In order to extract the processor name, use:

```
$ cat /proc/cpuinfo | sed -n 5p
```

The fifth line contains the processor name.

6. Print details about the memory or RAM as follows:

```
$ cat /proc/meminfo
```

Print the total memory (RAM) available on the system as follows:

```
$ cat /proc/meminfo | head -1
MemTotal:        1026096 kB
```

7. In order to list out the partitions information available on the system, use:

```
$ cat /proc/partitions
```

Or:

```
$ fdisk -l  #If you don't get any output, run as root
```

8. Get the entire details about the system as follows:

```
$ lshw   #Recommended to run as root
```

Using /proc for gathering information

/proc is an in-memory pseudo filesystem available with the GNU/Linux operating system. It was actually introduced to provide an interface to read several system parameters from the user space. It is very interesting and we can gather lots of information from it. Let's see how to.

How to do it...

If you look at /proc, you will see several files and directories, some of which are already explained in other recipes in this chapter. You can simply cat files in /proc and the subdirectories to get information. All of them are well-formatted text.

There will be a directory in /proc for every process that is running on the system, named after the PID of that process.

Suppose Bash is running with PID 4295 (pgrep bash), /proc/4295 will exist. Each of the directories corresponding to the process will contain a lot of information regarding to that process. Few of the important files in /proc/PID are as follows.

- ▶ environ: This contains environment variables associated with that process. cat /proc/4295/environ will display all the environment variables passed to that process.

- ▶ cwd: This is a symlink to a working directory of the process.

- ▶ exe: This is a symlink to the running executable for the current process.

  ```
  $ readlink /proc/4295/exe
  /bin/bash
  ```

- ▶ fd: This is the directory consisting of entries on file descriptors used by the process.

Scheduling with cron

It is a common requirement to schedule execution of scripts at a given time or at given time intervals. The GNU/Linux system comes with different utilities for scheduling tasks. cron is such a utility that allows tasks to automatically run in the background of the system at regular intervals using the cron daemon. The cron utility makes use of a file called **cron table** that stores a list of schedules of scripts or commands to be executed and the time at which they are to be executed. A common example usage is that you can schedule downloads of files from the Internet during the free hours (certain ISPs provide free usage hours, usually, at night time). This way you won't be required to wake up in the night to start the download. In addition to writing a cron entry and schedule the download, you can also schedule to drop the Internet connection automatically and shutdown the system when the free usage hours end.

Getting ready

The cron scheduling utility comes with all the GNU/Linux distributions by default. Once we write the cron table entry, the commands will be executed at the time specified for execution. The command crontab is used to add jobs to the cron table. The cron table is a simple text file and each user has a separate copy.

How to do it...

In order to schedule tasks, we should know the format for writing the cron table. A cron job specifies the path of a script or command to be executed and the time at which it is to be executed.

1. cron job to execute the test.sh script at the second minute of all hours on all days:

   ```
   02 * * * * /home/slynux/test.sh
   ```

2. In order to run the script at the fifth, sixth, and seventh hours on all days, use:

    ```
    00 5,6,7 * * /home/slynux/test.sh
    ```

3. Execute `script.sh` at every hour on Sundays as follows:

    ```
    00 */12 * * 0 /home/slynux/script.sh
    ```

4. Shutdown the computer at 2 A.M. everyday as follows:

    ```
    00 02 * * * /sbin/shutdown -h
    ```

5. Now, let us see how to schedule a cron job. You can execute the `crontab` command in multiple ways to schedule the scripts.

    Use the `-e` option to `crontab` to start editing the cron table:

    ```
    $ crontab -e
    02 02 * * * /home/slynux/script.sh
    ```

    When `crontab -e` is entered, the default text editor (usually vi) is opened up and the user can type the cron jobs and save it. The cron jobs will be scheduled and executed at specified time intervals.

6. There are two other methods we usually use when we invoke the crontab command inside a script for scheduling tasks:

    1. Create a text file (for example, `task.cron`) with the cron job in it, and then run the `crontab` with this filename as the command argument:

        ```
        $ crontab task.cron
        ```

    2. Or, specify the cron job inline without creating a separate file. For example:

        ```
        crontab<<EOF
        02 * * * * /home/slynux/script.sh
        EOF
        ```

        The cron job needs to be written in between `crontab<<EOF` and `EOF`.

How it works...

Each cron table consists of six sections in the following order:

  ▸ `Minute` (0 - 59)
  ▸ `Hour` (0 - 23)
  ▸ `Day` (1 - 31)
  ▸ `Month` (1 - 12)
  ▸ `Weekday` (0 - 6)
  ▸ `COMMAND` (the script or command to be executed at the specified time)

The first five sections specify the time at which an instance of the command is to be executed. There are a few additional options to specify the time schedule.

An asterisk (*) is used to specify that the command should be executed at every instance of time. That is, if * is written in the Hour field in the cron job, the command will be executed for every hour. Similarly, if you would like to execute the command at multiple instances of a particular time period, specify the time period separated by a comma in the corresponding time field (for example, for running the command at the fifth minute and tenth minute, enter 5,10 in the Minute field). We also have another nice option to run the command at particular divisions of time. Use */5 in the minutes field for running the command at every five minutes. We can apply this to any time field. A cron table can consist of one or more lines of cron jobs and each line in the cron table is a single job.

Cron jobs are executed with privileges with which the crontab command was executed. If you need to execute commands that require higher privileges, such as a command for shutting down the computer, run the crontab command as root.

The commands specified in a cron job are written with the full path to the command. This is because the environment in which a cron job is executed is different from the one that we execute on a terminal. Hence, the PATH environment variable may not be set. If your command requires certain environment variables to be set for running, you should explicitly set the environment variables.

There's more...

The crontab command has more options. Let's see a few of them.

Specifying environment variables

Many of the commands require environment variables to be set properly for execution. We can set environment variables by inserting a line with a variable assignment statement in the cron table of the user.

For example, if you are using a proxy server for connecting to the Internet, to schedule a command that uses the Internet you have to set the HTTP proxy environment variable http_proxy. It can be done as follows:

```
crontab<<EOF
http_proxy=http://192.168.0.3:3128
00 * * * * /home/slynux/download.sh
EOF
```

Running commands at system start up/boot

Running specific commands when the system starts (or, boots) is a common requirement at times. There are a lot of ways to achieve this, and using `cron` is one of them (the others being adding your commands to `/etc/rc.d` but that's not guaranteed to be the same across distros).

To run a command at boot, add the following line to your `crontab`:

```
@reboot command
```

This will run the command as your user at runtime. To run the command as root, edit root's `crontab`.

Viewing the cron table

We can list these existing cron jobs using the `-l` option:

```
$ crontab -l
02 05 * * * /home/user/disklog.sh
```

The `crontab -l` lists the existing entries in the cron table for the current user.

We can also view the cron table for other users by specifying a username with the `-u` option as follows:

```
$ crontab -l -u slynux
09 10 * * * /home/slynux/test.sh
```

You should run as root when you use the `-u` option to gain higher privilege.

Removing the cron table

We can remove the cron table for the current user using the `-r` option:

```
$ crontab -r
```

In order to remove `crontab` for another user, use:

```
# crontab -u slynux -r
```

Run as root to get higher privilege.

Writing and reading the MySQL database from Bash

MySQL is a widely used database management system used to manage databases for the storage systems for applications that are written in languages, such as PHP, Python, C++, and so on. Accessing and manipulating MySQL databases from shell scripts is also interesting, as we can write scripts to store contents from a text file or **Comma Separated Values** (**CSV**) into tables and interact with the MySQL database to read and manipulate data. For example, we can read all the e-mail addresses stored in a guestbook program's database by running a query from the shell script. In this recipe, we will see how to read and write to the MySQL database from Bash. Let's take this example problem:

I have a CSV file containing details of students. I need to insert the contents of the file to a database table. From this data, I need to generate a separate rank list for each department.

Getting ready

In order to handle MySQL databases, you should have `mysql-server` and `mysql-client` packages installed on your system. These tools do not come with a Linux distribution by default. As MySQL comes with a username and password for authentication, you should also set a username and password while installing the MySQL server.

How to do it...

The preceding problem can be solved using Bash utilities `sort`, `awk`, and so on. Alternately, we can also solve it by using an SQL database table. We will write three scripts for the purpose of creating a database and table, inserting student data into the table, and reading and displaying processed data from the table.

Create the database and table script as follows:

```
#!/bin/bash
#Filename: create_db.sh
#Description: Create MySQL database and table

USER="user"
PASS="user"

mysql -u $USER -p$PASS <<EOF 2> /dev/null
CREATE DATABASE students;
EOF

[ $? -eq 0 ] && echo Created DB || echo DB already exist
```

```
mysql -u $USER -p$PASS students <<EOF 2> /dev/null
CREATE TABLE students(
id int,
name varchar(100),
mark int,
dept varchar(4)
);
EOF

[ $? -eq 0 ] && echo Created table students || echo Table students
already exist

mysql -u $USER -p$PASS students <<EOF
DELETE FROM students;
EOF
```

The script for inserting data into the table is as follows:

```
#!/bin/bash
#Filename: write_to_db.sh
#Description: Read from CSV and write to MySQLdb

USER="user"
PASS="user"

if [ $# -ne 1 ];
then
  echo $0 DATAFILE
  echo
  exit 2
fi

data=$1

while read line;
do

  oldIFS=$IFS
  IFS=,
  values=($line)
  values[1]="\"`echo ${values[1]} | tr ' ' '#' `\""
  values[3]="\"`echo ${values[3]}`\""


  query=`echo ${values[@]} | tr ' #' ', ' `
```

```
    IFS=$oldIFS

    mysql -u $USER -p$PASS students <<EOF
INSERT INTO students VALUES($query);
EOF

done< $data
echo Wrote data into DB
```

The script for the query from the database is as follows:

```
#!/bin/bash
#Filename: read_db.sh
#Description: Read from the database

USER="user"
PASS="user"

depts=`mysql -u $USER -p$PASS students <<EOF | tail -n +2
SELECT DISTINCT dept FROM students;
EOF`

for d in $depts;
do

echo Department : $d

result="`mysql -u $USER -p$PASS students <<EOF
SET @i:=0;
SELECT @i:=@i+1 as rank,name,mark FROM students WHERE dept="$d" ORDER
BY mark DESC;
EOF`"

echo "$result"
echo

done
```

The data for the input CSV file (studentdata.csv) is as follows:

```
1,Navin M,98,CS

2,Kavya N,70,CS

3,Nawaz O,80,CS

4,Hari S,80,EC

5,Alex M,50,EC
```

```
6,Neenu J,70,EC
7,Bob A,30,EC
8,Anu M,90,AE
9,Sruthi,89,AE
10,Andrew,89,AE
```

Execute the scripts in the following sequence:

```
$ ./create_db.sh
Created DB
Created table students

$ ./write_to_db.sh studentdat.csv
Wrote data into DB

$ ./read_db.sh
Department : CS
rank  name   mark
1    Navin M  98
2    Nawaz O  80
3    Kavya N  70

Department : EC
rank  name   mark
1    Hari S  80
2    Neenu J 70
3    Alex M  50
4    Bob A   30

Department : AE
rank  name   mark
1    Anu M    90
2    Sruthi   89
3    Andrew   89
```

How it works...

We will now see the explanation of the preceding scripts one by one. The first script `create_db.sh` is used to create a database called `students` and a table named `students` inside it. We need the MySQL username and password to access or modify data in the DBMS. The variables USER and PASS are used to store the username and password. The `mysql` command is used for MySQL manipulations. The `mysql` command can specify the username by using `-u` and the password by using `-pPASSWORD`. The other command argument for the `mysql` command is the database name. If a database name is specified as an argument to the `mysql` command, it will use that for database operations, else we have to explicitly specify in the SQL query about which database is to be used with the use `database_name` query. The `mysql` command accepts the queries to be executed through standard input (`stdin`). The convenient way of supplying multiple lines through `stdin` is by using the `<<EOF` method. The text that appears in between `<<EOF` and `EOF` is passed to `mysql` as standard input. In the CREATE DATABASE query, we have redirected `stderr` to `/dev/null` in order to prevent displaying an error message. Also, in the table creation query, we have redirected `stderr` to `/dev/null` to ignore any errors that occur. Then, we check the exit status for the `mysql` command by using the exit status variable `$?` to know if a table or database already exists. If the database or table already exists, a message is displayed to notify that, else we will create them.

The next script `write_to_db.sh` accepts a filename of the student data CSV file. We read each line of the CSV file by using the `while` loop. So in each iteration, a line with comma separated values will be received. We then need to formulate the values in the line to an SQL query. For that, the easiest way to store data items in the comma-separated line is by using an array. We know that an array assignment is in the form `array=(val1 val2 val3)`. Here, the space character is the **Internal Field Separator** (**IFS**). We have a line with comma separated values, hence by changing the IFS to a comma, we can easily assign values to the array (`IFS=,`). The data items in the comma separated line are id, `name`, `mark`, and `department`. id and `mark` are integer values, whereas `name` and `dept` are strings (strings must be quoted). Also, the name can contain space characters. Space can conflict with the Internal Field Separator. Hence, we should replace the space in the name with a character (#) and replace it later after formulating the query. In order to quote the strings, the values in the array are reassigned prefix and suffix with `\"`. The `tr` is used to substitute space in the name to #. Finally, the query is formed by replacing the space character with a comma and replacing # with a space, and this query is executed.

The third script `read_db.sh` is used to find out the department and print the rank list of students for each department. The first query is used to find distinct names of departments. We use a `while` loop to iterate through each department and run the query to display student details in the order of highest marks. SET `@i=0` is an SQL construct used to set the variable `i=0`. On each row it is incremented and is displayed as the rank of the student.

User administration script

GNU/Linux is a multiuser operating system allowing many users to log in and perform several activities at the same time. There are several administration tasks that are handled with user management, which include setting the default shell for the user, disabling a user account, disabling a shell account, adding new users, removing users, setting a password, setting an expiry date for a user account, and so on. This recipe aims at writing a user management tool that can handle all of these tasks.

How to do it...

Let's go through the user administration script:

```bash
#!/bin/bash
#Filename: user_adm.sh
#Description: A user administration tool

function usage()
{
  echo Usage:
  echo Add a new user
  echo $0 -adduser username password
  echo
  echo Remove an existing user
  echo $0 -deluser username
  echo
  echo Set the default shell for the user
  echo $0 -shell username SHELL_PATH
  echo
  echo Suspend a user account
  echo $0 -disable username
  echo
  echo Enable a suspended user account
  echo $0 -enable username
  echo
  echo Set expiry date for user account
  echo $0 -expiry DATE
  echo
  echo Change password for user account
  echo $0 -passwd username
  echo
  echo Create a new user group
  echo $0 -newgroup groupname
```

```
   echo
   echo Remove an existing user group
   echo $0 -delgroup groupname
   echo
   echo Add a user to a group
   echo $0 -addgroup username groupname
   echo
   echo Show details about a user
   echo $0 -details username
   echo
   echo Show usage
   echo $0 -usage
   echo

   exit
}

if [ $UID -ne 0 ];
then
   echo Run $0 as root.
   exit 2
fi

case $1 in

   -adduser)  [ $# -ne 3 ] && usage ; useradd $2 -p $3 -m ;;
   -deluser)  [ $# -ne 2 ] && usage ; deluser $2 --remove-all-files;;
   -shell)    [ $# -ne 3 ] && usage ; chsh $2 -s $3 ;;
   -disable)  [ $# -ne 2 ] && usage ; usermod -L $2 ;;
   -enable)   [ $# -ne 2 ] && usage ; usermod -U $2  ;;
   -expiry)   [ $# -ne 3 ] && usage ; chage $2 -E $3 ;;
   -passwd)   [ $# -ne 2 ] && usage ; passwd $2 ;;
   -newgroup) [ $# -ne 2 ] && usage ; addgroup $2 ;;
   -delgroup) [ $# -ne 2 ] && usage ; delgroup $2 ;;
   -addgroup) [ $# -ne 3 ] && usage ; addgroup $2 $3 ;;
   -details)  [ $# -ne 2 ] && usage ; finger $2 ; chage -l $2 ;;
   -usage) usage ;;
   *) usage ;;
esac
```

A sample output is as follows:

```
# ./user_adm.sh -details test
Login: test                 Name:
Directory: /home/test               Shell: /bin/sh
Last login Tue Dec 21 00:07 (IST) on pts/1 from localhost
No mail.
No Plan.
Last password change          : Dec 20, 2010
Password expires        : never
Password inactive       : never
Account expires         : Oct 10, 2010
Minimum number of days between password change    : 0
Maximum number of days between password change    : 99999
Number of days of warning before password expires : 7
```

How it works...

The `user_adm.sh` script can be used to perform many user management tasks. You can follow the `usage()` text for the proper usage of the script which is called when any of the parameters given by the user is wrong or has the `-usage` parameter. A case statement is used to match the command arguments and execute the corresponding commands according to that. The valid command options for the `user_adm.sh` script are: `-adduser`, `-deluser`, `-shell`, `-disable`, `-enable`, `-expiry`, `-passwd`, `-newgroup`, `-delgroup`, `-addgroup`, `-details`, and `-usage`. When the `*)` case is matched, it means it is a wrong option and hence, `usage()` is invoked. For each match case, we have used `[ $# -ne 3 ] && usage`. It is used for checking the number of arguments. If the number of command arguments are not equal to the required number, the `usage()` function is invoked and the script will exit without executing further. In order to run the user management commands, the script needs to be run as root and hence, a check for the user ID 0 (root has user ID 0) is performed.

Let's explain each case one by one:

- ▶ `-useradd`: The `useradd` command can be used to create a new user. It has the following syntax:

  useradd USER -p PASSWORD

- ▶ The `-m` option is used to create the home directory. It is also possible to provide the full name of the user by using the `-c FULLNAME` option.

- ▶ `-deluser`: The `deluser` command can be used to remove the user. The syntax is as follows:

  deluser USER

- `--remove-all-files` is used to remove all files associated with the user including the home directory.

- `-shell`: The `chsh` command is used to change the default shell for the user. The syntax is:

chsh USER -s SHELL

- `-disable` and `-enable`: The `usermod` command is used to manipulate several attributes related to user accounts. `usermod -L USER` locks the user account and `usermod -U USER` unlocks the user account.

- `-expiry`: The `chage` command is used to manipulate user account expiry information. The syntax is:

chage -E DATE

There are additional options as follows:

  - `-m MIN_DAYS` (set the minimum number of days between password changes to `MIN_DAYS`)

  - `-M MAX_DAYS` (set the maximum number of days during which a password is valid)

  - `-W WARN_DAYS` (set the number of days of warning before a password change is required)

- `-passwd`: The `passwd` command is used to change passwords for the users. The syntax is:

passwd USER

The command will prompt to enter a new password.

- `-newgroup` and `addgroup`: The `addgroup` command will add a new user group to the system. The syntax is:

addgroup GROUP

In order to add an existing user to a group use:

addgroup USER GROUP

-delgroup

The `delgroup` command will remove a user group. The syntax is:

delgroup GROUP

- `-details`: The `finger USER` command will display the user information for the user which includes details such as user home directory path, last login time, default shell, and so on. The `chage -1` command will display the user account expiry information.

Bulk image resizing and format conversion

All of us use digital cameras and download photos from the cameras, as well as the Internet. When we need to deal with a large number of image files, we can use scripts to easily perform actions on the files in bulk. A regular task we come across with photos is resizing the file. Also, format conversion from one image format to another comes to use (for example, JPEG to PNG conversion). When we download pictures from a camera, the large resolution pictures take a large size. But we may need pictures of lower sizes that are convenient to store and e-mail over the Internet. Hence, we resize it to lower resolutions. This recipe will discuss how to use scripts for image management.

Getting ready

We will use the command `convert` from the **Imagemagick** suite, which contains excellent tools for manipulating images that can work across several image formats and different constructs with rich options. Most of the GNU/Linux distributions don't come with Imagemagick installed by default. You need to manually install the package. For more information, point your web browser to `www.imagemagick.org`.

How to do it..

In order to convert from one image format to another image format, use:

```
$ convert INPUT_FILE OUTPUT_FILE
```

For example:

```
$ convert file1.png file2.png
```

We can resize an image size to a specified image size either by specifying the scale percentage, or by specifying the width and height of the output image. Resize the image by specifying `WIDTH` or `HEIGHT` as follows:

```
$ convert image.png -resize WIDTHxHEIGHT image.png
```

For example:

```
$ convert image.png -resize 1024x768 image.png
```

It is required to provide either `WIDTH` or `HEIGHT`, so that the other will be automatically calculated and resized so as to preserve the image size ratio:

```
$ convert image.png -resize WIDTHx image.png
```

For example:

```
$ convert image.png -resize 1024x image.png
```

Resize the image by specifying the percentage scale factor as follows:

```
$ convert image.png -resize "50%" image.png
```

Let's see a script for image management:

```bash
#!/bin/bash
#Filename: image_help.sh
#Description: A script for image management

if [ $# -ne 4 -a $# -ne 6 -a $# -ne 8 ];
then
   echo Incorrect number of arguments
   exit 2
fi

while [ $# -ne 0 ];
do

   case $1 in
   -source) shift; source_dir=$1 ; shift ;;
   -scale) shift; scale=$1 ; shift ;;
   -percent) shift; percent=$1 ; shift ;;
   -dest) shift ; dest_dir=$1 ; shift ;;
   -ext) shift ; ext=$1 ; shift ;;
   *) echo Wrong parameters; exit 2 ;;
   esac;

done



for img in `echo $source_dir/*` ;
do
   source_file=$img
   if [[ -n $ext ]];
   then
     dest_file=${img%.*}.$ext
   else
     dest_file=$img
   fi

   if [[ -n $dest_dir ]];
   then
     dest_file=${dest_file##*/}
```

```
        dest_file="$dest_dir/$dest_file"
    fi

    if [[ -n $scale ]];
    then
        PARAM="-resize $scale"
    elif [[ -n $percent ]];    then
        PARAM="-resize $percent%"
    fi

    echo Processing file : $source_file
    convert $source_file $PARAM $dest_file

done
```

The following is a sample output, to scale the images in the directory `sample_dir` to `20%` size:

```
$ ./image_help.sh -source sample_dir -percent 20%
Processing file :sample/IMG_4455.JPG
Processing file :sample/IMG_4456.JPG
Processing file :sample/IMG_4457.JPG
Processing file :sample/IMG_4458.JPG
```

In order to scale the images to the width `1024`, use:

```
$ ./image_help.sh -source sample_dir -scale 1024x
```

Change the files to a PNG format by adding `-ext png` along with the preceding commands.

Scale or convert files with a specified destination directory as follows:

```
$ ./image_help.sh -source sample -scale 50% -ext png -dest newdir
# newdir is the new destination directory
```

How it works...

The preceding `image_help.sh` script can accept several command-line arguments, such as `-source`, `-percent`, `-scale`, `-ext`, and `-dest`. A brief explanation of each is as follows:

▶ The `-source` parameter is used to specify the source directory for the images.

▶ The `-percent` parameter is used to specify the scale percent and `-scale` is used to specify the scale width and height.

▶ Either `-percent` or `-scale` is used. Both of them do not appear simultaneously.

▶ The `-ext` parameter is used to specify the target file format. `-ext` is optional; if it is not specified, format conversion is not performed.

▶ The `-dest` parameter is used to specify the destination directory for scale or conversion of image files. `-dest` is optional. If `-dest` is not specified, the destination directory will be the same as the source directory. As the first step in the script, it checks whether the number of command arguments given to the script are correct. Either four, six, or eight parameters can appear.

Now, by using a `while` loop and case statement, we parse the command-line arguments corresponding to variables. `$#` is a special variable that returns the number of arguments. The `shift` command shifts the command arguments one position to the left, so that on each execution of shift, we can access command arguments one by one, by using the same `$1` variable rather than using `$1`, `$2`, `$3`, and so on. The case statement matches the value of `$1`; it is like a switch statement in the C programming language. When a case is matched, the corresponding statements are executed. Each match case statement is terminated with `; ;`. Once all the parameters are parsed in variables `percent`, `scale`, `source_dir`, ext, and `dest_dir`, a `for` loop is used to iterate through the path of each file in the source directory and the corresponding action to convert the file is performed.

If the variable `ext` is defined (if `-ext` is given in the command argument), the extension of the destination file is changed from `source_file.extension` to `source_file.$ext`. In the next statement, it checks whether the `-dest` parameter is provided. If the destination directory is specified, the destination file path is crafted by replacing the directory in the source path with the destination directory by using filename slicing. In the next statement, it crafts the parameter to the convert command for performing resize (`-resize widthx` or `-resize perc%`). After the parameters are crafted, the `convert` command is executed with proper arguments.

See also

▶ The *Slicing filenames based on extension* recipe of *Chapter 2, Have a Good Command*, explains how to extract a portion of the filename

Taking screenshots from the terminal

Taking screenshots is another common day-to-day activity for any computer user. It becomes even more important for administrators that maintain GUI applications running on computers and automate them. It is important to take screenshots when a particular event happens, to figure out what is going on in a GUI application.

Getting ready

We will be using a tool from the suite of programs called ImageMagick, which was used in the previous recipe as well. Install it using your package manager.

How to do it...

Let's get started with using the `import` command from ImageMagick to take screenshots:

1. Take the screenshot of the whole screen:

   ```
   $ import -window root screenshot.png
   ```

2. Manually select a region to take the screenshot:

   ```
   $ import screenshot.png
   ```

3. Take a screenshot of a specific window:

   ```
   $ import -window window_id screenshot.png
   ```

   To find out `window_id`, run the command `xwininfo` and click on the window you want. Then pass this `window_id` to the `-window` option of `import.x`.

Managing multiple terminals from one

If you have been using the shell extensively, you would have noticed that at times you will need to have access to more than one terminal at once. If you are using a graphical terminal emulator like Konsole, you might use multiple tabs to achieve this.

However, what to do when you want a solution without using a graphical terminal emulator? Or you are logged into a remote machine and want multiple shells? In the latter case, opening multiple `ssh` connections will basically waste network bandwidth and even slow down things. We will see how to achieve multiple shells while avoiding these problems.

Getting ready

To achieve this, we will be using a utility called **GNU screen**. If the screen is not installed on your distribution by default, install it using the package manager.

How to do it...

▸ **Creating screen windows**: To create a new screen, run the command screen from your shell. You will see a welcome message with some information about the screen. Press space or return to begin. You will be given a new shell to enter the commands. To create a new window (which basically means a new shell), press *Ctrl + A* and then *C* (these are case sensitive).

▸ **Viewing a list of open windows**: While running the screen, if you want to see a list of all open windows, use the keystrokes *Ctrl + A* and *"*.

▸ **Switching between windows**: A usual requirement while using the screen is to cycle through the open windows in a next/previous fashion. For this, use the keystrokes *Ctrl + A* and *Ctrl + N* for the next window and *Ctrl + A* and *Ctrl + P* for the previous window.

▸ **Attaching to and detaching screens**: A useful feature of the screen is that you can save and load screen sessions, called detaching and attaching in screen terminology. To detach from the current screen session, press *Ctrl + A* and *Ctrl + D*. When starting the screen, to attach to an existing screen use:

```
screen -r -d
```

▸ Which tells the screen to attach the last screen session. If you have more than one detached sessions, the screen will output a list of them and then you can use:

```
screen -r -d PID
```

▸ Where, `PID` is the pid of the screen session you want to attach to.

Index

Thank you for buying
Linux Shell Scripting Cookbook *Second Edition*

About Packt Publishing

Packt, pronounced 'packed', published its first book "*Mastering phpMyAdmin for Effective MySQL Management*" in April 2004 and subsequently continued to specialize in publishing highly focused books on specific technologies and solutions.

Our books and publications share the experiences of your fellow IT professionals in adapting and customizing today's systems, applications, and frameworks. Our solution based books give you the knowledge and power to customize the software and technologies you're using to get the job done. Packt books are more specific and less general than the IT books you have seen in the past. Our unique business model allows us to bring you more focused information, giving you more of what you need to know, and less of what you don't.

Packt is a modern, yet unique publishing company, which focuses on producing quality, cutting-edge books for communities of developers, administrators, and newbies alike. For more information, please visit our website: www.packtpub.com.

About Packt Open Source

In 2010, Packt launched two new brands, Packt Open Source and Packt Enterprise, in order to continue its focus on specialization. This book is part of the Packt Open Source brand, home to books published on software built around Open Source licences, and offering information to anybody from advanced developers to budding web designers. The Open Source brand also runs Packt's Open Source Royalty Scheme, by which Packt gives a royalty to each Open Source project about whose software a book is sold.

Writing for Packt

We welcome all inquiries from people who are interested in authoring. Book proposals should be sent to author@packtpub.com. If your book idea is still at an early stage and you would like to discuss it first before writing a formal book proposal, contact us; one of our commissioning editors will get in touch with you.

We're not just looking for published authors; if you have strong technical skills but no writing experience, our experienced editors can help you develop a writing career, or simply get some additional reward for your expertise.

[PACKT] open source
PUBLISHING   community experience distilled

CentOS 6 Linux Server Cookbook

A practical guide to installing, configuring, and administering the CentOS community-based enterprise server

Jonathan Hobson

CentOS 6 Linux Server Cookbook

ISBN: 978-1-84951-902-1   Paperback: 374 pages

A practical guide to installing, configuring, and administering the CentOS community-based enterprise server

1. Delivering comprehensive insight into CentOS server with a series of starting points that show you how to build, configure, maintain and deploy the latest edition of one of the world's most popular community based enterprise servers.

2. Providing beginners and more experienced individuals alike with the opportunity to enhance their knowledge by delivering instant access to a library of recipes that addresses all aspects of CentOS server and put you in control.

OpenStack Cloud Computing Cookbook

Over 100 recipes to successfully set up and manage your OpenStack cloud environments with complete coverage of Nova, Swift, Keystone, Glance, and Horizon

Kevin Jackson

OpenStack Cloud Computing Cookbook

ISBN: 978-1-84951-732-4   Paperback: 318 pages

Over 100 recipes to successfully set up and manage your OpenStack could environments with complete coverate of Nova, Swift, Keystone, Glance, and Horizon

1. Learn how to install and configure all the core components of OpenStack to run an environment that can be managed and operated just like AWS or Rackspace

2. Master the complete private cloud stack from scaling out compute resources to managing swift services for highly redundant, highly available storage

Please check **www.PacktPub.com** for information on our titles

OpenNebula 3 Cloud Computing

ISBN: 978-1-84951-746-1   Paperback: 314 pages

Set up, manage, and maintain your Cloud and learn solutions for datacenter virtualization with this step-by-step practical guide

1. Take advantage of open source distributed file-systems for storage scalability and high-availability

2. Build-up, manage, and maintain your Cloud without previous knowledge of virtualization and cloud computing

3. Install and configure every supported hypervisor: KVM, Xen, VMware

Advanced Penetration Testing for Highly-Secured Environments: The Ultimate Security Guide

ISBN: 978-1-84951-774-4   Paperback: 414 pages

Learn to perform professional penetration testing for highly-secured environment with this intensive hands-on guide

1. Learn how to perform an efficient, organized, and effective penetration test from start to finish

2. Gain hands-on penetration testing experience by building and testing a virtual lab environment that includes commonly found security measures such as IDS and firewalls

Please check **www.PacktPub.com** for information on our titles

CPSIA information can be obtained at www.ICGtesting.com
Printed in the USA
BVOW05s0737100913

330771BV00004B/39/P